LITERATURE OF

Spain AND THE Americas

TRADITIONS IN WORLD LITERATURE

National Textbook Company
a division of NTC/CONTEMPORARY PUBLISHING GROUP
Lincolnwood, Illinois USA

Cover Illustration: Funerary Mask
Teotihuacán Culture, Mexico
National Museum of Anthropology, Mexico City/Explorer, Paris
SuperStock

ISBN (student edition): 0-8442-1198-2 (hardbound); 0-8442-1199-0 (softbound)
ISBN (teacher's edition): 0-8442-1204-0 (softbound)

Acknowledgments begin on page 236, which is to be considered an extension of this copyright page.

Published by National Textbook Company,
a division of NTC/Contemporary Publishing Group, Inc.
4255 West Touhy Avenue,
Lincolnwood (Chicago), Illinois 60646-1975 U.S.A.
© 1999 NTC/Contemporary Publishing Group, Inc.

Library of Congress Cataloging-in-Publication Data

Literature of Spain and the Americas.
        p. 256   cm. 23 (Traditions in World Literature)
    Includes index.
    Summary: Presents selections from the writings of authors from Spain and Latin America, including Federico García Lorca, Carmen Laforet, Lope de Vega, Jorge Luis Borges, Carlos Fuentes, and Pablo Neruda, with biographical information, discussion questions, and writing prompts.
    ISBN 0-8442-1198-2 (hard), — ISBN 0-8442-1199-0 (soft)
    1. Spanish literature—translations into English. 2. Spanish American literature—20th century—translations into English. [1. Spanish literature—Translations into English. 2. Spanish American literature—Translations into English. 3. Spanish literature—Collections. 4. Spanish American literature—Collections.] I Series.
PQ6267.E1L58 1998
860.8—dc21   98-31287
                                                                                    CIP
                                                                                     AC

90 QB 0987654321

Contents

LITERATURE OF THE AMERICAS

INTRODUCTION

THE QUEST FOR AUTHENTICITY IN SPANISH AMERICAN WRITING

Angel Flores

The turbulence of World War I and its grim aftermath swept away the ivory towers in which Spanish American poets had been dreaming since the 1880s—a never-never world of princesses, fairies, and swans.

True enough, the "Modernist"* poets of this period had brought new sonorities and opened up new poetical horizons; and some of them stand among the loftiest composers of verse in the Spanish language. But a new generation of poets faced with the bitter reality of the postwar years could no longer inhabit the sublime dreamland of the Modernists and set out to return to the simple everyday America that their predecessors had sought assiduously to escape. Eschewing the romantic vocabulary, they cultivated rather a starkly photographic elementary expression, even the hitherto despised colloquial and native.

Something similar was happening in the novel. Works of fiction had been very late in making their appearance in Spanish America. The first, Fernández de Lizardi's *El periquillo sarniento* ["The Itching Parrot"] was not published until 1816, and it was predominantly an imitation of the Spanish romances of roguery. For one hundred years thereafter Spanish American novels copied, for the most part, Spanish models; but after World War I, writers of fiction in Spanish America began to think in terms of "the great American novel"; they sought authentically American characters and sites evocative of their conception of America. Writers from the River Plate area (Argentina and Uruguay) looked to their pampas and cowboys, or *gauchos,* as they were called, and instead of concentrating on their life in the open and mere picturesque elements in the landscape, they strove to capture the essence of their ecology: the gauchos in their intimate relationship with the land, and the economic forces that ultimately annihilated them in the name of progress. *Don Segundo Sombra* (1926), by the Argentine Ricardo Güiraldes, and other significant novels give a poignantly dramatic picture of the fate of the cowboys of the pampas.

About the same time, writers from the Andean countries of Peru, Bolivia, and Ecuador were focusing their attention on the Indians, enslaved by the Spanish conquerors and eking out, as they do to this day, a barely marginal, hopelessly precarious existence. What could be more "American" than these Indians? Again the goal of these novelists was not

---

*Modernist:** A literary movement that arose in Spanish America in the late 1800s. The Modernists displayed a verbal virtuosity and technical perfection that revolutionized Spanish literature.

primarily local color, but rather the violent exposé of a situation they wanted remedied with the return of the land to the Indians and their incorporation in our modern "civilization." Outstanding among this indigenist fiction were *Huasipungo* ["The Villagers," 1934] by the Ecuadorean Jorge Icaza and *El mundo es ancho y ajeno* ["Broad and Alien Is the World," 1941] by the Peruvian Ciro Alegría. These authors' passionate pleas often assume the proportions of a revolutionary call to insurrection.

When the jungle and rain forests of America were explored by our contemporary novelists, they found illustrious predecessors in the Uruguayan short-story writer Horacio Quiroga (1878–1937) and the Argentine W. H. Hudson (1841–1922), whose classic *Green Mansions* (1904) was written in English. The Colombian José E. Rivera (1888–1929) in *La vorágine* ["The Vortex," 1924] showed how foreign companies and scheming adventurers took advantage of peons and farmhands to expand their production of rubber and get bigger profits, while Rómulo Gallegos (1884–1968) drew a gruesome picture of the usurpation of power in the remote areas of his native Venezuela.

Thus it may be said that the most notable literary output of the 1920s and 1930s began and ended with social problems, that it was above all politically minded. Not only its themes and problems but its literary expression was realistic; though romantic patches do often appear, facts, disturbing facts, were piled up. Yet however laudable their intentions, as works of fiction they often lacked form, psychological penetration, style.

One of the most robust followers of this trend, recognized the world over since winning the Nobel Prize in 1967, was the Guatemalan Miguel Angel Asturias (1899–1974). As early as 1930 the French poet Paul Valéry had discovered him, writing an introduction to his *Leyendas de Guatemala,* lovely reconstructions of mythic tales from his native country's Indian population. Appalled by the political corruption of his country, Asturias then turned to the political novel. In *El Señor Presidente* ["Mr. President"] , which he finished in 1933 but could not publish until 1946, he depicted in lurid colors the reign of terror of the Guatemalan dictator Estrada Cabrera. Later he launched a powerful trilogy exposing the machinations of foreign fruit companies in Guatemala. In a more relaxed mood, he sent to press *Mulata de tal* ["Mulata," 1963].

Later Spanish American novelists respected the achievements of writers like Rivera and Gallegos without caring to imitate them. While sympathizing with their political implications and ideological drive, they found their works inflated, pretentious, inadequately motivated, and poorly structured. These novelists were more concerned with technique and better equipped to develop more complex plot structures, having gone beyond the traditional Spanish novel of the 1800s to study Freudian psychology, James Joyce, Marcel Proust, Franz Kafka, William Faulkner and the existentialists, especially Albert Camus and Jean-Paul Sartre, as well as the French new novel—Michel Butor, Alain Robbe-Grillet and Nathalie Sarraute, above all. Unquestionably the most substantial contribution of the these later Spanish American novelists has been the rich imaginative vein infused into their works. They insist on fluent means of expression and more flexible handling of time sequences. The writer is no longer bound by factual happenings: he moves freely in time and space. Photographic realism has gone by the board, and surprises, shifting viewpoints, mysteries abound, all of which are reminiscent of the old romances of chivalry. This approach is often described as "magic realism."

These "magic realists" are now as numerous as the Modernist poets of the poetry renascence of the late 1800s, but they are no longer enslaved to European literary fashions, On the contrary, after assimilating the latest techniques from Europe and the United States, they moved ahead to a point where they were part of the literary vanguard. European readers became familiar with the works of Spanish American writers such as the Argentine Jorge Luis Borges (1899–1986), whose short stories are enjoyed as much in France as in Japan. Although in the 1920s Borges' passion in his poetry and tales was for Argentine history and places, especially his native Buenos Aires, he gradually transcended the local in dramatizations of universal dilemmas and psychological labyrinths not unlike Kafka's, whom incidentally he had translated into Spanish. All his puzzling narratives are couched in an impeccable style, lean, clear-cut, functional, the very opposite of the flatulent rhetoric of the traditional Spanish and Spanish American fiction.

Influenced by Borges to some extent was another Argentine, Julio Cortázar (1914–1984), whose novel *Rayuela* ["Hopscotch," 1963] the sober *Times Literary Supplement* hailed as "the greatest novel to have come out of Latin America." Amalgam of humor and tragic pathos, this is a sophisticated allegory of man's predicament in contemporary society, bringing up to date the quest begun by Joyce in *Ulysses* and by Kafka in *The Castle.* Earlier Cortázar had shown his inventiveness as short-story writer—one of his yarns was used by Michelangelo Antonioni for his film *Blow-Up*—and as the author of the poignantly satiric novel *Los Premios* ["The Winners," 1965], similar in setting and approach to Katherine Anne Porter's *Ship of Fools,* but quite different in its philosophy.

Ten years older than Cortázar, the Cuban Alejo Carpentier (1904–1980) wrote several novels widely different in scope and subject matter but all suspenseful and exciting. In *El reino de este mundo* ["The Kingdom of This World," 1949] he dramatized episodes in the life of the Negro ruler Henri Christophe of Haiti, against a world of voodoo, legends, and superstitions; and in *Los pasos perdidos* ["The Lost Steps," 1953], perhaps his most memorable achievement, the "civilized" man of today faces the mysteries of the jungle.

The constant preoccupation of Mexican writers has been the Mexican Revolution of 1910–1920, which, with *Los de abajo* ["The Underdogs," 1915] by Mariano Azuela (1873–1952), gave birth to the modern Mexican novel and opened up the sluices of literary creativeness to the extent that to this day the Mexican novel is identified with the Mexican Revolution. In the case of Juan Rulfo (1918–1986) the revolution serves as background of some of his short stories, *El llano en llamas* ["The

Burning Plain," 1933] and, more remotely, of his novelette *Pedro Páramo* (1955). What made his art unique was his understanding grasp of the Mexican man, of the Mexican quintessence, through his uncanny control of dialogue, psychological penetration, and masterful ability in evoking a somber atmosphere wherein a very specific, tangible reality runs into a most disquieting nightmarish stream.

Though born years after the revolution, Carlos Fuentes (1928–), another leading Mexican storyteller, has never ceased weighing its impact on Mexican life. Through a lens that views Mexican society past and present simultaneously, he shows how the revolution failed to fulfill its goals. Fuentes won recognition with his first novel, *La región más transparente* ["Where the Air Is Clear," 1958], the region sarcastically referred to as "transparent" being Mexico City. Here the novelist described the sham of the city's intellectuals, the mendacity of its politicos—in short, the hypocrisy and corruption of its "great" men. Obsessed with finding the cause of Mexico's illness, Fuentes in *La muerte de Artemio Cruz* ["The Death of Artemio Cruz," 1962] drew a magnificent portrait of an erstwhile revolutionist turned, by dint of opportunist moves, into a tycoon.

Another novelist who explored the puzzling present was the Chilean José Donoso (1924–), who with humor and verve draws a magnificent portrait of social decay in *Coronación* ["Coronation," 1957], projected with equal amplitude and adroitness in *Este domingo* ["This Sunday," 1965].

This social awareness combined with a gift for analyzing human motivations was again found in the Peruvian Mario Vargas Llosa (1936–), whose first novel, *La ciudad y los perros* ["The Time of the Hero," 1962] fixed a steady eye on the activities of teenagers in a military school in Lima, revealing at the same time the failings of the Peruvian Establishment. This satire was found so harrowing that it aroused public indignation and one thousand copies were publicly burned. In 1966 Vargas Llosa reaffirmed his literary reputation with *La Casa verde* ["The Green House," 1969], a longer, more ambitious novel, with a double setting: the town of Piura and a remote village in the Amazonian region. This powerful saga, though complex in its rhetoric, faithfully mirrors much of the poverty, lust, and crime of our age.

Another novelist who has attracted readers the world over is the Colombian Gabriel García Márquez (1928-). Using a lean, precise style, Marquez created the imaginary Colombian village of Macombo, run by a bunch of scoundrels, whose inhabitants, ignorant, illiterate and browbeaten, grope through life in a nightmarish trance. In intrinsic veracity and mythic density García Márquez is unsurpassed even by Faulkner, and he evinces a keener political awareness. His masterpiece, *Cien años de soledad* ["One Hundred Years of Solitude," 1970], brings Macombo to life with incredible vividness; here all his literary virtues converge: his comic spirit, his satire, his myth-making, and his fertile fantasy. *Cien años de soledad* has found its place among the foremost novels of modern Spanish America: Cortázar's *Rayuela*, Fuentes' *La muerte de Artemio Cruz* and Vargas Llosa's *La Casa verde*.

READING TRANSLATIONS

Since every language is a unique and complex structure of sounds and meanings, translation cannot be a simple matter of substituting a word from one language for a word in another. When a work of literature is being translated, the challenge is even greater. In that case the translator must attempt to create something that is both faithful to the work in the original language but also reads well in the language into which the work is being translated.

Below is a passage from a classic of Spanish drama, *La vida es sueño* ["Life Is a Dream"], by Pedro Calderón de la Barca (1600–1682), one of Spain's greatest Renaissance playwrights. The text in Spanish is followed by two English translations.

In this speech the play's hero, Segismundo, speculates on the drama's central theme, that life is a dream from which only death awakens us.

LA VIDA ES SUEÑO (1636)

> . . . Y sí haremos, pues estamos
> En mundo tan singular,
> Que el vivir sólo es soñar;
> Y la experiencia me enseña,
> 5   Que el hombre que vive, sueña
> Lo que es, hasta despertar,
>   Sueña el rey que es rey, y vive
> Con este engaño mandando,
> disponiendo y gobernando;
> 10   Y este aplauso, que recibe
> Prestado, en el viento escribe;
> Y en cenizas le convierte
> La muerte (¡desdicha fuerte!):
> ¿Que hay quien intente reinar
> 15   Viendo que ha de despertar
> En el sueño de la muerte?
>   Sueña el rico en su riqueza,
> Que más cuidado le ofrece;
> Sueña el pobre que padece
> 20   Su miseria y su pobreza;
> Sueña el que a medrar empieza,
> Sueña el que afana y pretende,
> Sueña el que agravia y ofende,
> Y en el mundo, en conclusión,
> 25   Todos sueñan lo que son,
> Aunque ninguno lo entiende.
>   Yo sueño que estoy aquí,
> Destas prisiones cargado;

Y soñé que en otro estado
30   Más lisonjero me vi.
¿Qué es la vida? Un frenesí.
¿Qué es la vida? Una ilusión,
Una sombra, una ficción,
Y el mayor bien es pequeño;
35   Que toda la vida es sueño,
Y los sueños sueños son.

DENIS FLORENCE MacCARTHY (1873)

. . . And we'll do so, since 'tis plain,
In this world's uncertain gleam,
That to live is but to dream:
Man dreams what he is, and wakes
5   Only when upon him breaks
Death's mysterious morning beam.
The king dreams he is a king,
And in this delusive way
Lives and rules with sovereign sway;
10   All the cheers that round him ring,
Born of air, on air take wing.
And in ashes (mournful fate!)
Death dissolves his pride and state;
Who would wish a crown to take,
15   Seeing that he must awake
In the dream beyond death's gate?
And the rich man dreams of gold,
Gilding cares it scarce conceals,
And the poor man dreams he feels
20   Want and misery and cold,
Dreams he too who rank would hold,
Dreams who bears toil's rough-ribbed hands,
Dreams who wrong for wrong demands,
And in fine, throughout the earth,
25   All men dream, whate'er their birth,
And yet no one understands,
'Tis a dream that I in sadness
Here am bound, the scorn of fate;
'Twas a dream that once a state
30   I enjoyed of light and gladness.
What is life? 'Tis but a madness.
What is life? A thing that seems,
A mirage that falsely gleams,
Phantom joy, delusive rest,
35   Since is life a dream at best,
And even dreams themselves are dreams.

ARTHUR SYMONS (1902)

We live, while we see the sun,
Where life and dreams are as one;
And living has taught me this,
Man dreams the life that is his,
5   Until his living is done.
The king dreams he is king, and he lives
In the deceit of a king,
Commanding and governing;
And all the praise he receives
10   Is written in wind, and leaves
A little dust on the way
When death ends all with a breath.
Where then is the gain of a throne,
That shall perish and not be known
15   In the other dream that is death?
Dreams the rich man of riches and fears
The fears that his riches breed;
The poor man dreams of his need,
And all his sorrows and tears;
20   Dreams he that prospers with years
Dreams he that feigns and foregoes,
Dreams he that rails on his foes;
And in all the world, I see,
Man dreams whatever he be,
25   And his own dream no man knows.
And I too dream and behold,
I dream and I am bound with chains,
And I dreamed that these present pains
Were fortunate ways of old.
30   What is life? a tale that is told;
What is life? a frenzy extreme,
A shadow of things that seem;
And the greatest good is but small,
That all life is a dream to all,
35   And that dreams themselves are a dream.

Literature of Spain

MAX AUB

(1903–1972)

Born in Paris of a French mother and German father, Max Aub moved to Spain when he was about ten years old. He was educated in Valencia, on the eastern coast of Spain, and eventually achieved success as a novelist, playwright, and filmmaker. In addition to writing, he served as Director of Theaters and Movies, as Secretary of the National Council of Theaters, and as Cultural Assistant at the Spanish Embassy in Paris. In 1942, Aub moved to Mexico City, where he wrote most of his novels and short stories.

Aub's most famous fictional work is a long novel about the Spanish Civil War entitled *The Magic Labyrinth*, which is made up of five books published between 1943 and 1963. He also wrote two panoramic novels about life in Madrid, *Good Intentions* and *Valverde Street*. His works are often characterized by slow, dreamlike sequences, psychological introspection, and characters with strong inner conflicts. Because his novels tend to deal with constantly changing scenes and characters, they are sometimes said to be kaleidoscopic in effect. ■

THE LAUNCH

Translated by Elizabeth Mantel

He said he was born in Bermeo,[1] but the truth was that he came from a little town across the mouth of the Mundaca river, a settlement which was known by no name, or by many names, which is the same thing. The beaches and cliffs of this area were all that he knew of the world. For him, the Machichaco, Potorroari and Uguerriz marked Ultima Thule;[2] for him, Sollube was Olympus; Bermeo, Paris; and the Atalaya mall, the Elysian Fields.[3] The wide expanse of his world, his Sahara, was the Laida, and the end of his world to the east was the steep, flat-topped, reddish Ogoño. Beyond was Elanchove and the gentlemen of Lequeitio, in hell. His mother was the daughter of an overseer in an arms factory in Guernica. His father was a miner from Matamoros: he did not live long. They called him "El Chirto," perhaps because he was half crazy. When he became ill he left the Franco-Belgian mines of Somorrostro, and went to work in a sawmill factory. There, among the woodplaning and dovetailing machines, Erramón Churrimendi grew up.

---

1. **Bermeo:** a fishing port in northern Spain on the Bay of Biscay. All other towns, unless otherwise noted, are in the vicinity of Bermeo.
2. **Ultima Thule:** the end of the world.
3. **Elysian Fields:** paradise in Greek mythology.

He was fond of the little steamboats, the tunny boats, the pretty little sardine fishing smacks; the fishing tackle: the trotlines, the sieves, the fish traps, the nets. The world was the sea, and the only living beings were the hake, the eels, the sea bass, and the tunny. And he loved to catch moving fish in the water with a deep fisherman's net, to fish for anchovies and sardines with a light, or at dusk; and to catch the bonito and tuna with a spinning tackle.

But he no sooner put his feet in a boat than he became seasick. And there was nothing he could do about it. He tried all the official medicines, and all the recondite ones, and all advice, spoken and whispered. He followed the advice of Don Pablo, of the drugstore; of Don Saturnio, of the City Council; of Cándida, Don Timoteo's maid; of the doctor from Zarauz, who was a native of Bermeo. To no avail. He had only to put one foot in a boat, and he became seasick. He tried a hundred stratagems: he would get aboard on an empty stomach, or after a good breakfast, sober, or drunk, or without having slept; he even tried the magic cures of Sebastiana, the woman from the edge of town; he tried crosses, lemons, the right foot, the left foot, at 7:00 A.M. on the dot, at low tide and at high tide, on the right day of the week. He went after Mass, after several "Our Fathers," and he tried pure will power and even in his sleep he heard: "I'll never be seasick again, I'll never be seasick again. . . ." But nothing helped. As soon as he put his foot on a moving plank, his insides turned round and round, he lost all sense of balance, and he was forced to huddle in the corner of the boat to keep out of the others' way, hoping to stay unnoticed. He spent some terrible moments. But he was not among those who despair, and for many years he repeatedly dared the adventure. Because, naturally, the people were laughing at him—not much, but they were laughing at him. He took to wine. What else could he do? Chacolí wine is a remedy. Erramón never married, the idea never even occurred to him. Who would marry him? He was a good man. Everyone admitted that. He was not even guilty of anything. But he got seasick. The sea made sport of him, and without any right.

He slept in a cabin by the estuary. It belonged to him. There was a beautiful oak there—if I say *there was,* it's for a good reason.

It *was* really a splendid tree, with a tall trunk and high branches. A tree the likes of which there are not many. It was his tree, and every day, every morning, every evening, on passing by, the man would touch it as if it were a horse's croup or the side of a beautiful woman. Sometimes he even spoke to it. It seemed to him that the bark was warm and that the tree was grateful to him. The roughness of the tree perfectly matched the rough skin on the man's hand. There was a perfect understanding between him and the tree.

Erramón was a methodical man. So long as there was variety in his work he did whatever he was asked, willingly and tidily. He was asked to do a hundred odd chores: to repair nets, to dig, to help in the sawmill, which had been his father's; to him it was all the same whether he raised a thatch or caulked, or earned his few pesetas[4] by helping to bring in the

4. **pesetas:** The peseta is the monetary unit of Spain.

fish. He never said no to anything. Erramón also sang, and sang well. He was greatly respected in the tavern. One of his Basque[5] songs went something like this:

> All the Basques[5] are alike.
> All save one.
> And what's the matter with that one?
> That's Erramón.
> And he's like all the rest.

One night Erramón dreamed that he was not seasick. He was alone in a little boat, far out on the sea. He could see the coastline clearly in the distance. Only the red Ogoño shone like a fake sun which was sinking in the middle of the earth. Erramón was happier than he had ever been in his life. He lay down in the bottom of the boat and began to watch the clouds. He could feel the incessant rocking motion of the sea. The clouds were flying swiftly by, pushed by a wind which greeted him without stopping; and the circling seagulls were shouting his welcome:
"Erramón, Erramón!"
And again:
"Erramón, Erramón!"
The clouds were like lace doves. Erramón closed his eyes. He was on the water and he was not seasick. The waves rocked him in their hammock back and forth, back and forth, up and down, in a sweet cradling motion. All his youth was about his neck, and yet, at that moment, Erramón had no memories, no other desire than to continue forever just as he was. He caressed the sides of his boat. Suddenly his hands were speaking to him. Erramón raised his head in surprise. He was not mistaken! His boat was made of the wood of his oak tree!
So shocking was the effect that he woke up.
From that moment on, Erramón's life began to change completely. It entered his head that if he made a boat out of his tree he would never again become seasick. In order to prevent himself from committing this crime, he drank more chacolí than usual; but he could not sleep. He turned over and over in his bed, hounded by the stars. He listened to his dream. He tried to convince himself of the absurdity of all this:
"If I've always been seasick, I'll continue being seasick."
He turned over on his left side.
He got up to look at his tree, and caressed it.
"Will I end by winning or losing?"
But deep inside he knew he should not do it, that it would be a crime. Was it his tree's fault that he got seasick? But Erramón could not resist the temptation for long. One morning he himself, aided by Ignacio, the one from the sawmill, cut down the tree. When the tree fell, Erramón felt very sad and alone as if the most beloved member of his family had died. It was

---

5. **Basque**: member of a people of northern Spain and southern France.

hard for him now to recognize his cabin, it was so lonely. Only with his back to it, facing the estuary, did he feel easy.

Every afternoon he went to see how his tree was changing into a boat. This took place on the beach where his friend Santiago, the boatwright, was building it. The whole thing was made of the trunk; the keel, the floor timbers, the frame, the stem, the beams, even the seats and the oars, and a mast, just in case.

And so it was that one August morning when the sea did not seem like one, it was so calm, Erramón plowed outward on it with his new boat. It was a marvelous boat, it flew at the slightest urging of the man; he dipped the oars gently, throwing back his shoulders before he slightly contracted his arms, which made the boat fly. For the first time Erramón felt drunk, ecstatic. He drew away from the shore. He dipped the right oar a few times to make a turn, then the other in order to zigzag through the water. Then he drew the oars in and began to caress the wood of his boat. Slowly, the boards were letting in a little water. Erramón raised his hands to his forehead to dampen it a little. The silence was absolute; not a cloud, not a breeze, not even a seagull. The land had disappeared, submerged. Erramón put his hands on the gunwale to caress it. Again he removed his hands wet. He was a little surprised: splashes on the wood had long since dried in the sun. He glanced over the inside of the boat: from every part water was slowly seeping in. On the bottom there was already a small puddle. Erramón did not know what to do. Again he passed his hands over the sides of his boat. There was no question about it; the wood was gradually letting water in. Erramón looked around; a slight uneasiness was beginning to gnaw his stomach. He had himself helped in caulking the boat and was sure that the work had been well done. He bent down to inspect the seams: they were dry. It was the wood that was letting the water in! Without thinking, he raised his hand to his mouth. The water was sweet!

Desperately, he began to row. But despite his frantic efforts the boat did not move. It seemed to him that his boat was caught among the branches of a giant underwater tree, held as if in a hand. He rowed as hard as he could, but the boat did not budge. And now he could see with his own eyes how the wood of his tree was exuding clean, fresh water! Erramón fell to his knees and began to bail with his hands, because he had no bucket.

But the hull continued to ooze more and more water. It was already a spring with a thousand holes. And the sea seemed to be sprouting branches.

Erramón crossed himself.

He was never seen again on the shores of Biscay. Some said that he had been seen around San Sebastian, others that he was seen in Bilbao.[6] A sailor spoke of an enormous octopus which had been seen about that

---

6. **San Sebastian . . . Bilbao:** major seaports on the Bay of Biscay.

time. But no one could give any information about him with any certainty. The oak tree began to grow again. The people shrugged their shoulders. The rumor spread that he was in America. Then, nothing.

DISCUSSION QUESTIONS

1. What two conflicting human needs are represented by the tree and the ocean? What is significant about the fact that Erramón can travel on the ocean only by sacrificing the tree?

2. What details does the author provide to indicate Erramón's lack of connection to everything but the tree?

3. As he sets out to sea, there are strong indications that Erramón's experience in the new boat will be different from the experience in his dream. What details does Aub supply to suggest this difference?

4. What images make it clear that Erramón is thinking of the tree during his final moments?

5. What general comment on human relationships is suggested by the last three sentences of this story?

6. In some ways "The Launch" resembles a parable or allegory—short, simple story forms that point out a moral. Do you think this story carries a moral? If so, how would you express that moral?

SUGGESTION FOR WRITING

This story is told with almost no dialogue (conversation between characters). Imagine that it is your job to help turn this story into a play. Choose a scene that you consider crucial, and write a script for that scene, providing a description of the stage setting and the appropriate dialogue. You might show Erramón talking with people in the tavern, with the boatwright, or even to the tree, in which case you would write a monologue. Try to create a dialogue or monologue that reveals Erramón's thoughts and feelings about the conflict he is experiencing.

EMILIA PARDO BAZÁN

(1852–1921)

The only daughter of a count, Emilia Bazán was a precocious child who had read the Greek classics, the Bible, and *Don Quixote* by the time she was 15 years old. A year later she married and moved to Madrid with her husband. She continued to read widely and eventually opened a literary salon to discuss contemporary issues, such as Darwinism and feminism. Bazán wrote and campaigned actively for women's rights, eventually causing her scandalized husband to separate from her.

The author of over 500 short stories, Bazán believed that literature should be a close study of social problems and should be based on actual observation. In preparation for her early novel, *The Platform*, which centers on a female worker in a tobacco factory, Bazán directly observed factory conditions for two months. A later novel about the decay of an aristocratic family, *The Manors of Ulloa*, is generally regarded as her masterpiece. In 1916 she was given a position as professor of literature at Central University of Madrid, an honor not usually offered to women at that time. ∎

THE FIRST PRIZE

Translated by Armando Zegri

In the time of Godoy,[1] the fortune of the Torres-nobles de Fuencar[2] was placed among the most powerful of the Spanish monarchy. Political vicissitudes and other reverses reduced their revenues and put an end to the dissolute mode of living of the last Marqués de Torres-nobles, a dissolute spendthrift whose conduct had induced much gossip in the court when Narváez[3] was young. He was close to seventy years when the Marqués de Torres-nobles adopted the resolution to retire to his farm at Fuencar, the only remaining property which was unmortgaged. There he devoted himself to the task of building up his body, which was no less ruined than his house; and as Fuencar was able to let him enjoy a modicum of comfort, he organized his life so that nothing was wanting. He had a priest who, in addition to saying Mass on Sundays and conducting the festivals, played

---

1. **Godoy:** Manuel de Godoy (1767–1851), Spanish statesman who secured peace with France in 1795. His alliance with Napoleon in 1805 involved Spain in a war against England that led to a Franco-Spanish defeat.

2. **Torres-nobles de Fuencar . . . Marqués de Torres-nobles:** the marqués' name and the name of his family estate in the country, probably in the town of Fuentcarrel, six miles north of Madrid, are the same.

3. **Narváez:** Ramón Mar'a de Narváez (1800–1868), authoritarian Spanish premier and Duke of Valencia.

cards with him and would read and comment to him on the most reactionary political periodicals; a major-domo, in charge of the estate, who skillfully directed the crops; an obese coachman who solemnly drove the two mules of his carriage; a reserved and solicitous governess, too old to tempt him and yet not sufficiently old to be repulsive in his eyes; a butler that he brought from Madrid, the only remaining relic of his past dissolute life, and now converted to the master's reformed life, as discreet and punctual now as in the past; and finally, a female cook, clean as gold, with delicate hands for all the plates of the ancient national kitchen, who could satisfy the stomach without irritating it, and could delight the palate without perverting it. With such excellent wills, the Marqués' house functioned like a well-wound clock, and the master more and more congratulated himself on having left the Gulf of Madrid and found port in Fuencar, where he might dock for repairs. His health recuperated; the sleep and digestion of that poor threadbare tunic which serves as the jail to the spirit, was renovated; and in a few months the Marqués de Torresnobles grew fat without losing his agility, his back straightened a bit, and his fresh breath testified to the fact that his ferocious gastric malady no longer bothered his stomach.

But if the Marqués lived well, so did his servants. In order to keep them in his service, he paid them more generously than any one else in the province, and frequently gave them presents. So they were quite happy: little work to do, but that little, methodical and unchanging; a high salary, an occasional pleasant surprise from the generous Marqués.

The month of December, the year before last, was colder than usual, and the farm and environs of Fuencar were covered with about five inches of snow. Bored with the solitude of his huge study, the Marqués descended one night to the kitchen, instinctively seeking sociability—the companionship of fellowmen. He drew near to the fire, warmed the palms of his hands, snapped his fingers, and even laughed at the tales of Andalusian humor narrated by the major-domo and the shepherd. He even observed that the eyes of the cook were most attractive. Among other talk, more or less of a rustic nature, that amused him, he heard that all his servants were planning to club together so as to buy a tenth of a ticket in the Navidad lottery.[4]

The following day, very early, the Marqués dispatched his butler to the next town. And that same night the condescending señor entered the kitchen, waving a number of papers, and announced to the domestics, with a benign expression, that he had carried out their wishes, by purchasing a whole ticket for the coming lottery, of which he meant to present them with a two-tenth share, reserving for himself the remaining eight-tenths, so as to tempt his luck. Upon hearing the news, everyone in the kitchen burst out into loud bravos and extravagant blessings; all save the shepherd, an old white-haired fellow, low-speaking and sententious, who shook his head, and affirmed that no good could come of playing

---

4. **Navidad lottery:** Christmas lottery.

with gentlemen, and that it killed luck. This so enraged the Marqués, that he forbade the shepherd from sharing in the two-tenth share of the ticket in question.

That night the Marqués slept less soundly than he had done since coming to Fuencar; some of those ideas which mortify bachelors kept him awake. He had not relished the grasping avidity with which his servants spoke of the money they might win. "These fellows," the Marqués reflected, "are only waiting to fill their pockets, before they forsake me. And what plans they have! Celedonio (the coachman) talked of setting up a tavern . . . probably to get drunk on his own wine. And that dolt of a Doña Rita (she was the governess) is thinking of nothing else but of keeping a boarding house! Jacinto (the butler) kept mighty silent, but I could see him squinting in the direction of that Pepa (the cook) who, let us be frank, has some charm. . . . I would swear that they are planning to get married. Bah!" As he uttered this exclamation, the Marqués de Torres-nobles turned in his bed the better to cover himself, for a cold gust of wind had attacked his neck. "And after all, what is all this to me? We won't win the big prize . . . and if we do, they will have to wait till I leave them the money in my will."

A moment later, the good man was snoring.

Two days later, the lottery was held, and Jacinto, who was more resourceful than Celedonio, arranged matters so that his master should send him to town in order to purchase some needed items. Night fell, there was a heavy fall of snow, and Jacinto had not yet returned, in spite of the fact that he had left the house at dawn.

The servants were gathered in the kitchen, as usual; suddenly they heard the muffled hoofbeats of a horse over the new-fallen snow, and a man, whom they recognized as their friend Jacinto, entered like a bomb. He was pallid, trembling and transformed, and with a catch in his voice, let fall these words:

"The first prize!"

At this precise moment, the Marqués was in his study and, his legs wrapped in a thick poncho and smoking a fragrant cigar, was listening to the priest reading the political gossip of *El Siglo Futuro*.[5] Both suddenly paused and listened to the outburst issuing from the kitchen. At first the Marqués thought there was a row among his servants, but ten minutes of listening convinced him that these were voices of jubilation, so unmeasured and crazy were the sounds; and the Marqués, angry and feeling that his dignity was compromised, dispatched the priest to learn what was happening, and to command silence. Within three minutes the messenger returned, and falling on the divan, huskily exclaimed, "I am choking!" Then he wrenched his collar loose and tore his vest in the effort to open it.

The Marqués ran to his assistance and, fanning his face with *El Siglo Futuro*, finally succeeded in forcing a few fragmentary phrases out of the priest's mouth.

---

5. *El Siglo Futuro: The Future Century*, a periodical published from 1875 to 1936 that supported Don Carlos's and his successors' claims to the Spanish throne.

"The first prize! We have won . . . n . . . the prize . . . !"

In spite of his years, the Marqués rushed to the kitchen with unwonted agility; reaching the door, he suddenly stopped, stupefied by the unusual scene that presented itself to his eyes. Celedonio and Doña Rita were dancing—I don't know if it was the *jaleo* or the *cachucha*,[6]—with a thousand and one different stampings, leaping about like mannikins that have been electrified. Jacinto, amorously embracing a chair, was waltzing round and round the room. Pepa was drumming with a pan handle on a frying pan, producing a horrible cacophony, and the major-domo, stretched out on the floor, was rolling around, shouting, or rather ululating: "Long live the Virgin!" Hardly did they perceive the Marqués than the crazy loons rushed at him with outstretched arms and, before he could offer any resistance, they hoisted him on their shoulders, and singing and dancing and passing him around from one to the other, like a rubber ball, they gave him a free ride all round the kitchen, until they perceived that he was in a towering rage, and put him back on the ground. And then things grew worse, for the cook, Pepa, seizing the Marqués by the waist, willy-nilly rushed him into a dizzying gallop, while the major-domo, presenting a bottle of wine, insisted that he sample it, assuring his employer that the liquor was very fine, since he had sent most of the blood of the bottle into his stomach, and therefore knew what he was talking about.

As soon as the Marqués could make his escape, he rushed to his room, anxious to divulge to someone the terrible happenings; to the priest he described the audacities of his servants, and then discussed the matter of the first prize. To his grand surprise, he observed that the priest was ready to leave the house, wrapped in his cape, and putting on his cap.

"Where can you be going, Don Calixto, for the love of God?" the astonished Marqués exclaimed.

Well, with his permission, Don Calixto was going to Seville to visit his family, give them the glad tidings, and collect in person his share of the tenth of the prize, a matter of several thousand *duros*.[7]

"And you are going to leave me now? And the Mass? And . . ."

While he was still talking, the butler introduced his face through the door. If the Marqués would let him, he also wished to go and collect his part of the prize. The Marqués raised his voice, and told them they must be unnatural monsters to wish to leave the house at such an ungodly hour, and with so much snow on the ground; to this both Don Calixto and Jacinto answered that the train would be leaving at midnight, at the next station, to which place they would wend on foot, as best they could. The Marqués was about to open his mouth, to declare: "Jacinto will remain here, for I have need of him," when just then the ruddy face of the coachman appeared framed in the door, and without authorization, and with insolent joy, came to bid adieu to his master, since he too was about to collect his winnings.

---

6. *jaleo* (hä lā′ ō) . . . *cachucha* (kä chü′ chä): Spanish dances.

7. *duros:* The *peso duro,* or piece of eight, was formerly the Spanish dollar.

"And the mules?" shouted the master. "And pray tell me, who will take care of the coach?"

"Anyone your Grace wishes to put on the job. I'm not going to drive any more!" the coachman answered, presenting his back, and making room for Doña Rita who entered, not as was her wont, as if she were gingerly treading over eggs, but with disheveled hair, an excited manner, and a smile on her mouth. Brandishing a heavy bunch of keys, she handed them to the Marqués, with these words:

"Your Grace must know that these belong to the pantry . . . this to the closet . . . and that one . . ."

"That one is the key of the devil who will get you and your family, you witch of hell! You want me to fetch the bacon, the beans, eh? Go to the . . ."

Doña Rita failed to hear the final imprecation, for she sailed out whistling, and behind her went the others, and after all of them went the Marqués himself, angrily following them through the rooms and almost overtaking them in the kitchen; but he could not muster up enough courage to follow them into the courtyard, for fear of the cold. By the light of the moon that silvered the snowy expanse, the Marqués beheld them depart: first came Don Calixto, then Celedonio and Doña Rita arm in arm, and last of all Jacinto walking close to a feminine form which he made out to be Pepa, the cook. "Pepilla, too!" The Marqués gazed into the abandoned kitchen, and saw the dying embers, and heard a sort of animal grunt. At the foot of the chimney, sprawling his full length, the major-domo was sleeping off his spree.

The following morning, the shepherd, who had not cared "to kill his luck," prepared a mess of soup, made out of bread and garlic, for the Marqués de Torres-nobles de Fuencar, so that the noble señor might have something to eat on the day he awoke a millionaire.

It is unnecessary for me to describe the sumptuous installation of the Marqués in Madrid, but I must relate that he acquired a cook whose dishes were gastronomical poems. It is declared that the delicacies of this excellent artist, whose offerings were relished so much by the Marqués, produced that illness which sent him to the grave. Nevertheless, I believe that his death was caused by his fright, when he fell from a magnificent English horse, that became panicky; this happened shortly after he came to live in the palace he furnished in the Alcala Street.

When they opened the Marqués' will, they found that he made the shepherd of Fuencar his heir.

DISCUSSION QUESTIONS

1. What would you do if you won a fortune in the lottery? Consider not only what you would buy, but also the lifestyle decisions you would make.

2. The Marqués is upset when he learns that his servants are deserting him immediately after winning the lottery. Do your sympathies lie more with the Marqués or with the servants?

3. Why does the Marqués buy a lottery ticket for his servants? How does his plan backfire?

4. Bazán slowly builds the character of the Marqués and his household through small details, such as the fact that he selects a governess who is "too old to tempt him yet not sufficiently old to be repulsive in his eyes." What kind of household does the Marqués want to establish? What other details reveal the kind of man he is?

5. Who turns out to be the Marqués' heir? Why is this an ironic ending to the story?

SUGGESTION FOR WRITING

It is easy to think of the benefits of winning a lottery, but sometimes there are drawbacks as well. Write a short story in a modern setting about someone who, like the Marqués, discovers the down side to winning the lottery.

GUSTAVO ADOLFO BÉCQUER

(1836–1870)

A poet whose works have been widely admired for over a hundred years, Bécquer lived his short life under a cloud of misery. Orphaned as a young boy, he went to Madrid at the age of 18 to become a writer. He contributed poems to newspapers, often anonymously, and eked out a living as a translator and writer of miscellaneous pieces. Plagued by constant illness and poverty, he never succeeded in publishing any poetry during his lifetime. After his death, however, a group of friends financed the publication of a volume of his poems with the understanding that any profits would go to his widow and children. Gradually his fame grew and more poems were submitted for publication. Bécquer's works generally focus on private feelings, such as love, solitude, and emotional pain. His poems often have a haunting, mysterious quality. ∎

THEY CLOSED HER EYES

Translated by John Masefield

> They closed her eyes
> That were still open;
> They hid her face
> With a white linen,
> 5   And, some sobbing
> Others in silence,
> From the sad bedroom
> All came away.
>
> The nightlight in a dish
> 10 Burned on the floor;
> It threw on the wall
> The bed's shadow,
> And in that shadow
> One saw sometime
> 15 Drawn in sharp line
> The body's shape.

The dawn appeared.
At its first whiteness
With its thousand noises
20 The town awoke.
Before that contrast
Of light and darkness,
Of life and strangeness
I thought a moment.
25 *My God, how lonely*
The dead are!

On the shoulders of men
To church they bore her,
And in a chapel
30 They left her bier.
There they surrounded
Her pale body
With yellow candles
And black stuffs.

35 At the last stroke
Of the ringing for the Souls,
An old crone finished
Her last prayers.
She crossed the narrow nave,
40 The doors moaned,
And the holy place
Remained deserted.

From a clock one heard
The measured ticking,
45 And from a candle
The guttering.
All things there
Were so dark and mournful,
So cold and rigid,
50 That I thought a moment:
My God, how lonely
The dead are!

From the high belfry
The tongue of iron
55 Clanged, giving out
A last farewell.
Crêpe on their clothes,
Her friends and kindred
Passed in a line
60 In homage to her.

In the last vault
Dark and narrow,
The pickaxe opened
A niche at one end;
65 They laid her away there.
Soon they bricked the place up,
And with a gesture
Bade grief farewell.

Pickaxe on shoulder
70 The gravedigger,
Singing between his teeth,
Passed out of sight.
The night came down,
It was all silent.
75 Alone in the darkness
I thought a moment,—
My God, how lonely
The dead are!

In the dark nights
80 Of bitter winter,
When the wind makes
The rafter creak,
When the violent rain
Lashes the windows,
85 Lonely I remember
That poor girl.

There falls the rain
With its noise eternal,
There the northwind
90 Fights with the rain.
Stretched in the hollow
Of the damp bricks,
Perhaps her bones
Freeze with the cold.

95 Does the dust return to dust?
Does the soul fly to heaven?
Or is all vile matter,
Rottenness, filthiness?
I know not, but
100 There is something—something—
Something which gives me
Loathing, terror,—
To leave the dead
So alone, so wretched.

DISCUSSION QUESTIONS

1. How would you describe the mood of this poem?

2. Why do you think Bécquer does not give the girl a name or tell us anything about her life and the circumstances of her death?

3. This poem moves through three settings, each one colder and darker than the previous one. What are these settings? What action is repeated in each setting?

4. How many times does the refrain occur in this poem? How does the intensity of the refrain change with each repetition?

SUGGESTION FOR WRITING

Make a diagram in which you classify the images of this poem into three groups: visual images (appealing to the sense of sight), auditory images (appealing to the sense of sound), and tactile images (appealing to the sense of touch).

CAMILO JOSÉ CELA

(born 1916)

An influential novelist and short story writer, Cela served in the Spanish Civil War and then attended the University of Madrid. His fictional works focus on impoverished and ignoble characters whose lives are marked by ugliness, brutality, and selfishness. Cela's first important work was *The Family of Pascual Duarte*, a novel whose main character is a man whose life was scarred by the cruelty of society and who is eventually executed for murdering his mother. Another significant novel, *The Hive*, is a panoramic view of society with a cast of 116 characters.

Cela's novels and short stories clearly reflect his belief that writers of fiction should lash out against deceit, oppression, hypocrisy, and conformity. His narrative style is an intriguing blend of grotesque imagery and modern psychological insights. In 1989 Cela was awarded the Nobel Prize for Literature. ∎

THE VILLAGE IDIOT

Translated by Beatrice P. Patt

The name of the village idiot was Blas. Blas Herrero Martínez. Before the death of Perejilondo, the previous village idiot who had managed to forget that Hermenegildo was his real name, Blas was a rather dull boy who stole pears, and who served as the victim of everyone's useless blows and ill temper. He was a pale boy, long-legged, solitary, and tremulous. The village did not warrant more than one idiot; it was too small to accommodate more than one, and Blas Herrero Martínez, who was aware of this and had a high regard for tradition, was content to roam about the pine groves and meadows stealing whatever he could, without ever coming too close. In this way he patiently waited for the now aged Perejilondo to be taken away in a wooden box with his feet in front of him and the priests behind. Custom was custom and had to be respected; there was a saying in the town to the effect that custom was more important than the king and no less important than the law. Blas Herrero Martínez, who understood life intuitively and with the same accuracy as a well-trained hound following a scent, knew that his time had not yet come, and courageously resigned himself to waiting. Even though the contrary may appear to be true, in this life there is always time for everything.

Blas Herrero Martínez had a small, bald, pointed head, a narrow chest, spindly legs, freckles, and buckteeth; he was cross-eyed and he drooled. The lad was an obvious sort of idiot, with every requirement scrupulously fulfilled; considered carefully, as one should consider him, Blas played the role of village idiot to perfection. He was unmistakably an idiot and not just a run-of-the-mill type whose idiocy could not be established without a doctor's diagnosis.

He was good-natured and gentle, and always smiled like a sick calf even when he had just been hit with a stone, a frequent occurrence, since the villagers were not exactly what one might call sensitive. Blas Herrero Martínez of the little ferret face would wiggle his ears—one of his talents—and nurse his latest wound, which bled a watery pale pink, smiling all the while in a manner hard to describe: perhaps he was imploring his tormentors not to hit him with the second stone on the sore made by the first.

In the time of Perejilondo, on Sundays, which were the only days when Blas felt he had some right to walk through the village streets, our village idiot would sit down after Mass at the door of Louise's café and wait the two or three hours required for the customers to finish their aperitifs and go home to dinner. When Louise's café was entirely empty or nearly so, Blas would go in smiling and slip under the tables to pick up the cigarette butts. Sometimes there were very good days; two years before, for example, there had been a very gay party and Blas had managed to fill his tin with about seven hundred cigarette stubs. The pride and joy of Blas Herrero Martínez was this deep, beautiful, shiny yellow tin on which were painted a shell and some words in English.

When Blas finished his task he ran breathlessly to see Perejilondo, who by this time was very old and scarcely able to move. He said to him: "Perejilondo, look what I've brought. Are you satisfied?"

Perejilondo answered in his best falsetto: "Yes. . . . Yes. . . ."

Then he gloated over the butts with a miserly smile, and, seizing half a dozen in a haphazard way, gave them to Blas.

"Did I do the right thing? Are you satisfied?"

"Yes. . . . Yes. . . ."

Blas Herrero Martínez took his stubs and, unrolling them, made whatever kind of cigarette happened to come out. Sometimes the result was a rather thick cigarette but at other times it came out so thin that it was almost impossible to smoke, worse luck. Blas always gave the butts he found in Louise's café to Perejilondo, because Perejilondo was the rightful owner of all the butts in the village. After all, it was not for nothing that he was the ranking village idiot. Once it became Blas's turn to dispose of the butts at will, he would not allow any newcomer to cheat him either. That was hardly to be expected! Fundamentally, Blas was a conservative with a great regard for tradition, and he was aware of the fact that Perejilondo was the official village idiot.

Nonetheless, on the day of Perejilondo's death Blas could not restrain a spontaneous feeling of joy and began to jump and gambol about like a lamb in the meadow where he usually went to drink. Shortly thereafter he realized that he had done wrong and then he went to the cemetery to do penance and to weep over the mortal remains of Perejilondo, a man over whose grave nobody else had ever done penance, nor wept, nor was ever destined to weep. For a few weeks he brought the butts to the cemetery;

after setting aside his half-dozen he carefully buried the rest over the grave of his mentor. Later on he gradually stopped doing this and finally did not even bother to collect all the butts; he merely picked up as many as he needed and left the rest for whoever came after him and wanted them. He forgot Perejilondo and observed that something strange was happening: it was an unfamiliar sensation to bend down to pick up a butt and not wonder whether or not it really belonged to him.

DISCUSSION QUESTIONS

1. What is your general opinion of the villagers in this story? Why do you think they need to have someone in the role of village idiot? Are there any negative social roles at your school?

2. How does Blas feel about being the village idiot? What are some of the "traditions" that go with playing the role of village idiot?

3. How would you describe the relationship between Blas and Perejilondo? How does Blas change after Perejilondo's death?

4. What is Cela's attitude toward the traditions described in "The Village Idiot"? How would you characterize the tone of this story?

SUGGESTION FOR WRITING

List the slang terms currently in use at your school that designate what could be considered a social role, such as *preppie, punk,* or *jock.* (You may use your own lingo.) When you are through with the list, select one item and explain briefly the benefits and drawbacks of playing that particular social role. Be as objective as you can. Refer only to the role and not to individuals.

FEDERICO GARCÍA LORCA

(1898–1936)

Born and raised near Granada on a prosperous estate, García Lorca attended the Residencia de Estudiantes, a college in Madrid. There he remained for almost ten years, mixing with a group of artists that included the famous painter, Salvador Dali, and the film director, Luis Buñuel. Although he was a complex and sophisticated writer, many of his finest works were inspired by the simple gypsy folklore of his native region. His best-known collection of poetry is probably the *Gypsy Ballads*, which made him an instant celebrity. These poems treat themes such as beauty, violence, passion, and gloom.

After leaving the Residencia de Estudiantes, García Lorca spent a year in New York City at Columbia University, where he wrote a series of complicated poems that reflect his suicidal mood at the time. These poems, published after his death under the title *The Poet in New York*, are a torrent of strange surrealistic metaphors. García Lorca returned to Spain to direct a traveling theater, and his finest plays—*Blood Wedding, Yerma,* and *The House of Bernarda Alba*—grew out of his work with this company of players. When the Spanish Civil War broke out, García Lorca, though not politically involved, was arrested by the fascist authorities and executed. ∎

THE LAMENT

Translated by Stephen Spender and J. L. Gili

> I have shut my balcony
> because I do not want to hear the lament,
> but from behind the gray walls
> I hear nothing else but the lament.
>
> 5   There are very few angels that sing,
> there are very few dogs that bark,
> a thousand violins fit into the palm of the hand:
> but the lament is an immense angel,
> the lament is an immense violin,
> 10   the tears muzzle the wind,
> and I hear nothing else but the lament.

SONG

Translated by Stephen Spender and J. L. Gili

The girl with the beautiful face
is gathering olives.
The wind, that gallant of towers,
takes her by the waist.
5   Four riders passed
on Andalusian ponies,
with suits of blue and green,
with long dark cloaks.
"Come to Córdoba, lass."
10   The girl pays no heed.
Three young bullfighters passed,
slender of waist,
with orange-colored suits
and swords of antique silver.
15   "Come to Seville, lass."
The girl pays no heed.
When the evening became
purple, with diffused light,
a youth passed bringing
20   roses and myrtle of moon.
"Come to Granada, lass."
And the girl pays no heed.
The girl with the beautiful face
goes on gathering olives,
25   with the gray arm of the wind
encircling her waist.

THE GUITAR

Translated by Stephen Spender and J. L. Gili

The lament
of the guitar begins.
The wine cups of the day-break
are broken.
5   The lament
of the guitar begins.
It is useless
to hush it.
10   It is impossible
to hush it.
It weeps monotonous

as the water weeps,
as the wind weeps

15　over the snowfall.
It is impossible
to hush it.
It weeps for things
far away.

20　Sands of the warm South
which ask for white camellias.
Weeps, arrow without target,
the evening without morning,
and the first bird dead

25　upon the branch.
Oh guitar!
Heart stabbed
by five swords.

THE ARREST OF ANTOÑITO EL CAMBORIO ON THE ROAD TO SEVILLE

Translated by A. L. Lloyd

Antonio Torres Heredia,
son and grandson of Camborios,
with a willow wand in his hand
goes to Seville to see the toros.[1]

5　Swarthy as the green moon,
slowly he goes, and with grace,
his blue-polished ringlets
shining between his eyes.
He cut some round lemons

10　in the middle of the road
and kept throwing them in the water
till he turned it to gold.[2]
And in the middle of the road,
beneath the branches of an elm,

15　the Civil Guard came marching,
and bore him off arm in arm.

Slowly the day goes by,
the evening with one shoulder hanging
makes a wide pass with the cape

---

1. the toros: the bullfights.

2. lemons . . . gold: possibly a reference to the sun reflecting on puddles of water.

20 over the sea and the streamlets.
The olive trees are awaiting
the night of Capricorn,[3]
and over the leaden mountains
a sharp breeze leaps like a horse.
25 Antonio Torres Heredia,
son and grandson of Camborios,
comes without wand of willow
between the five tricorns.[4]

—Antonio, what sort of man are you?
30 If you're called Camborio's son,
you should have made of them
a five-jetted fountain of blood.
You are neither a real Camborio
nor anyone else's son.
35 There are no more gypsies left
that walked on the mountain alone!
The old knives they once wielded
are shivering under the dust.

At nine o'clock at night
40 they bring him to the jail,
while the *guardias civiles*[5]
are all drinking lemonade.
And at nine o'clock at night
they shut him in the jail,
45 while the sky is shining
like the croup of a foal.

---

3. **night of Capricorn:** December twenty-second.

4. **tricorns:** probably a reference to the three-cornered hats worn by the Spanish rural police.

5. *guardias civiles*: Spanish rural police.

THE DEATH OF ANTOÑITO EL CAMBORIO

Translated by Stephen Spender and J. L. Gili

Voices of death resounded
near the Guadalquivir.[6]
Ancient voices which surround
voice of manly carnation.[7]
5   He nailed through their boots
bites of wild boar.
In the fight he leapt
like the slippery dolphin.
He bathed in enemy blood
10   his crimson tie,
but there were four daggers
and he could only succumb.
When the stars nail
spears on the gray water,
15   when the yearlings dream
verónicas[8] of gillyflowers,
voices of death resounded
near the Guadalquivir.

—Antonio Torres Heredia,
20   an authentic Camborio,
dark of green moon,
voice of manly carnation:
Who took your life away
near the Guadalquivir?
25   —My four cousins the Heredias,
sons of Benamejí.[9]
They did not envy in others
what they envied in me.
Raisin-colored shoes,
30   ivory medallions
and this skin kneaded
of olive and jasmine.
—Ah, Antoñito of the Camborios
worthy of an Empress!

---

6. **Guadalquivir** (gwä′ THäl kē bēr′): a river flowing from southern Spain to the Atlantic.

7. **manly carnation:** The red carnation is symbolic of courage.

8. *verónica*: a pass in bullfighting in which the matador stands still and swings the cape away
from the charging bull.

9. **Benamejí** (bā nä mā hē′): a town in southern Spain.

35   Remember the Virgin
      because you are to die.
      —Ah, Federico García,
      call the Guardia Civil!
      Already my waist has snapped
40   like a stalk of maize.

      Three gushes of blood,
      and he died in profile.
      Living coin which never
      will be repeated.
45   A swaggering angel places
      his head on a cushion.
      Others with a wearied blush
      lighted an oil lamp.
      And when the four cousins
50   arrive at Benamejí,
      voices of death ceased
      near the Guadalquivir.

THE DAWN

Translated by Rolfe Humphries

      Dawn in New York contains
      Four columns of mire,
      A hurricane of dark doves
      Dabbling in rotten water.
5   Dawn in New York goes wailing
      Over tremendous stairs
      Seeking among the awns[10]
      Spikenard of painted pain.
      Dawn comes, no one receives it on his mouth,
10   For here no morning or hope is possible:
      Sometimes the coins in furious angry swarms
      Sting, pierce, devour abandoned children.
      The first to go out realize in their bones
      No Paradise ever, no loves bereft of leaves;
15   They know they go to a heaven of law and number,
      Games without skill, sweat without reward,
      Light is buried among the links of noise
      In a shameless challenge of unrooted science.
      In the wards are people, staggering and sleepless,
20   Like late survivors of a bloody shipwreck.

---

10. awns: the delicate bristles or "beards" of some cereal and other grass plants.

NEW YORK (OFFICE AND ARRAIGNMENT)

Translated by Rolfe Humphries

For Fernando Vela

    Under the multiplications
    There is a drop of duck's blood;
    Underneath the divisions
    A drop of sailor's blood;
5   Under the sums, a river of tender blood.
    A river that sings as it comes
    By dormitory and suburb
    And is silver, cement or breeze
    In the false dawn of New York.
10   Mountains exist. I know.
    And spectacles for the learned,
    I know. But I did not come
    To look at the beautiful sky,
    But the muddy river of blood,
15   Engine over the falls, spirit to cobra's tongue.
    Daily New York slaughters
    Four million ducks, five million pigs,
    Two thousand doves for the satisfaction of the dying,
    A million cows, a million lambs,
20   Two million roosters leaving the skies in pieces,

    Better to sob, whetting the edge of the knife,
    Or murder the dogs in the dazzling hunt
    Than resist, in the dawn,
    The endless trains of milk,
25   The endless trains of blood,
    The trains of roses, shackled
    By dealers in perfumes.
    The ducks and the doves and the hogs and the sheep
    Shed their drops of blood
30   Underneath multiplication
    And the terrible outcries of cattle, jammed together
    Fill with grief the valley
    Where the Hudson rolls, drunk on oil.

    I damn all the people
35   Who ignore the other half
    The half beyond salvation
    Raising the concrete mountains
    Where little forgotten beasts
    Know the beat of their hearts,
40   And where we shall all go down
    In the final feast of the drill.

I spit in your face, I say.
The other half hears me out,
Eating, excreting, and flying
45   In purity like the children
Who live in the janitor's lodge
Probing with fragile straws
The holes where the insects live
Burning antennae off.
50   This is not hell, but the street.
Not death, but a market for fruit.
There's a world of broken rivers, infinite distances
In the little paw of the cat crushed by the automobile,
And I hear the earthworm's song
55   In the heart of many girls.
Rust and ferment, and land
Terribly tossed and shaken
Floating by numbered stores.
What shall I do, then? rearrange the landscape?
60   Line up the loves to be mere photographs?
To be like blocks of wood, or bloody puffballs?
No, no; I damn all this,
I exorcise the spell
Of those deserted shops
65   Where agony never shines,
Which erase the scheme of the woods,
And I offer myself to be eaten
By the cattle, densely jammed,
Whose outcries fill the valley
70   Where the Hudson rolls, drunk on oil.

SEVILLE

Translated by Rolfe Humphries

> Seville is a tower
> Full of subtle archers.
>
> Trust Seville to wound.
> Cordova to die in.
> 5   City that lies in wait
> To catch the ample rhythm
> And twist and coil and wind it
> To labyrinthine patterns,
> Enkindled withe and tendril.
>
> 10   Trust Seville to wound.
>
> Beneath the arch of heaven
> Over the open country,
> She looses forever,
> Her arrowy river.
>
> 15   Cordova to die in.
>
> Crazy with horizons,
> She mingles in her wine
> The pure and the bitter,
> Don Juan and Dionysus.[11]
>
> 20   Seville to wound, always.

---

11. **Don Juan and Dionysus:** Don Juan was a legendary Spanish nobleman and a libertine. Dionysus was the Greek god of wine.

DISCUSSION QUESTIONS

1. List five adjectives that reflect the main impressions created by García Lorca's poetry.

2. In "The Lament," what is the poet trying to shut out? Why does he finally conclude that it is impossible?

3. In "Song," what might "the girl with the beautiful face" represent? Why does she not respond to all the glamorous invitations that come her way?

4. In "The Guitar," what associations does García Lorca have with this musical instrument? What do you think is meant by "arrow without target" and "evening without morning"? What particular feature of guitar playing might have inspired the image, "Heart stabbed/by five swords"?

5. Trace the passage of time in "The Arrest of Antoñito el Camborio on the Road to Seville." What images does García Lorca use to indicate the time of day?

6. Contrast the use of brilliant color in the first stanza of "The Arrest . . ." with the grayness of the remainder of the poem. What is the effect of this contrast?

7. The poet expresses no sympathy for Antoñito in the third stanza of "The Arrest . . ." In fact, he sharply criticizes this character. What is the basis for his criticism?

8. What is García Lorca's attitude toward Antoñito in "The Death of Antoñito el Camborio"? How does it differ from his attitude toward the same character in the previous poem?

9. In "The Dawn" and "New York (Office and Arraignment)," what are García Lorca's feelings toward New York City? What images does he use to communicate these feelings? What, in particular, do you think the following images mean: "Four columns of mire," "Dawn in New York goes wailing / Over tremendous stairs," and "Dawn comes, no one receives it on his mouth"?

10. Seville is a colorful, flamboyant, historical, and highly romantic city—a center for bullfighting, processions, and other dramatic events. Why might such a place be viewed as a place "to wound"?

SUGGESTION FOR WRITING

García Lorca reveals his feelings about New York City by creating a torrent of negative images. Select a place that you have strong feelings about, either positive or negative. Create a list of images that help to communicate the flavor of this place. Then use these images to construct a short poem that reveals your feelings about the place.

JUAN RAMÓN JIMÉNEZ

(1881-1958)

A poet known for his delicate, melodic, and elegant works, Jiménez was born in Andalusia in southern Spain, the son of wealthy winegrowers. After studying law for a time, he went to Madrid to join a group of modernist poets. There he published two volumes of poems, *Violet Souls* and *Water Lilies,* which received savage criticism for their unconventional form and melancholy subject matter. This setback, in combination with the financial ruin of his family and his father's death, caused him to suffer a mental breakdown. After months spent in clinics, he returned to Andalusia, where he began writing again. Always acutely sensitive, he did his best to shut out the intrusions of the world, composing in a soundproof room and drawing on his own inner resources. Jiménez' marriage in 1916 was an important turning point, as his wife provided a comfortable buffer against the world. Moving to Madrid after his marriage, he produced more than 25 volumes of poetry, his most frequent themes being solitude, beauty, love, and death. Jiménez was extremely fastidious about each poem, and his dedication is suggested by his famous statement that "a poem is not finished, it is abandoned." His most famous work is *Platero and I,* a series of poems addressed to a donkey whose companionship he enjoyed in his youth.

In 1936 Jiménez' many-years' residence in Madrid was ended by the Spanish Civil War, which forced him into exile. He and his wife spent their remaining years traveling and teaching in the United States and South America. Jiménez was awarded the Nobel Prize for Literature in 1956. ∎

POEMS

Translated by Eloise Roach

WHAT HAPPENS TO A MELODY

What happens to a melody
when the playing stops; what
to a breeze that stops
blowing, and what
5 to a light that goes out?

Tell me, death, what are you but a silence,
calm, and shadow?

I SHALL NOT RETURN

I shall not return. And night,
mildly warm, serene and silent,
will lull the world, under beams
of its solitary moon.

5   My body will not be there,
and through the wide-open window,
a refreshing breeze will come
inquiring for my soul.

I don't know if any await
10   the end of my double absence,
or who will kiss my memory
amidst caresses and weeping.

But there will be stars and flowers,
there will be sighs and hopes,
15   and love in the avenues
in the shadows of the trees.

And that piano will be playing
as in this untroubled night,
and no one there to listen,
20   pensive, by my window frame.

HAND AGAINST THE LIGHT

We are nothing but a feeble bag
of blood and bones,
and a pin, it is true, can kill us;
but in us flows the seed
5   that may produce
the one butterfly,
of light only and of shadow only and only ours,
without skin, network, or frame,
nor possibility of being caught
10   by human or divine;
the invulnerable being,
incorporeal, as long as the world,
that brims, free, the infinite
and goes on to the impossible.

IS IT I, PACING MY ROOM

       Is it I, pacing my room
tonight, or is it the tramp
who was prowling in my garden
at the fall of dusk?

5   I look
around and find everything
is the same and not the same . . .
Was the window left wide open?
Had I not fallen asleep?
10 Was not the garden in green
of moonlight? . . . The sky was clear
and blue . . . Now there are clouds and wind
and all the garden is dark . . .
I believe my beard was
15 black . . . And I was wearing gray.
And now my beard is white
and I wear mourning. Is this
my walk? Does this voice
I now utter have the rhythms
20 of the voice I used to have?
Am I myself, or am I
the beggar prowling my garden
at the fall of night?

                I look
25 around . . . There are clouds and winds . . .
The garden is full of gloom . . .
     . . . I walk up and down . . . Had I
already fallen asleep?
My beard is white . . . All things
30 are the same and not the same.

FORGERS OF SWORDS

    Forgers
of swords:
here is
the word!

THE LAMB BAAED GENTLY

The lamb baaed gently.
The tender donkey showed its joy
in lusty bray.
5   The dog barked playfully almost
talking to the stars.

I could not sleep. I went outdoors
and saw heavenly tracks upon the ground
all flower-decked
10   like a sky
turned upside down.

A warm and fragrant mist
hovered over the grove;
the moon was sinking low
15   in a soft golden west
of divine orbit.

My breast beat without pause,
as if my heart had wined . . .

I opened wide the stable door to see
20   if He were there.
                              He was!

THIS OTHER I

This other I that spies
all that I do
is he the noble human
or the evil one?

5   Does he lift me or subdue me;
is he my conscience
or my white serpent
(black temptress)?

Must I respect him
10   like myself,
or overthrow him,
as an enemy?

I FIRED AT THE IDEAL

     I fired at the ideal,
thinking that I would not hit.
—Black shot, how your recoil
shattered my soul!

5   The evening, after the shot
that split its very being,
hushed, of a sudden, turned
dark green, its forehead pallid.

     And I heard, deep in my heart,
10   that, throbbing, awaited it,
the abrupt thud of the dead
sky, with its folded wings.

I WISH MY BOOK MIGHT BE

     I wish my book might be
as is the sky at night,
all present truth, without history.

     That, as the sky, it might give itself
5   at every moment, with all its stars; nor
should childhood, youth, old age detract
or add in charm to its great beauty.

     Tremor, flash of light, music
present and total!
10   Tremor, flash of light, music in the mind
—heaven of the heart—of the pure book!

DISCUSSION QUESTIONS

1. "What Happens to a Melody" and "I Shall Not Return" are both poems dealing with the subject of death. How would you describe the poet's attitude toward death in these poems? Do thoughts of death make him fearful, resistant, hostile, or hopeful—or do they arouse other feelings?

2. What is the relevance of the title "Hand Against the Light"? What do you think is meant by the "butterfly" that is characterized as "invulnerable" and "incorporeal"?

3. In "Is It I, Pacing My Room," what does the poet mean when he says, "All things are the same and not the same"?

4. In "The Lamb Baaed Gently," what is the implication of the last stanza?

5. Who is "This Other I" in the poem of the same name, and why does the poet have such mixed feelings toward this individual?

6. In "I Fired at the Ideal," Jiménez makes use of a highly unusual comparison to describe the end of evening and the dawning of a new day. What metaphor does he create to indicate the end of evening?

7. In "I Wish My Book Might Be," the poet expresses a wish that his writing might be like the night sky. What does he mean by this comparison?

SUGGESTION FOR WRITING

"Forgers of Swords" is an interesting sort of protest poem that presents the problem in three words and the solution in four words. Using this poem as a model, write your own brief protest poem in ten words or less. In the first part of the poem, define the problem, and in the second part of the poem, either offer a solution or suggest some likely consequences. The subject may be as light or as serious as you wish.

CARMEN LAFORET

(born 1921)

A novelist and short story writer, Carmen Laforet grew up in the Canary Islands, where her mother died, leaving her in the care of a stepmother. This stepmother became a hated figure that appears in many of Laforet's works in one form or another. When she was 18, Laforet went to Barcelona to study fine arts and law, She later moved to Madrid, where she met and married a journalist. Her first novel, *Nothing,* published in 1944, was an instant success and gained her international recognition for its passion and striking imagery. Her next two novels were entitled *The Island and the Devils* and *Sunstroke.*

Laforet's fiction generally presents characters struggling in an empty world without permanent values. These works powerfully dramatize the conflict between the hopes of individuals and the dreary, alien world around them. Writers who deal with human alienation in a meaningless world are often called existential writers, and Laforet is credited with writing the first Spanish existential novel. Her existential world view is also evident in the short story that appears below. ■

THE RETURN

Translated by Martin Nozick

It was a bad idea, thought Julian as he pressed his forehead against the windowpane and felt the wet cold go right through to the bones that stood out so clearly under his transparent skin. It was a bad idea, sending him home for Christmas. Besides, they were sending him home for good; he was completely cured.

Julian was a tall man, encased in a nice black overcoat. He was blond, with prominent eyes and cheekbones that emphasized his thinness. But Julian was looking well these days. His wife marveled how well he looked every time she visited him. There was a time when Julian had been a handful of blue veins, legs like long sticks and big gnarled hands. That was two years ago when they committed him to the institution, which, strangely enough, he was reluctant to leave.

"Very impatient, aren't you? They'll be coming for you soon. The four o'clock train is due very shortly and you'll be able to take the five-thirty back. And tonight you will be home, celebrating Christmas Eve. . . . Julian, please do not forget to take your family to Midnight Mass, as an act of grace. . . . If our House weren't so far away . . . It would be pleasant to have all of you here tonight. . . . Your children are very handsome, Julian, especially the youngest; he looks like a Christ Child, or a little Saint John, with his curls and blue eyes. I think he would make a fine acolyte, because he has a very bright face. . . ."

Julian listened to the nun's prattle in adoration. Julian loved Sister María de la Asunción very much, for she was fat and short with a smiling face and cheeks like apples. Waiting in that enormous forbidding visitors' room, ready for departure and plunged in thought, he had not heard her footsteps. . . . He had not heard her come in, because the nuns, despite their tiers of skirts and their wimples, have a tread as light and silent as a sailboat. But when he noticed her, his heart jumped with joy. The last joy he would derive from this stage of his life. His eyes filled with tears; he had always been inclined to sentimentality, but now it was almost a disease.

"Sister María de la Asunción . . . I should like to attend Midnight Mass here with you this year. I think it would be all right if I stayed here until tomorrow. It would be enough to be with my family on Christmas Day. In a certain sense, you are also my family. I . . . I am very grateful to all of you."

"Don't be foolish; that is impossible. Your wife is waiting for you right now. As soon as you have rejoined your family and are working, you will forget all this; it will be like a dream. . . ."

Then Sister María de la Asunción left too, and Julian felt dejected again, for he did not like leaving the asylum. It was a place of death and despair, but for him it had been a place of refuge, of salvation. . . . And even the last few months, when the authorities felt he had fully recovered, it had been a place of happiness. They had even let him drive! And not just going through the motions. He had driven the Mother Superior herself and Sister María de la Asunción to the city to do some shopping. And Julian knew how brave these women had been, putting themselves like that into the hands of a lunatic . . . or a former lunatic: he had once been considered dangerous. But he did not disappoint them. The car had run perfectly under his expert control. The nuns had not even been shaken by the deep ruts in the road. When they got back, they congratulated him and he had felt himself blushing.

"Julian . . ."

Sister Rosa was standing in front of him, the nun with the round eyes and oval mouth. He did not like Sister Rosa very much; in fact, he did not like her at all. And he could not understand why. At the beginning, he was told, they had been obliged to put him into a strait jacket more than once for having tried to attack her. Sister Rosa always seemed frightened of Julian. Now, suddenly, as he gazed at her, he realized whom she resembled. She resembled poor Herminia, his wife whom he loved so much. Life was so full of puzzles. Sister Rosa looked like Herminia, and yet, perhaps because of that, Julian could not abide her.

"Julian, a call for you. Will you come to the phone? Mother asked me to tell you to answer it."

"Mother" was the Mother Superior herself. They all called her that. It was an honor for Julian to answer the telephone.

It was Herminia on the line, asking him in a shaky voice to take the train by himself, if he didn't mind.

"Your mother is not feeling well; no, nothing serious—another of her liver attacks. . . . But I didn't dare leave her alone with the children. I couldn't call you earlier; she was in too much pain and I couldn't go out. . . ."

Julian still held the phone in his hand, but he was no longer thinking about his family. All he could think of was that he would have an opportunity to stay here for the night; that he would help them light the lights before the shrine of the Nativity, he would have a wonderful Christmas Eve dinner and sing carols with the rest of them. It all meant so much to Julian.

"Then I'll probably come tomorrow. Don't be frightened. No, nothing wrong; but since you are not coming, I thought I would help the sisters a bit; they have so much to do at Christmas time. Yes, I'll be there for dinner sure. . . . Yes, I'll be home for Christmas Day."

Sister Rosa was at his side, staring at him with her round eyes and oval mouth. She was the only unpleasantness he was glad to be leaving forever. . . . Julian lowered his eyes and humbly requested an audience with "Mother"; he wanted to ask her humbly a special favor.

The next day, Julian was riding in a train through a gray sleet on his way to the city. In a third-class coach he was wedged in between turkeys, chickens, and their owners, all bursting with optimism. All of Julian's property that morning consisted of a battered suitcase and the good black-dyed overcoat that kept him pleasantly warm. As they approached the city, as its smell struck his nostrils and he looked out upon the enormous rows of depressing factories and workmen's flats, Julian began to feel he had had no right to enjoy himself so fully the evening before; he should not have eaten so much of so many choice things; he should not have sung in the voice which, during the war, had helped the other soldiers in the trenches through long hours of boredom and sadness.

Julian felt he should not have spent such a warm, cozy Christmas Eve, because for several years now they had had no such celebrations at home, Poor Herminia had probably managed some shapeless nougats made of sweet-potato paste and painted in gay colors, and the children had spent half an hour chewing on them eagerly after an everyday dinner. At least, that is what had happened the last Christmas Eve he had spent at home. He had been out of work for months. He had always been a good provider, but then came the gasoline shortage and things came to a standstill. Herminia scrubbed stairs. She scrubbed countless stairs every day until the poor thing couldn't talk of anything but stairs and the food she could not buy. At the time Herminia was pregnant again and her appetite was something terrific. She was a thin woman, as tall and blonde as Julian; she was easygoing and wore thick glasses despite her youth. . . . Julian could not swallow his own food as he watched her devour her watery soup and sweet potatoes. Watery soup and sweet potatoes: that was what they ate every day at Julian's house all that winter, morning and evening. Breakfast was only for the children. Herminia looked greedily at the hot bluish milk they drank before going off to school. . . . Julian, who, according to his family, had always been a glutton, left off eating entirely. . . . But that was much worse for everybody, because his mind started to go and he became aggressive. Then he began imagining that his poor flat was a garage and that the beds crammed into all the rooms were luxurious automobiles. And one day he tried to kill Herminia and his mother, and they had to drag him out in a strait jacket. . . . But all that was part of the past. The relatively recent past. Now he was going back, completely recovered. He had been fine for several months now. But the nuns had sympathized with him and let him linger on a little while longer, just a little while . . . until the Christmas holidays. Suddenly he realized what a coward he had been, putting it off. The streets leading home were full of brilliantly lighted shop windows. He stopped at a pastry shop and bought a tart. He had some money and spent it on that. He had eaten so many the last few days that it did not tempt him, but his family would not feel that way.

It was not easy, climbing the stairs to his flat, his suitcase in one hand, the sweet in the other. It was very high up and he was eager to see them all, to kiss his mother, the old lady who always smiled and pretended nothing was the matter so long as her pains were not too bad.

There were four doors, formerly green, now nondescript. One of them was his. He knocked.

He was in Herminia's skinny arms; the children were shouting. A pleasant smell wafted in from the kitchen. Something good was cooking.

"Papa, we've got turkey!"

That was the first thing they told him. He looked at his wife. He looked at his mother; she had aged greatly and was very pale from her last illness, but she had a nice new woolen shawl over her shoulders. The little dining room boasted a basket brimful of sweets, gewgaws and ribbons.

"Did you win the lottery?"

"No, Julian, when you went off, some ladies came. . . . From a welfare organization, you know. . . . They took good care of us; they found me work and they are going to get you a job too, in a garage."

In a garage? Of course, a former madman could not be a taxi driver. A mechanic, perhaps. Julian gazed at his mother again and saw her eyes were full of tears. . . . But she was smiling, smiling as always.

Suddenly Julian felt his shoulders sag again under a load of responsibilities and worries. He had come back to the large family standing around him and it was his business to rescue them from the clutches of Charity. They would go hungry again, of course. . . .

"But Julian, aren't you glad? . . . We're all together again, all together at Christmas. . . . And what a Christmas we're going to have! Look!"

And again they pointed to the gift basket, to the children eager and wide-eyed. They were doing it for his benefit as he stood there, a sad, thin man with bulging eyes and a black overcoat. And it was as if he had left childhood behind again that Christmas Day so that he might look once more upon life—with all the cruelty that, beneath those gifts, it would have forever.

DISCUSSION QUESTIONS

1. Why is Julian reluctant to leave the asylum? Do you think his feelings represent universal human feelings, or only the mentality of a disturbed individual?

2. Julian has a strong attachment to Sister María de la Asunción and an equally strong dislike for Sister Rosa. How can these feelings be explained?

3. What details does the author provide to reveal Julian's state of dependency?

4. What impression are we given of Julian's wife and mother? Why do you think he tried to kill them?

5. In the concluding sentence of the story, the author writes that Julian "left childhood behind again that Christmas." What is the meaning of this statement?

SUGGESTION FOR WRITING

At one point in the story, Julian says that the asylum is "also my family." Write an essay in which you compare Julian's two families. How are the atmospheres of these two homes different? How do the two families' expectations of Julian differ? Be sure to support your main points with plenty of specific details.

ANTONIO MACHADO
(1875–1939)

Federico García Lorca and Antonio Machado are generally considered the most important Spanish poets of their generation. Born in Seville, Machado was a member of a well-known family that included several radical intellectuals who permanently influenced his thinking. Machado was educated in both Madrid and Paris, where he met some of the leading writers and philosophers of the day. His early poetry, which is best represented by a collection called *The Plains of Castille,* is characterized by very personal, intimate themes. His later poetry is more political and social in its orientation.

Machado was a lifelong socialist and a staunch defender of the Spanish Republic. In 1936 a civil war began between the supporters of Spain's socialist government and fascists led by General Francisco Franco. The Spanish Civil War, which resulted in the collapse of the Republic in 1939, also brought about Machado's death. His flight from Spain proved to be too much for his health, and he died shortly after crossing the French border. His final poems were laments on the damage done by the Civil War. The poem that appears below is a lament for the death of the poet Federico García Lorca, who was viciously executed in mysterious circumstances during the early part of the war. ■

THE CRIME WAS IN GRANADA
Translated by Willis Barnstone

I

He was seen walking between rifles
down a long street,
coming upon the cold field
which still held stars of early dawn.
5   They killed Federico
when daylight came.
The squad of executioners
dared not look upon his face.
All had shut their eyes.
10   They prayed: Not even God can save you!
Dead fell Federico—
blood on his forehead and lead in his entrails.
. . . Oh, that the crime was in Granada.
Let all know it! Poor Granada! In his Granada!

II

THE POET AND DEATH

15 He was seen walking alone with her,
without fear of her scythe.
The sun was already on the towers; hammers
on the anvils, anvils and anvils of the forges.
Federico spoke,
20 flirting with death. She listened.
"Because the clapping of your dry palms
sounded yesterday in my verse, companion,
and you gave ice to my song and the edge
of your silver sickle to my tragedy,
25 I will sing you the flesh you do not have,
the eyes you lack,
the hair the wind was ruffling,
the red lips where they kissed you.
Today as before, gypsy,[1] my death,
30 how good it is alone with you
in these winds of Granada, my Granada!"

III

He was seen walking . . .
      My friends, build
of stone and dream in the Alhambra,[2]
35 a tomb for the poet,
over a fountain where water weeps
and says eternally:
The crime was in Granada, in his Granada!

----

1. **gypsy:** García Lorca often wrote of gypsies and their way of life. Here the gypsy is a personification of death.

2. **Alhambra:** palace of the Moorish kings at Granada.

DISCUSSION QUESTIONS

1. If you were planning to do a public reading of this poem, what piece of music might you select for background music? Explain why you think your chosen piece would be appropriate.

2. Stanza 2 is an imaginary dialogue between the poet and death, which is portrayed as a gypsy. What characteristics of gypsies, as they are traditionally depicted, might make them appropriate figures of death?

3. What do you think Machado means by the metaphors "without fear of her scythe" and "you gave ice to my song"?

4. What is the effect of the concluding line of each stanza?

SUGGESTION FOR WRITING

For centuries Granada has been regarded as a Spanish ideal, a lovely city that people do not associate with injustice and crime. Do some research on the city and write a description of some of the features that contribute to the romantic image that Granada has enjoyed over the years. Or, if you prefer, make a visual display that communicates the unique atmosphere of Granada.

LOPE de RUEDA

(1510–1565)

An early playwright and actor, Lope de Rueda was born in Seville. He began work as a goldsmith but soon left to join a band of strolling actors. At that time Spanish drama was dominated by highly formal religious dramas, but Rueda helped give it a new direction. His plays introduced comic roles that included fools and rascals and used natural, everyday speech. These changes, along with the joyful vitality of his plays, helped to popularize drama and move it into the marketplace, where it could be widely enjoyed by the common people.

Perhaps Rueda's most significant contribution was his creation of the *paso*, a short skit performed between the acts of longer plays. These skits were usually comedies that featured peasants and displayed a delightful spirit of absurdity. The short play that appears below, called *The Olives,* is an example of a *paso*. With these little comedies, performed during intermissions, Rueda fathered the one-act play, the most popular dramatic form in Spain. ■

THE OLIVES

Translated by Angel Flores

CHARACTERS

TORUBIO, *an old man*

AGUEDA DE TORUEGANO, *his wife*

MENCIGUELA, *their daughter*

ALOJA, *a neighbor*

TORUBIO. Good Lord, the storm certainly has razed the fields! All the way to the mountain clearing yonder! I remember how the bottom simply dropped out of the sky and clouds came crashing down.
    Well now, I wonder what that wife of mine has up her sleeve for supper—a pox on her! (*calling*) Agueda, Menciguela, Agueda de Toruegano! (*He bangs furiously at the door.*) (*Enter* MENCIGUELA.)

MENCIGUELA. Mercy, father! Do you always have to smash doors?

TORUBIO. There's a sharp tongue for you! Where's your mother, Miss Chatterbox?

MENCIGUELA. She's next door, helping out with the sewing.

TORUBIO. Blast her sewing and yours! Go call her! (*Enter* AGUEDA.)

AGUEDA. Well, well! Just look at our lord and master, in one of his nasty moods. What a wretched little bundle of fagots he's loaded on his back!

TORUBIO. Wretched, is it, my fine lady? Why, it took two of us—me and your godson together—to lift it from the ground!

AGUEDA. Hmm—well, maybe! Oh, my, you're soaking wet!

TORUBIO. Drenched to the bone! But for God's sake, bring me something to eat!

AGUEDA. What the devil do you expect? There's not a thing in the house.

MENCIGUELA. How wet this wood is, father!

TORUBIO. Of course it is. But you know your mother; she'll say it's only dew!

AGUEDA. Run, child, go cook your father a couple of eggs, and make his bed.

(*Exit* MENCIGUELA.)

AGUEDA. I suppose you forgot all about the olive-shoot I asked you to plant?

TORUBIO. If not for that, I'd be home before this.

AGUEDA. You don't say! And where did you plant it?

TORUBIO. Close to the new-bearing fig tree; you remember, where I kissed you long, long ago . . . (*Enter* MENCIGUELA.)

MENCIGUELA. Come, father, everything's ready!

AGUEDA. Know what I was thinking? In six or seven years we'll have seven or eight bushels of olives, and if we plant a shoot here and a shoot there every now and then we'll have a wonderful grove in another twenty-five years.

TORUBIO. Right you are, Agueda, a fine-looking grove!

AGUEDA. And you know what? I'll gather the olives, you'll cart them off on your little donkey, and Menciguela will sell them in the market. (*turning to* MENCIGUELA) But listen to me, Menciguela, don't you dare sell them for less than two Castilian reals[1] a half peck!

TORUBIO. Good gracious, woman! What are you talking about? Two Castilian reals? Why, such a price would give us nightmares.

---

1. **Castilian reals:** former Spanish coins, eight of which made the piece of eight or Spanish dollar, which was roughly equivalent to the U. S. dollar.

Besides, the market-inspector would never allow it! Fourteen, or at most fifteen dineros[2] a half peck is quite enough to ask.

AGUEDA. Bosh, Torubio! You're forgetting that our olives are the finest Cordovans in Spain!

TORUBIO. Even if they are from Cordova, my price is just right.

AGUEDA. Bother your prices! Menciguela, don't you sell our olives for less than two Castilian reals a half peck!

TORUBIO. What do you mean, "Two Castilian reals"? Come here, Menciguela, how much are you going to ask?

MENCIGUELA. Whatever you say, father.

TORUBIO. Fourteen or fifteen dineros.

MENCIGUELA. So be it, father.

AGUEDA. What do you mean, "So be it, father"? Come here, Menciguela, how much are you going to ask?

MENCIGUELA. Whatever you say, mother.

AGUEDA. Two Castilian reals.

MENCIGUELA. Two Castilian reals.

TORUBIO. What do you mean, "Two Castilian reals"? Let me tell you that if you disobey my orders, you'll surely get two hundred lashes from me. How much are you going to ask, Menciguela?

MENCIGUELA. Whatever you say, father,

TORUBIO. Fourteen or fifteen dineros.

MENCIGUELA. So be it, father.

AGUEDA. What do you mean, "So be it, father"? (*striking* MENCIGUELA) Here, take this "so-be-it" and that "so-be-it," and this, and that—that will teach you!

TORUBIO. Leave the child alone!

MENCIGUELA. Ouch, mamma, stop! Father, she's killing me! . . . Help! Help! . . . (*Enter* ALOJA.)

ALOJA. What's wrong, neighbors? Why are you beating your daughter?

AGUEDA. Oh, good sir, this awful man is giving things away. He has made up his mind to send his family to the poorhouse. Imagine, olives as big as walnuts!

---

2. **dineros:** former Spanish coins.

TORUBIO. I swear by the bones of my ancestors that they're no bigger than pistachio nuts!

AGUEDA. They certainly are!

TORUBIO. They are not!

ALOJA. Very well, my dear lady, please do me the favor of going inside and I'll try to settle the matter.

AGUEDA. You mean muddle it up worse! (*Exit* AGUEDA.)

ALOJA. Now, dear neighbor, how about the olives? Show them to me and I'll buy them all—up to thirty bushels worth.

TORUBIO. But you don't understand at all! You see, my friend, the olives are not here at home, they're there, out in the fields.

ALOJA. If that's the case, you'll harvest them and I'll give you a fair price for the whole lot of them.

MENCIGUELA. Mother says she must get two Castilian reals a half peck.

ALOJA. My, my, but that's high!

TORUBIO. See what I mean?

MENCIGUELA. My father wants fifteen dineros a half peck.

ALOJA. Show us a sample.

TORUBIO. In God's name, señor, you don't seem to understand! Today I planted the shoot of an olive-tree and my wife claims that in six or seven years she'll gather seven or eight bushels. Then I'll take them to market and our daughter will sell them. She wants her to ask for two Castilian reals per half peck. But I object. My wife insists; so what with one word leading to the next, it turned into a squabble.

ALOJA. A squabble, bah! The trees aren't even planted and you fools beat this poor child for quoting the wrong price!

MENCIGUELA. What shall I do, señor?

TORUBIO. Don't cry, darling! She's pure gold, sir. Run and set the table, and as soon as I make the first sale I'll see to it that you get the prettiest skirt in town.

ALOJA. And you, neighbor, go in and make peace with your wife.

TORUBIO. Good-bye, señor.

(*Exeunt* TORUBIO *and* MENCIGUELA.)

ALOJA. O Lord, what strange things one has to witness in life! The trees haven't even been planted but everyone's up in arms about the olives! A good reason for me to put an end to my mission!

DISCUSSION QUESTIONS

1. How would you describe the mood of this play? If you were directing it, what stage devices (such as scenery and props) might you use to communicate this mood?

2. This entire play centers on an argument between a husband and wife. In the opening lines of the play how does the author prepare us for the likelihood of an argument? What is the subject of the argument?

3. How would you describe Menciguela, the daughter of the old couple? What does her presence add to the play?

4. Has Torubio learned anything by the end of the play? How do you know?

SUGGESTION FOR WRITING

The Olives is obviously based on an old proverb, which is variously expressed as "Don't count your chickens before they hatch," "Don't cross that bridge until you come to it," and (in Spanish) "Don't sell the bearskin before you kill the bear." Select one of the following proverbs and write a short skit that dramatizes the truth of the saying:

- All that glitters is not gold.

- United we stand, divided we fall.

- The pot should not call the kettle black.

- A stitch in time saves nine.

LOPE de VEGA

(1562–1635)

Probably Spain's greatest dramatist, Lope de Vega was born in Madrid and lived an adventurous and turbulent life. In addition to being a writer, he was a scholar, soldier, priest, and famous lover. As a result of his first love affair, he was imprisoned and banished from Madrid for eight years. After several other mistresses and wives, he eventually met the love of his life, Marta de Nevares. This relationship ended tragically, as she was eventually afflicted with blindness, followed by insanity and death. Shortly afterward, Lope de Vega's son drowned and his daughter was abducted. Engulfed in personal grief and believing that he was being punished for his wild past, he did penance by whipping himself on a regular basis for the rest of his life.

Lope de Vega was an extremely productive writer, with estimates of his dramatic works running as high as 2,000, of which fewer than 500 survive. His plays, which were written primarily for the common people, usually feature playful dialogue, exciting situations, and a complex plot containing a rapid succession of lively scenes. His most frequent themes involve conflicts of passion and honor. The first dramatist to draw on traditions that were uniquely Spanish, Lope de Vega made wide use of Spanish history, folklore, and values in his works. ■

FUENTE OVEJUNA

Translated by Angel Flores and Muriel Kittel

CHARACTERS

QUEEN ISABELLA OF CASTILE

KING FERDINAND OF ARAGON

RODRIGO TÉLLEZ GIRÓN, *Master of the religious and military Order of Calatrava*

FERNAN GÓMEZ DE GUZMÁN, *Commander of the Order of Calatrava*

DON MANRIQUE

A JUDGE

TWO COUNCILMEN OF CIUDAD REAL

FLORES
ORTUNO } *servants of the Commander*

ESTEBAN
ALONZO } *Mayors of Fuente Ovejuna*

LAURENCIA ⎤
JACINTA ⎬ *Peasant Girls*
PASCUALA ⎦

JUAN ROJO, *Councilman of Fuente Ovejuna, a peasant*

ANOTHER COUNCILMAN OF FUENTE OVEJUNA

FRONDOSO ⎤
MENGO ⎬ *Peasants*
BARRILDO ⎦

LEONELO, *Licentiate of Law*

CIMBRANOS, *a soldier*

A BOY

PEASANTS, MEN AND WOMEN

MUSICIANS

TIME: 1476

ACT ONE

SCENE 1: *Hall of the* MASTER OF THE ORDER OF CALATRAVA, *in Almagro.*

(*Enter the* COMMANDER *and his servants,* FLORES *and* ORTUNO.)

COMMANDER. Does the Master know that I am here?

FLORES. He does, my lord.

ORTUNO. The Master is becoming more mature.

COMMANDER. Does he know that I am Fernan Gómez de Guzmán?

FLORES. He's only a boy—you mustn't be surprised if he doesn't.

COMMANDER. Nevertheless he must know that I am the Comendador.

ORTUNO. There are those who advise him to be discourteous.

COMMANDER. That will win him little love. Courtesy is the key to good will, while thoughtless discourtesy is the way to make enemies.

ORTUNO. If we but realized how it makes us hated and despised by everyone we would rather die than be discourteous.

FLORES. What a nuisance discourtesy is: among equals it's foolish and toward inferiors it's tyrannical. In this case it only means that the boy has not learned what it is to be loved.

COMMANDER. The obligation he took upon himself when he accepted his sword and the Cross of Calatrava[1] was placed on his breast should have been enough to teach him courtesy.

FLORES. If he has been prejudiced against you you'll soon find out.

ORTUNO. Why don't you leave if you're in doubt?

COMMANDER. I wish to see what he is like.

(*Enter the master of* CALATRAVA *and* RETINUE.)

MASTER. Pardon me, Fernan Gómez de Guzmán; I only just heard that you had come. Forgive me if I have kept you waiting.

COMMANDER. I have just cause for complaint. Both my love for you and my rank entitle me to better treatment—for you are the Master of Calatrava and I your Commander and your servant.

MASTER. I did not know of your welcome arrival—let me embrace you again.

COMMANDER. You owe me a great deal; I have risked my life to settle your many difficulties. I even managed to persuade the Pope to increase your age.[2]

MASTER. That is true, and by the holy cross which we both proudly bear on our breasts I shall repay you in love, and honor you as my own father.

COMMANDER. I am satisfied that you will.

MASTER. What news of the war?

COMMANDER. Listen carefully, and I will tell you where your duty lies.

MASTER. I am listening; tell me.

COMMANDER. Master Don Rodrigo Téllez Girón, I need hardly remind you how your brave father resigned his high position as Master to you eight years ago, and appointed Don Juan Pacheco, the Grand Master of Santiago, to be your coadjutor, nor how kings and commanders confirmed and swore to his act, and the Pope and his successor Paul agreed to it in their bulls;[3] no, what I have come to tell you is this: now that Pacheco is dead and you, in spite of

---

1. **Cross of Calatrava:** The Order of Calatrava, a military knighthood founded in 1158, commanded the Territory of Campo de Calatrava, of which Almagro was the capital city. The order's symbol was a red cross.

2. **persuade the Pope to increase your age:** The government of Spain at this time was a mixture of territorial kings and nobles, all of whom swore allegiance to the Pope. Thus the Pope's official sanction of the youth's right to govern enhanced Girón's power.

your youth, have sole control of the government, now is the time for you to take up arms for the honor of your family. Since the death of Henry IV your relatives have supported the cause of Don Alonso, King of Portugal, who claims the throne of Castile through his wife Juana.[4] Ferdinand, the great prince of Aragon, makes a similar claim through his wife Isabella. But your relatives do not consider Ferdinand's rights to be as clear as those of Juana—who is now in your cousin's power. So I advise you to rally the knights of Calatrava in Almagro and to capture Ciudad Real, which stands on the frontier between Andalusia and Castile. You will not need many men, because the enemy can count only on their neighbors and a few noblemen who support Isabella and consider Ferdinand their legitimate king. It will be wonderful if you, Rodrigo, if you, a youth, can astonish those who say that this cross is too heavy for your young shoulders. Emulate the counts of Uruena from whom you spring, and who from the height of their fame seem to be challenging you with the laurels they have won; emulate the marquises of Villena and those other captains who are so numerous that the wings of fame are not strong enough to bear them. Unsheathe your white sword, dye it red in battle till it matches the cross upon your breast. For I cannot call you the Master of the Red Cross as long as your sword is white: both the sword you bear and the cross you wear must be red. And you, mighty Girón, must add the crowning glory to the immortal fame of your ancestors.

MASTER. Fernan Gómez, you may be sure that I side with my family in this dispute, for I am convinced that they are right. And as I translate my conviction into action at Ciudad Real you will see me tearing the city walls down with the violence of a thunderbolt. I know that I am young—but do not think that my courage died with my uncle's death. I will unsheathe my white sword and its brilliance shall become the color of the cross, bathed in red blood.
But tell me, where do you live, and do you have any soldiers?

COMMANDER. A few—but they are faithful and they will fight like lions. I live in Fuente Ovejuna,[5] where the people are skilled in agriculture and husbandry rather than in the arts of war.

MASTER. And you live there, you say?

---

3. **bulls:** formal announcements from the Pope.

4. **Henry IV . . . Juana:** Henry IV was king of Castile from 1454 to his death in 1474. Since there was no rule of succession to the throne of Castile, at Henry's death both Ferdinand of Aragon and Don Alonso of Portugal claimed it through their wives: Ferdinand by his marriage to Henry's sister, Isabella, and Don Alonso by his marriage to Henry's daughter, Juana.

5. **Fuente Ovejuna:** the name means "sheep wash," the place where sheep are cleaned before they are sheared.

COMMANDER. I do. I chose a house on my estate to stay in during these troubled times. Now see that all your people go into action with you—let no man stay behind!

MASTER. You shall see me today on horseback, bearing my lance on high.

(*Exeunt* COMMANDER *and* MASTER.)

SCENE 2: *A public square in Fuente Ovejuna.*

(*Enter* LAURENCIA *and* PASCUALA.)

LAURENCIA. I hoped he would never come back.

PASCUALA. I must say I thought you'd be more distressed at the news.

LAURENCIA. I hoped to God I'd never see him again.

PASCUALA. I have seen women just as adamant as you, Laurencia, if not more so—and yet, underneath, their hearts were as soft as butter.

LAURENCIA. Well, is there an oak tree as hard as I am?

PASCUALA. Be careful. No one should boast that he'll never thirst for water.

LAURENCIA. But I do. And I'll maintain it against the world. What good would it do me to love Fernan? Do you think I would marry him?

PASCUALA. Of course not.

LAURENCIA. Well then, I condemn infamy. Too many girls hereabouts have trusted the Commander only to be ruined by him.

PASCUALA. All the same it will be a miracle if you escape him.

LAURENCIA. You don't understand, Pascuala. He has been after me for a month now, but he has only been wasting his time. His emissary, Flores, and that blustering fool Ortuno have come to show me a blouse, a necklace, a hat, and have told me so many wonderful stories about their lord and master that they have succeeded in frightening me but not in moving my heart.

PASCUALA. Where did they talk to you?

LAURENCIA. Down there by the brook, about six days ago.

PASCUALA. It looks as if they are trying to deceive you, Laurencia.

LAURENCIA. Deceive me?

PASCUALA. If not you, then the priest.

LAURENCIA. I may be a young chicken, but I'm too tough for His Highness. Pascuala, I would far rather put a slice of ham on the fire in the early morning and eat it with my homemade bread and a glass of wine stolen from my mother, and then at noon to smell a piece of beef boiling with cabbage and eat it ravenously, or, if I have had a trying day, marry an eggplant to some bacon; and in the evening, while cooking the supper, go and pick a handful of grapes from the vines (God save them from the hail) and afterwards dine on chopped meat with oil and pepper, and so happily to bed murmuring "Lead us not into temptation"—I would much rather this than all the wiles and tricks of scoundrels. For after all, all they want after giving us so much trouble is their pleasure at night and our sorrow in the morning.

PASCUALA. You are right, Laurencia, for as soon as they tire of love they are more ungrateful than the sparrows are to the peasants. In winter when the fields are frozen hard the sparrows fly down from the roofs, and saying "Sweet Sweet," hop right on to the dining table for crumbs, but as soon as the cold is over and the fields are again in bloom they no longer come down saying "Sweet Sweet," but stay hopping on the roof, mocking us with their calls. Men are the same; when they need us nothing can be sweeter than they— we are their life, their soul, their heart, their all—but as soon as they tire of us their sweetness disappears and their wooing phrases become a mockery.

LAURENCIA. The moral of which is: trust no man, Pascuala.

PASCUALA. That's what I say.

(*Enter* FRONDOSO, BARRILDO, *and* MENGO.)

FRONDOSO. You are wrong, Barrildo, in this argument.

BARRILDO. Well never mind, here's somebody who will settle the matter.

MENGO. Let's have an understanding before we reach them: if I'm right, then each of you gives me a present as a reward.

BARRILDO. All right. But if you lose, what will you give?

MENGO. I'll give my boxwood rebec,[6] which I value more than a barn.

BARRILDO. That's fine.

FRONDOSO. Let's approach them. God bless you, fair ladies.

LAURENCIA. You call us ladies, Frondoso?

---

6. boxwood rebec: a pear-shaped string instrument.

FRONDOSO. We want to keep up with the times. In these days all bachelors are licentiates; the blind are one-eyed; the cross-eyed merely squint; and the lame have only a sprained ankle. The unscrupulous are called honest; the ignorant, clever; and the braggart, brave. A large mouth is described as luscious, a small eye as sharp. The pettifogger is called diligent; the busybody, charming; the charlatan, sympathetic; the deadly bore, gallant. The cowardly become valiant; the hard-headed, vivacious; coxcombs are comrades; fools, broad-minded; malcontents, philosophers. Baldness is identified with authority, foolish chatter with wit. People with tumors have only a slight cold, and those who are arrogant are circumspect; the shifty are constant; and the humpbacked, just slightly bent. This, in short—the enumeration could go on indefinitely—was the sort of thing I did in calling you ladies. I merely followed the fashion of the day.

LAURENCIA. In the city, Frondoso, such words are used in courtesy; discourteous tongues use a severer and more acrimonious vocabulary.

FRONDOSO. I should like to hear it.

LAURENCIA. It's the very opposite of yours. The serious-minded are called bores; the unfortunate, lucky; the even-tempered, melancholy; and anyone who expresses disapproval is hateful. Those who offer good advice are importunate; the liberal-minded are dull-witted; the just, unjust; and the pious, weak-kneed. In this language the faithful become inconstant; the courteous, flatterers; the charitable, hypocrites; and the good Christians, frauds. Anyone who has won a well-deserved reward is called fortunate; truth becomes impudence; patience, cowardice; and misfortune, retribution. The modest woman is foolish; the beautiful and chaste, unnatural; and the honorable woman is called . . . But enough! This reply should be sufficient.

MENGO. You little devil!

LAURENCIA. What an elegant expression.

MENGO. I bet the priest poured handfuls of salt[7] on her when he christened her.

LAURENCIA. What was the argument that brought you here, if we may ask?

FRONDOSO. Listen, Laurencia.

LAURENCIA. Speak.

---

7. **handfuls of salt:** During the rite, the priest would put a few grains of salt, symbolic of wisdom and incorruption, on the infant's tongue.

FRONDOSO. Lend me your ear, Laurencia.

LAURENCIA. Lend it to you? Why, I'll give it to you right now.

FRONDOSO. I trust your discretion.

LAURENCIA. Well, what was the wager about?

FRONDOSO. Barrildo and I wagered against Mengo.

LAURENCIA. And what does Mengo claim?

BARRILDO. It is something that he insists on denying, although it is plainly a fact.

MENGO. I deny it because I know better.

LAURENCIA. But what is it?

BARRILDO. He claims that love does not exist.

LAURENCIA. Many people think that.

BARRILDO. Many people do, but it's foolish. Without love not even the world could exist.

MENGO. I don't know how to philosophize; as for reading, I wish I could! But I say that if the elements of Nature live in eternal conflict, then our bodies, which receive from them food, anger, melancholy, phlegm, and blood, must also be at war with each other.

BARRILDO. The world here and beyond, Mengo, is perfect harmony. Harmony is pure love, for love is complete agreement.

MENGO. As far as the natural world goes, I do not deny it. There is love which rules all things through an obligating interrelationship. I have never denied that each person has love proportionate to his humor—my hand will protect me from the blow aimed at my face, my foot will protect me from harm by enabling me to flee danger, my eyelids will protect my eyes from threatening specks— such is love in nature.

PASCUALA. What are you trying to prove, then?

MENGO. That individuals love only themselves.

PASCUALA. Pardon me, Mengo, for telling you that you lie. For it is a lie. The intensity with which a man loves a woman or an animal its mate . . .

MENGO. I call that self-love, not love. What is love?

LAURENCIA. A desire for beauty.

MENGO. And why does love seek beauty?

LAURENCIA. To enjoy it.

MENGO. That's just what I believe. Is not such enjoyment selfish?

LAURENCIA. That's right.

MENGO. Therefore a person seeks that which brings him joy.

LAURENCIA. That is true.

MENGO. Hence there is no love but the kind I speak of, the one I pursue for my personal pleasure, and which I enjoy.

BARRILDO. One day the priest said in a sermon that there was a man named Plato who taught how to love, and that this man loved only the soul and the virtues of the beloved.

PASCUALA. You have raised a question which the wise men in their schools and academies cannot solve.

LAURENCIA. He speaks the truth; do not try to refute his argument. Be thankful, Mengo, that Heaven made you without love.

MENGO. Are you in love?

LAURENCIA. I love my honor.

FRONDOSO. May God punish you with jealousy.

BARRILDO. Who has won the wager then?

PASCUALA. Go to the sacristan with your dispute, for either he or the priest will give you the best answer. Laurencia does not love deeply, and as for me, I have little experience. How are we to pass judgment?

FRONDOSO. What can be a better judgment than her disdain?

(*Enter* FLORES.)

FLORES. God be with you!

PASCUALA. Here is the Commander's servant.

LAURENCIA. His goshawk,[8] you mean. Where do *you* come from, my good friend?

FLORES. Don't you see my soldier's uniform?

LAURENCIA. Is Don Fernan coming back?

FLORES. Yes, the war is over, and though it has cost us some blood and some friends, we are victorious.

FRONDOSO. Tell us what happened.

FLORES. Who could do that better than I? I saw everything. For his campaign against this city, which is now called Ciudad Real, the

---

8. goshawk: a powerful hawk used in falconry.

valiant Master raised an army of two thousand brave infantry from among his vassals and three hundred cavalry from laymen and friars. For even those who belong to Holy Orders are obliged to fight for their emblem of the red cross—provided, of course, that the war is against the Moors.[9] The high-spirited youth rode out to battle wearing a green coat embroidered with golden scrolls; the sleeves were fastened with six hooks, so that only his gauntlets showed beneath them. His horse was a dappled roan, bred on the banks of the Betis, drinking its waters and grazing on its lush grass. Its tailpiece was decorated with buckskin straps, the curled panache[10] with white knots that matched the snowflakes covering its mane. Our lord, Fernan Gómez, rode at the Master's side on a powerful honey-colored horse with black legs and mane and a white muzzle. Over a Turkish coat of mail he wore a magnificent breast-and-back plate with orange fringes and resplendent with gold and pearls. His white plumes seemed to shower orange blossoms on his bronze helmet. His red and white band flashed on his arm as he brandished an ash tree for a lance, making himself feared even in Granada. The city rushed to arms; the inhabitants apparently did not come out to fight but stayed within the city walls to defend their property. But in spite of the strong resistance the Master entered the city. He ordered the rebels and those who had flagrantly dishonored him to be beheaded, and the lower classes were gagged and whipped in public. He remained in the city and is so feared and loved that people prophesy great things for him. They say that a young man who has fought so gloriously and punished so severely all in a short time must one day fall on fertile Africa like a thunderbolt, and bring many blue moons under the red cross.[11] He made so many gifts to the Commander and his followers that he might have been disposing of his own estate rather than despoiling a city. But now the music sounds. The Commander comes. Welcome him with festivity, for good will is one of the most precious of a victor's laurels.

(*Enter the* COMMANDER *and* ORTUNO; MUSICIANS; JUAN ROJO, ESTEBAN, *and* ALONZO, *elders of the town.*)

MUSICIANS (*singing*).

Welcome, Commander,
Conqueror of lands and men!
Long live the Guzmánes!

---

9. **Moors:** Arab invaders of Spain. At this time Spain was in the last stage of Moorish influence. The Moors were finally driven out in 1492.

10. **panache** (pə nash´): tuft of feathers used as a headdress.

11. **blue moons . . . red cross:** emblems of the Moors and the Order of Calatrava, respectively.

Long live the Girónes!
In peacetime gracious,
Gentle his reasoning,
When fighting the Moors
Strong as an oak.
From Ciudad Real
He comes victorious,
Bearing to Fuente Ovejuna
Its banners in triumph.
Long live Fernan Gómez,
Long live the hero!

COMMANDER. Citizens of Fuente Ovejuna, I am most grateful to you for the love you show me.

ALONZO. It is but a small part of the love we feel, and no matter how great our love it is less than you deserve.

ESTEBAN. Fuente Ovejuna and its elders, whom you have honored with your presence, beg you to accept a humble gift. In these carts, sir, we bring you an expression of gratitude rather than a display of wealth. There are two baskets filled with earthenware, a flock of geese that stretch their heads out of their nets to praise your valor in battle; ten salted hogs, prize specimens, more precious than amber; and a hundred pairs of capons and hens, which leave the cocks of the neighboring villages desolate. You will find no arms, no horses, no harnesses studded with pure gold. The only gold is the love your vassals feel towards you. And for purity you could find nothing greater than those twelve skins of wine. That wine could give warmth and courage to your soldiers even unclothed in the dead of winter; it will be as important as steel in the defense of your walls. I leave unmentioned the cheese and other victuals: they are a fitting tribute from our people to you. May you and yours enjoy our gifts.

COMMANDER. I am very grateful to you for all of them. Go now and rest.

ESTEBAN. Feel at home in this town, my lord! I wish the reeds of mace and sedge that we placed on our doors to celebrate your triumphs were oriental pearls. You deserve such tribute and more.

COMMANDER. Thank you, gentlemen. God be with you.

ESTEBAN. Singers, sing again.

MUSICIANS (*singing*).

Welcome, Commander,

Conqueror of lands and men!

(*Exeunt* ELDERS *and* MUSICIANS.)

COMMANDER. You two wait.

LAURENCIA. What is Your Lordship's pleasure?

COMMANDER. You scorned me a few days ago, didn't you?

LAURENCIA. Is he speaking to you, Pascuala?

PASCUALA. I should say not—not to me!

COMMANDER. I am talking to you, beautiful wildcat, and to the other girl too. Are you not mine, both of you?

PASCUALA. Yes, sir, to a certain extent.

COMMANDER. Go into the house. There are men inside, so you need not fear.

LAURENCIA. If the elders accompany us—I am the daughter of one of them—it will be all right for us to go in too, but not otherwise.

COMMANDER. Flores!

FLORES. Sir?

COMMANDER. Why do they hesitate to do what I command?

FLORES. Come along, girls, come right in.

LAURENCIA. Let me go!

FLORES. Come in, girl, don't be silly.

PASCUALA. So that you can lock us in? No thank you!

FLORES. Come on. He wants to show you his spoils of war.

COMMANDER (*aside to* ORTUNO). Lock the door after them,

(*Exit* COMMANDER.)

LAURENCIA. Flores, let us pass.

ORTUNO. Aren't you part of the gifts of the village?

PASCUALA. That's what you think! Out of my way, fool, before I . . .

FLORES. Leave them alone. They're too unreasonable.

LAURENCIA. Isn't your master satisfied with all the meat given him today?

ORTUNO. He seems to prefer yours.

LAURENCIA. Then he can starve!

(*Exeunt* LAURENCIA *and* PASCUALA.)

FLORES. A fine message for us to bring! He'll swear at us when we appear before him empty-handed.

ORTUNO. That's a risk servants always run. When he realizes the situation he'll either calm down or else leave at once.

SCENE 3: *Chamber of the Catholic Kings, in Medina del Campo.*

(*Enter* KING FERDINAND OF ARAGON, QUEEN ISABELLA, MANRIQUE *and* ATTENDANTS.)

ISABELLA. I think it would be wise to be prepared, Your Majesty— especially since Don Alfonso of Portugal is encamped there. It is better for us to strike the first blow than to wait for the enemy to attack us.

KING. We can depend on Navarre and Aragon for assistance, and I'm trying to reorganize things in Castile so as to ensure our success there.

ISABELLA. I'm confident your plan will succeed.

MANRIQUE. Two councilmen from Ciudad Real seek audience with Your Majesty.

KING. Let it be granted them.

(*Enter* TWO COUNCILMEN *of Ciudad Real.*)

FIRST COUNCILMAN. Most Catholic King of Aragon, whom God has sent to Castile to protect us, we appear as humble petitioners before you to beg the assistance of your great valor for our city of Ciudad Real. We are proud to consider ourselves your vassals, a privilege granted us by a royal charter but which an unkind fate threatens to take away. Don Rodrigo Téllez Girón, famous for the valiant actions that belie his youth, and ambitious to augment his power, recently laid close siege to our city. We prepared to meet his attack with bravery, and resisted his forces so fiercely that rivers of blood streamed from our innumerable dead. He finally conquered us—but only because of the advice and assistance given him by Fernan Gómez. Girón remains in possession of our city, and unless we can remedy our disaster soon we will have to acknowledge ourselves his vassals against our will.

KING. Where is Fernan Gómez now?

SECOND COUNCILMAN. In Fuente Ovejuna, I think. That is his native town and his home is there. But the truth is, his subjects are far from contented.

KING. Do you have a leader?

SECOND COUNCILMAN. No, we have none, Your Majesty. Not one nobleman escaped imprisonment, injury, or death.

ISABELLA. This matter requires swift action, for delay will only work to the advantage of the impudent Girón. Furthermore the King of Portugal will soon realize that he can use him to gain entry to Extremadura, and so cause us much damage.

KING. Don Manrique, leave at once with two companies. Be relentless in avenging the wrongs this city has suffered. Let the Count of Cabra go with you. The Cordovan is recognized by everyone as a brave soldier. This is the best plan for the moment.

MANRIQUE. I think the plan is an excellent one. As long as I live, his excesses shall be curbed.

ISABELLA. With your help we are sure to succeed.

SCENE 4: *The countryside near Fuente Ovejuna.*

(Enter LAURENCIA and FRONDOSO.)

LAURENCIA. You are very stubborn, Frondoso. I left the brook with my washing only half wrung out, so as to give no occasion for gossip— yet you persist in following me. It seems that everyone in town is saying that you are running after me and I after you. And because you are the sort of fellow who struts about and shows off his clothes, which are more fashionable and expensive than other people's, all the girls and boys in the countryside think there must be something between us. They are all waiting for the day when Juan Chamorro will put down his flute and lead us to the altar. I wish they would occupy their minds with things that are more their business—why don't they imagine that their granaries are bursting with red wheat, or that their wine jars are full of dregs? Their gossip annoys me, but not so much that it keeps me awake at night.

FRONDOSO. Your disdain and beauty are so great, Laurencia, that when I see you and listen to you I fear they will kill me. You know that my only wish is to become your husband: is it fair then to reward my love in this way?

LAURENCIA. I know no other way.

FRONDOSO. Can you feel no pity for my troubled mind, no sympathy for my sad condition when you know I cannot eat or drink or sleep for thinking of you? Is it possible that such a gentle face can hide so much unkindness? Heavens! You'll drive me mad.

LAURENCIA. Why don't you take medicine for your condition, Frondoso?

FRONDOSO. You are the only medicine I need, Laurencia. Come with me to the altar, and let us live like turtledoves, billing and cooing, after the church has blessed us.

LAURENCIA. You had better ask my uncle, Juan Rojo. I'm not passionately in love with you . . . but there is hope that I might be in time.

FRONDOSO. Oh—here comes the Commander!

LAURENCIA. He must be hunting deer. Hide behind these bushes.

FRONDOSO. I will. But I'll be full of jealousy.

(*Enter the* COMMANDER.)

COMMANDER. This is good luck. My chase of the timid fawn has led me to a lovely doe instead.

LAURENCIA. I was resting a bit from my washing. By Your Lordship's leave I'll return to the brook.

COMMANDER. Such disdain, fair Laurencia, is an insult to the beauty Heaven gave you; it turns you into a monster. On other occasions you have succeeded in eluding my desires—but now we are alone in these solitary fields where no one can help you. Now, with no one to witness, you cannot be so stubborn and so proud, you cannot turn your face away without loving me. Did not Salustiana, the wife of Pedro Redondo, surrender to me—and Martin del Pozo's wife, too, only two days after her wedding?

LAURENCIA. These women, sir, had had others before you and knew the road to pleasure only too well. Many men have enjoyed *their* favors. Go, pursue your deer, and God be with you. You persecute me so that were it not for the cross you wear I should think you were the devil.

COMMANDER. You little spitfire! (*Aside.*) I had better put my bow down and take her by force.

LAURENCIA. What? . . . What are you doing? Are you mad?

(*Enter* FRONDOSO, *who picks up the bow.*)

COMMANDER. Don't struggle. It won't help you.

FRONDOSO (*aside*). I'll pick up his bow, but I hope I don't have to use it.

COMMANDER. Come on, you might as well give in now.

LAURENCIA. Heaven help me now!

COMMANDER. We are alone. Don't be afraid.

FRONDOSO. Generous Commander, leave the girl alone. For much as I respect the cross on your breast, it will not stop me from aiming this bow at you if you do not let her go.

COMMANDER. You dog, you peasant slave!

FRONDOSO. There's no dog here. Laurencia, go quickly now.

LAURENCIA. Take care of yourself, Frondoso.

FRONDOSO. Run . . .

(*Exit* LAURENCIA.)

COMMANDER. What a fool I was to put down my sword so as not to frighten my quarry!

FRONDOSO. Do you realize, sir, that I have only to touch this string to bring you down like a bird?

COMMANDER. She's gone. You damned, treacherous villain. Put that bow down, put it down, I say.

FRONDOSO. Put it down? Why? So that you can shoot me? No, love is deaf, remember, and hears nothing when it comes into its own.

COMMANDER. Do you think a knight surrenders to a peasant? Shoot, you villain, shoot and be damned or I'll break the law of chivalry.

FRONDOSO. No, not that. I'm satisfied with my station in life, and since I must preserve my life, I'll take your bow with me.

(*Exit* FRONDOSO.)

COMMANDER. What a strange experience! But I'll avenge this insult and remove this obstacle . . . But to let him go! My God, how humiliating!

ACT TWO

SCENE 1: *The Plaza of Fuente Ovejuna.*

(*Enter* ESTEBAN *and* FIRST COUNCILMAN.)

ESTEBAN. I don't think any more grain should be taken out of our community granaries, even though they are full right now. It's getting late in the year, and the harvest looks poor. I think it's better to have provisions stored up in case of emergency—though I know some people have other ideas.

FIRST COUNCILMAN. I agree with you. And I've always tried to administer the land along such peaceable ways.

ESTEBAN. Well, let's tell Fernan Gómez what we think about it. We shouldn't let those astrologers, who are so ignorant of the future, persuade us that they know all the secrets that are only God's business. They pretend to be as learned as the theologians the way they mix up the past and the future—but if you ask them anything about the immediate present they are completely at a loss. Do they have the clouds and the course of the sun, the moon, and the stars locked up at home that they can tell us what is happening up there and what is going to bring us grief? At seed time they levy tax on us; give us just so much wheat, oats and vegetables, pumpkins, cucumbers, mustard . . . Then they tell us someone has died, and later we discover it happened in Transylvania; they tell us that wine will be scarce and beer plentiful—somewhere in Germany; that cherries will freeze in Gascony, or hordes of tigers will prowl through Hircania. Their final prophecy is that whether we sow or not the year will end in December!

(*Enter the licentiate* LEONELO *and* BARRILDO.)

LEONELO. You won't be awarded the hickory stick to beat the other students with, for it's already been won by somebody else.

BARRILDO. How did you get on at Salamanca?

LEONELO. That's a long story.

BARRILDO. You must be a very learned man by now.

LEONELO. No, I'm not even a barber. The things I was telling you about happen all the time in the school I was at.

BARRILDO. At least you are a scholar now.

LEONELO. Well, I've tried to learn things that are important.

BARRILDO. Anyone who has seen so many printed books is bound to think he is wise.

LEONELO. Froth and confusion are the chief results of so much reading matter. Even the most voracious reader gets sick of seeing so many titles. I admit that printing has saved many talented writers from oblivion, and enshrined their works above the ravages of time. Printing circulates their books and makes them known. Gutenberg, a famous German from Mainz, is responsible for this invention. But many men who used to have a high reputation are no longer taken seriously now that their works have been printed. Some people put their ignorance in print, passing it off as wisdom; others inspired by envy write down their crazy ideas and send them into the world under the name of their enemies.

BARRILDO. That's a disgraceful practice.

LEONELO. Well, it's natural for ignorant people to want to discredit scholars.

BARRILDO. But in spite of all this, Leonelo, you must admit that printing is important.

LEONELO. The world got on very well without it for a good many centuries—and no Saint Jerome or Saint Augustine has appeared since we have had it.

BARRILDO. Take it easy, Leonelo. You're getting all worked up about this printing business.

(*Enter* JUAN ROJO *and another* PEASANT.)

JUAN ROJO. Four farms put together would not raise one dowry, if they're all like the one we've just seen. It's obvious that both the land and the people are in a state of chaos.

PEASANT. What's the news of the Commander?—don't get excited now.

JUAN ROJO. How he tried to take advantage of Laurencia in this very field!

PEASANT. That lascivious brute! I'd like to see him hanging from that olive tree! . . .

(*Enter* COMMANDER, ORTUNO, *and* FLORES.)

COMMANDER. Good day to you all!

COUNCILMAN. Your Lordship!

COMMANDER. Please don't get up.

ESTEBAN. You sit down, my lord. We would rather stand.

COMMANDER. Do sit down.

ESTEBAN. Honor can only be rendered by those who have it themselves.

COMMANDER. Sit down, and let us talk things over calmly.

ESTEBAN. Has Your Lordship seen the hound I sent you?

COMMANDER. Mayor, my servants are all amazed by its great speed.

ESTEBAN. It really is a wonderful animal. It can overtake any culprit or coward who is trying to escape.

COMMANDER. I wish you would send it after a hare that keeps eluding me.

ESTEBAN. I'd be glad to. Whereabouts is this hare?

COMMANDER. It's your daughter.

ESTEBAN. My daughter!

COMMANDER. Yes.

ESTEBAN. But is she worth your while?

COMMANDER. Intervene in my favor, Mayor, for God's sake.

ESTEBAN. What has she done?

COMMANDER. She's determined to hurt me—while the wife of a nobleman here in town is dying for an opportunity to see me.

ESTEBAN. Then she would do wrong—and you do yourself no good to talk so flippantly.

COMMANDER. My, my, what a circumspect peasant! Flores, give him a copy of the *Politics* and tell him to read Aristotle.

ESTEBAN. My lord, the town's desire is to live peaceably under you. You must remember that there are many honorable persons living in Fuente Ovejuna.

LEONELO. Did you ever hear such impudence as this Commander's?

COMMANDER. Have I said anything to offend you, Councilman?

COUNCILMAN. Your pronouncements are unjust, my lord, and not worth uttering. It is unfair to try to take away our honor.

COMMANDER. Honor? Do you have honor? Listen to the saintly friars of Calatrava!

COUNCILMAN. Some people may boast of the cross you awarded them, but their blood is not as pure as you may think.

COMMANDER. Do I sully mine by mixing it with yours?

COUNCILMAN. Evil will sully it rather than cleanse it.

COMMANDER. However that may be, your women are honored by it.

ESTEBAN. Such words are dishonorable.

COMMANDER. What boors these peasants are! Ah, give me the cities, where nobody hinders the pleasures of lofty men. Husbands are glad when we make love to their wives.

ESTEBAN. They certainly should not be. Do you expect us to suffer such tribulations as readily? There is a God in the cities too, and punishment falls swiftly.

COMMANDER. Get out of here!

ESTEBAN. Are you talking to us?

COMMANDER. Get off the Plaza immediately. I don't want to see any of you around here.

ESTEBAN. We're going.

COMMANDER. Not in a group like that . . .

FLORES. I beg of you to control yourself.

COMMANDER. These peasants will gossip in groups behind my back.

ORTUNO. Have a little patience.

COMMANDER. I marvel that I have so much. Let each man go alone to his own house.

LEONELO. Good Heavens! Will the peasants stomach that?

ESTEBAN. I'm going this way.

(Exeunt PEASANTS.)

COMMANDER. What do you think of those fellows?

ORTUNO. You don't seem to be able to hide your emotions, yet you refuse to sense the ill feeling around you.

COMMANDER. But are these fellows my equals?

FLORES. It's not a question of equality.

COMMANDER. Is that peasant to keep my bow unpunished?

FLORES. Last night I thought I saw him by Laurencia's door and I gave him a slash from ear to ear—but it was someone else.

COMMANDER. I wonder where that Frondoso is now?

FLORES. They say he's around.

COMMANDER. So that's it. The villain who tried to murder me is allowed to go about scot-free.

FLORES. Don't worry. Sooner or later he'll fall into the snare like a stray bird, or be caught on the hook like a fish.

COMMANDER. But imagine—a peasant, a boy, to threaten me with my own crossbow, me, a captain whose sword made Cordova and Granada tremble! Flores, the world is coming to an end!

FLORES. Blame it on love.

ORTUNO. I suppose you spared him for friendship's sake.

COMMANDER. I have acted out of friendship, Ortuno, else I should have ransacked the town in a couple of hours. However, I plan to withhold my vengeance until the right moment arrives. And now—what news of Pascuala?

FLORES. She says she's about to get married.

COMMANDER. Is she going to that length?

FLORES. In other words, she's sending you to where you'll be paid in cash.

COMMANDER. What about Olalla?

ORTUNO. Her reply is charming.

COMMANDER. She's a gay young thing. What does she say?

ORTUNO. She says her husband follows her around all the time because he's jealous of my messages and your visits, but as soon as she manages to allay his fears you'll be the first to see her.

COMMANDER. Fine! Keep an eye on the old man.

ORTUNO. You'd better be careful.

COMMANDER. What news from Ines?

FLORES. Which Ines?

COMMANDER. The wife of Anton.

FLORES. She's ready when you are. I spoke to her in her backyard, through which you may go whenever you wish,

COMMANDER. Easy girls I love dearly and repay poorly. Flores, if they only knew their worth! . . .

(*Enter* CIMBRANOS, *a soldier.*)

CIMBRANOS. Is the Commander here?

ORTUNO. Don't you see him before you?

CIMBRANOS. Oh, valiant Fernan Gómez! Change your green cap for your shining helmet, and your cloak for a coat of mail! For the Master of Santiago and the Count of Cabra are attacking Rodrigo Girón, and laying siege to Ciudad Real in the name of the Queen of Castile. All that we won at so much cost in blood and men may soon be lost again. Already the banners of Aragon with their castles, lions, and bars, can be seen above the high towers of the city. Though the King of Portugal has paid homage to Girón, the Master of Calatrava may have to return to Almagro in defeat. Mount your horse, my lord, your presence alone will force the enemy back to Castile.

COMMANDER. Stop. That's enough. Ortuno, order a trumpet to sound at once in the Plaza. Tell me, how many soldiers do I have?

ORTUNO. Fifty, I believe, sir.

COMMANDER. Order them to horse.

CIMBRANOS. Ciudad Real will fall to the King if you do not hurry.

COMMANDER. Never fear, that shall not happen!

(*Exeunt all.*)

SCENE 2: *Open country near Fuente Ovejuna.*

(*Enter* MENGO, LAURENCIA, *and* PASCUALA, *running.*)

PASCUALA. Please don't leave us.

MENGO. Why? What are you afraid of?

LAURENCIA. Well, Mengo, we prefer to go to the village in groups when we don't have a man to go with us. We're afraid of meeting the Commander.

MENGO. What a cruel and importunate devil that man is.

LAURENCIA. He never stops pestering us.

MENGO. I wish God would strike him with a thunderbolt and put an end to his wickedness.

LAURENCIA. He's a bloodthirsty beast that poisons and infects the whole countryside.

MENGO. I hear that in trying to protect you, here in the meadow, Frondoso aimed his crossbow at the Commander

LAURENCIA. I used to hate men, Mengo, but since that day I've looked at them with different eyes. Frondoso acted so gallantly! But I'm afraid it may cost him his life.

MENGO. He'll be forced to leave the village.

LAURENCIA. I keep telling him to go away, although I love him dearly now. But he answers all such counsel with anger and contempt— and all the while the Commander threatens to hang him by the feet.

PASCUALA. I'd like to see that Commander carried off by the plague!

MENGO. I'd rather kill him with a mean stone. By God, if I threw a stone at him that I have up at the sheepfold, it would hit him so hard it would crush his skull in. The Commander is more vicious than that old Roman, Sabalus.

LAURENCIA. You mean Heliogabalus,[1] who was more wicked than a beast.

MENGO. Well, Galvan or whoever it was—I, don't know too much about history—the Commander surpasses him in wickedness. Can anyone be more despicable than Fernan Gómez?

PASCUALA. No one can compare with him. You'd think he'd sucked his cruelty from a tigress.

(*Enter* JACINTA.)

JACINTA. If friendship means anything, in God's name help me now!

LAURENCIA. What's happened, Jacinta, my friend?

PASCUALA. Both of us are your friends.

JACINTA. Some of the Commander's attendants are trying to take me to him. They're on their way to Ciudad Real, but they're acting more like villains than soldiers.

LAURENCIA. May God protect you, Jacinta! If the Commander is bold with you he'll be cruel to me.

(*Exit* LAURENCIA.)

PASCUALA. Jacinta, I'm not a man, so I can't defend you.

(*Exit* PASCUALA.)

MENGO. But I have both strength and reputation. Stand beside me, Jacinta.

JACINTA. Have you any arms?

MENGO. Yes, those that Nature gave me.

JACINTA. I wish you were armed.

MENGO. Never mind, Jacinta. There are plenty of stones around here.

(*Enter* FLORES *and* ORTUNO.)

FLORES. So you thought you could get away from us, did you?

JACINTA. Mengo, I'm dead with fear.

---

1. **Heliogabalus:** Roman emperor (A.D. 218–222) known for his debauchery and cruelty. He was also called Sabalus and Galvan.

MENGO. Gentlemen, this is a poor peasant girl . . .

ORTUNO. Oh, have you decided to defend young women?

MENGO. I'm merely asking for mercy. I'm her relative, and I hope to be able to keep her near me.

FLORES. Kill him off!

MENGO. By God, if you make me mad and I take out my sling, your life will be in danger!

(*Enter the* COMMANDER *and* CIMBRANOS.)

COMMANDER. What's all this? Do I have to get off my horse for some petty quarrel?

FLORES. You ought to destroy this miserable village for all the joy it brings you. These wretched peasants have dared to challenge our arms.

MENGO. My lord, if injustice can move you to pity, punish these soldiers who in your name are forcing this girl to leave her husband and honest parents. Grant me permission to take her home.

COMMANDER. I will grant them permission to punish you. Drop that sling!

MENGO. My lord!

COMMANDER. Flores, Ortuno, Cimbranos, tie his hands with it.

MENGO. Is this your justice?

COMMANDER. What do Fuente Ovejuna and its peasants think of me?

MENGO. My lord, how have I or Fuente Ovejuna offended you?

FLORES. Shall I kill him?

COMMANDER. Don't soil your arms with such trash. Keep them for better things.

ORTUNO. What are your orders?

COMMANDER. Flog him. Tie him to that oak tree and beat him with the reins.

MENGO. Pity, my lord, have pity, for you are a nobleman!

COMMANDER. Flog him till the rivets fall from the leather.

MENGO. My God. For such ugly deeds, uglier punishments!

(*Exeunt* MENGO, FLORES, *and* ORTUNO.)

COMMANDER. Now my girl, why were you running away? Do you prefer a peasant to a nobleman?

JACINTA. Can you restore the honor which your attendants have taken from me in bringing me to you?

COMMANDER. Do you mean to say your honor has been lost because I wanted to take you away?

JACINTA. Yes. For I have an honest father who, if he does not equal you in birth, surpasses you in virtue.

COMMANDER. All these troubles around this village, where peasants defy their betters, scarcely help to soothe my temper. Come along here now!

JACINTA. With whom?

COMMANDER. With me.

JACINTA. You had better think over what you're doing.

COMMANDER. I have thought it over, and it's so much the worse for you. Instead of keeping you for myself, I shall give you to my whole army.

JACINTA. No power on earth can inflict such an outrage on me while I live.

COMMANDER. Get a move on now, girl.

JACINTA. Sir, have pity!

COMMANDER. There is no pity.

JACINTA. I appeal from your cruelty to divine justice.

(*Exit* COMMANDER, *hauling her out.*)

SCENE 3: *Esteban's house.*

(*Enter* LAURENCIA *and* FRONDOSO.)

LAURENCIA. Are you unaware of your danger, that you dare to come here?

FRONDOSO. My daring is proof of my love for you. From that hill I saw the Commander riding away, and since I have complete confidence in you all my fear left with him. I hope he never comes back!

LAURENCIA. Don't curse him—for the more one wishes a person to die the longer he lives.

FRONDOSO. In that case may he live a thousand years, and so by wishing him well let's hope his end will be certain . . . Tell me, Laurencia, has my fondness for you affected you at all? Is my loyalty safely entrusted? You know that the entire village thinks we are made for each other. Won't you forget your modesty and say definitely yes or no?

LAURENCIA. My answer to you and to the village is—yes!

FRONDOSO. I could kiss your feet for such an answer! You give me new life . . . let me tell you now how much I love you.

LAURENCIA. Save your compliments and speak to my father, Frondoso, for that's the important thing now. Look, there he comes with my uncle. Be calm and confident, Frondoso, for this meeting will determine whether I'm to be your wife or no.

FRONDOSO. I put my trust in God.

(LAURENCIA *hides herself. Enter* ESTEBAN *and the* COUNCILMAN.)

ESTEBAN. The Commander's visit has aroused the whole town. His behavior was most regrettable, to say the least. Everybody was shocked, and poor Jacinta is bearing the brunt of his madness.

COUNCILMAN. Before long Spain will be rendering obedience to the Catholic Kings, as they are called. The Master of Santiago has been appointed Captain General, and is coming on horseback to free Ciudad Real from Girón . . . I'm very sorry about Jacinta, who is an honest girl.

ESTEBAN. The Commander also had Mengo flogged.

COUNCILMAN. Yes. His flesh is darker than ink or a black cloth.

ESTEBAN. Please, no more—it makes my blood boil when I think of his disgusting behavior and reputation. What good my Mayor's staff against that?

COUNCILMAN. It was his servants who did it. Why should you be so upset?

ESTEBAN. Shall I tell you something else? I have been told that one day Pedro Redondo's wife was found down there in the depth of the valley. He had abused her and then turned her over to his soldiers.

COUNCILMAN. Listen, I hear something . . . Who's there?

FRONDOSO. It is I, Frondoso, waiting for permission to come in.

ESTEBAN. You need no permission, Frondoso, to enter my house. You owe your life to your father, but your upbringing to me. I love you like my own son.

FRONDOSO. Sir, trusting that love, I want to ask a favor. You know whose son I am.

ESTEBAN. Did that crazy Fernan Gómez hurt you?

FRONDOSO. Not a little.

ESTEBAN. My heart told me so.

FRONDOSO. You have shown me so much affection that I feel free to make a confession to you. I love Laurencia, and wish to become her husband. Forgive me if I have been too hasty. I'm afraid I've been very bold.

ESTEBAN. You have come just at the right moment, Frondoso, and you will prolong my life, for this touches the fear nearest my heart. I thank God that you have come to save my honor, and I thank you for your love and the purity of your intentions. But I think it only right to tell your father of this first. As soon as he approves I will give my consent too. How happy I shall be if this marriage takes place.

COUNCILMAN. You should ask the girl about him before you accept him.

ESTEBAN. Don't worry about that. The matter is settled; for they discussed it beforehand, I'm sure. If you like, Frondoso, we might talk about the dowry, for I'm planning to give you some *maravedies*.[2]

FRONDOSO. I'm not concerned about that. I don't need a dowry.

COUNCILMAN. You should be grateful that he doesn't ask you for it in wineskins.

ESTEBAN. I'll ask Laurencia what she would like to do and then let you know.

FRONDOSO. That's fair. It's a good idea to consult everybody concerned.

ESTEBAN. Daughter! . . . Laurencia!

LAURENCIA. Yes, father.

ESTEBAN. You see how quickly she replies. Laurencia, come here a minute. What would you say if your friend Gila were to marry Frondoso, who is as honest a young man as one could find in Fuente Ovejuna?

LAURENCIA. Is Gila thinking of getting married?

ESTEBAN. Why yes, if someone can be found who would be a worthy match for her.

LAURENCIA. My answer is yes.

----

2. *maravedies*: Spanish copper coins.

ESTEBAN. I would say yes too—except that Gila is ugly, and it would be much better if Frondoso became your husband, Laurencia.

LAURENCIA. In spite of your years, you are still a flatterer, father.

ESTEBAN. Do you love him?

LAURENCIA. I am fond of him, and he returns my affection, but you were saying . . .

ESTEBAN. Shall I say yes to him?

LAURENCIA. Yes, say it for me, sir.

ESTEBAN. I? Well, then I have the keys. It's settled then. Let's go to his father.

COUNCILMAN. Yes, let's go.

ESTEBAN. What shall we tell him about the dowry, son? I can afford to give you 4,000 *maravedies.*

FRONDOSO. Do you want to offend me, sir?

ESTEBAN. Come, come, my boy, you'll get over that attitude in a day or two. Even if you don't need it now, a dowry will come in handy later on.

(*Exeunt* ESTEBAN *and* COUNCILMAN.)

LAURENCIA. Tell me, Frondoso, are you happy?

FRONDOSO. Happy? I'm afraid I'll go crazy with so much joy and happiness. My heart is so overflowing that my eyes are swimming with joy when I look at you, Laurencia, and realize that you, sweet treasure, will be mine.

(*Exeunt* LAURENCIA *and* FRONDOSO.)

SCENE 4: *Meadow near Ciudad Real.*

(*Enter the* MASTER, *the* COMMANDER, FLORES, *and* ORTUNO.)

COMMANDER. Fly, sir! There's no hope for us.

MASTER. The walls were weak and the enemy strong.

COMMANDER. They have paid dearly for it, though, in blood and lives.

MASTER. And they will not be able to boast that our banner of Calatrava is among their spoils. That alone would have been enough to honor their enterprise.

COMMANDER. Your plans are ruined now, Girón.

MASTER. What can I do if Fate in its blindness raises a man aloft one day only to strike him down the next?

VOICES BACKSTAGE. Victory for the Kings of Castile!

MASTER. They're decorating the battlements with lights now, and hanging out pennants of victory from the windows in the high towers.

COMMANDER. They do that because they have paid heavily in blood—it's really more a sign of tragedy than a celebration.

MASTER. Fernan Gómez, I'm going back to Calatrava.

COMMANDER. And I to Fuente Ovejuna. Now you have to think of either defending your relatives or paying homage to the Catholic King.

MASTER. I'll write to you about my plans.

COMMANDER. Time will tell you what to do.

MASTER. Ah, years full of the bitterness of time's betrayals!

(*Exeunt.*)

SCENE 5: *A meadow near Fuente Ovejuna.*

(*Enter the wedding train:* MUSICIANS, MENGO, FRONDOSO, LAURENCIA, PASCUALA, BARRILDO, ESTEBAN, *and* JUAN ROJO.)

MUSICIANS (singing).
Long live the bride and groom!
Many long and happy years to them.

MENGO. It has not been very difficult for you to sing.

BARRILDO. You could have done better yourself, couldn't you?

FRONDOSO. Mengo knows more about whippings now than songs.

MENGO. Don't be surprised if I tell you that there's someone in the valley to whom the Commander . . .

BARRILDO. Don't say it. That brutal assassin has assailed everyone's honor.

MENGO. It was bad enough for a hundred soldiers to whip me that day when all I had was a sling. It must have been unbearable for that man to whom they gave an enema of dye and herbs—I won't mention his name, but he was an honorable man.

BARRILDO. It was done in jest, I suppose . . .

MENGO. This was no joke. Enemas are desirable sometimes, but I would rather die than undergo one like that.

FRONDOSO. Please sing us a song—if you have anything worth listening to.

MENGO.
God grant the bride and groom long life
Free from envy and jealous strife,
And when their span of years is past,
May they be united at the last.
God grant the bride and groom long life!

FRONDOSO. Heaven curse the poet who conceived such a poem!

BARRILDO. It was a rather poor job.

MENGO. This makes me think of something about the whole breed of poets. Have you seen a baker making buns? He throws the pieces of dough into the boiling oil until the pot is full. Some buns come out puffed up, others twisted and funnily shaped, some lean to the left, others to the right, some are well fried, others are burnt. Well, I think of a poet composing his verses in much the same way that the baker works on his dough. He hastily throws words into his pot of paper, confident that the honey will conceal what may turn out ridiculous or absurd. But when he tries to sell his poem no one wants it and the confectioner is forced to eat it himself.

BARRILDO. Stop your foolishness now, and let the bride and groom speak.

LAURENCIA. Give us your hands to kiss.

JUAN ROJO. Do you ask to kiss my hand, Laurencia? You and Frondoso had better ask to kiss your father's first.

ESTEBAN. Rojo, I ask Heaven's blessing on her and her husband for ever.

FRONDOSO. Give us your blessing, both of you.

JUAN ROJO. Let the bells ring, and everyone celebrate the union of Laurencia and Frondoso.

MUSICIANS (*signing*).
To the valley of Fuente Ovejuna
Came the maid with the flowing hair.
A knight of Calatrava
Followed her to the valley here.
Amid the shrubs she hid herself,
Disturbed by shame and fear.
With the branches she covered herself,
Feigning she had not seen him,
But the knight of Calatrava drew near:
"Why are you hiding, fair maiden,

Know you not that my keen desire
Can pierce the thickest wall?"
She made curtains of the branches
Confused by shame and fear.
But love passes sea and mountain:
"Why are you hiding, fair maiden,
Know you not that my keen desire
Can pierce the thickest wall?"

(*Enter the* COMMANDER, FLORES, ORTUNO, *and* CIMBRANOS.)

COMMANDER. Silence! You will all remain quietly where you are.

JUAN ROJO. This is not a game, my lord, and your orders will be obeyed. Won't you join us? Why do you come in such a bellicose manner? Are you our conqueror? But what am I saying . . .

FRONDOSO. I'm a dead man. Heaven help me!

LAURENCIA. Quickly, Frondoso, escape this way.

COMMANDER. No. Arrest him, and tie him up.

JUAN ROJO. Yield to them, my boy, and go quietly to prison.

FRONDOSO. Do you want them to kill me?

JUAN ROJO. Why?

COMMANDER. I am not a man to murder people without reason. If I were, these soldiers would have run him through by now. I'm ordering him to be taken to jail where his own father will pronounce sentence on him.

PASCUALA. Sir, a wedding is in progress here now.

COMMANDER. What is that to me? Is he the only person in town who counts?

PASCUALA. If he offended you, pardon him, as becomes your rank.

COMMANDER. Pascuala, it is nothing that concerns me personally. He has offended the Master Téllez Girón, whom God preserve. He acted counter to his orders and his honor, and must be punished as an example. Otherwise others may rebel too. Don't you know that one day this boy aimed a crossbow at the very heart of the Commander, Mayor? Loyal vassals you are indeed!

ESTEBAN. As his father-in-law I feel I must come to his defense. I think it only natural that a man, especially a man in love, should challenge you for trying to take away his girl—what else could he do?

COMMANDER. You are a fool, Mayor.

ESTEBAN. In your opinion, my lord!

COMMANDER. I had no intention of taking away his girl—for she was not his.

ESTEBAN. You had the thought, and that is enough. There are kings in Castile who are drawing up new rules to prevent disorder. And they will do wrong if, after the wars, they tolerate in the towns and country districts such powerful men wearing those huge crosses on their chests. Those crosses were meant for royal breasts, and only kings should wear them.

COMMANDER. Wrest the mayor's staff from him!

ESTEBAN. Take it, sir, it is yours to keep.

COMMANDER. I'll strike him with it as if he were an unbroken horse.

ESTEBAN. You are my lord, and I must bear it: strike, then.

PASCUALA. Shame on you! Striking an old man!

LAURENCIA. You strike him because he is my father—what injury do you avenge in this way?

COMMANDER. Arrest her, and let ten soldiers guard her.

(*Exeunt* COMMANDER *and his men.*)

ESTEBAN. May Heaven visit justice upon him!

(*Exit* ESTEBAN.)

PASCUALA. The wedding has become a mourning.

(*Exit* PASCUALA.)

BARRILDO. Is there not one of us who can speak?

MENGO. I've already had a sound whipping and I'm covered with wales—let someone else anger him this time.

JUAN ROJO. Let us all take counsel.

MENGO. I advise everybody to keep quiet. He made my posterior look like a piece of salmon.

(*Exeunt all.*)

ACT THREE

SCENE 1: *A room in the Town Hall of Fuente Ovejuna.*

(*Enter* ESTEBAN, ALONZO, *and* BARRILDO.)

ESTEBAN. Has everybody come to the meeting?

BARRILDO. Some people are absent.

ESTEBAN. Then our danger is more serious.

BARRILDO. Nearly all the town has been warned.

ESTEBAN. With Frondoso imprisoned in the tower, and my daughter Laurencia in such peril, if God, in his mercy, does not come to our help . . .

(*Enter* JUAN ROJO *and the* COUNCILMAN.)

JUAN ROJO. What are you shouting about, Esteban? Don't you know secrecy is all important now?

ESTEBAN. I wonder I'm not shouting even louder!

(*Enter* MENGO.)

MENGO. I want to join in this meeting.

ESTEBAN. With tears streaming down my beard, I ask you, honest farmers, what funeral rites can we give to a country without honor—a country that is lost? And if our honor is indeed lost, which of us can perform such rites, when there is not one among us who has not been dishonored? Answer me now, is there anyone here whose life, whose deep life of honor, is still intact? Are we not all of us in mourning for each other now? If all is lost, what is there to wait for? What is this misfortune that has overtaken us?

JUAN ROJO. The blackest ever known . . . But it has just been announced that the Kings of Castile have concluded a victorious peace, and will soon arrive in Cordova. Let us send two councilmen to that city to kneel at their feet and ask their help.

BARRILDO. But King Ferdinand, who has conquered so many enemies, is still busy making war, and will not be able to help us now while he's in the midst of battles. We must find some other way out.

COUNCILMAN. If you want my opinion, I suggest we leave the town.

JUAN ROJO. But how can we do that on such short notice?

MENGO. If I understand the situation at all, this meeting will cost us a good many lives.

COUNCILMAN. The mast of patience has been torn from us, and now we are a ship driven before a storm of fear. They have brutally abducted the daughter of the good man who rules our community, and unjustly broken the staff of office over his head. What slave was ever treated worse?

JUAN ROJO. What do you want the people to do?

COUNCILMAN. Die, or give death to the tyrants, for we are many and they are few.

BARRILDO. What? Raise our weapons against our lord and master!

ESTEBAN. Except for God, the King's our only lord and master, not these inhuman, barbarous men. If God is behind our rightful anger, what have we to lose?

MENGO. Let us be a little more cautious. I'm here to speak for the humblest peasants who always have to bear the brunt of any trouble—and I want to represent their fears prudently.

JUAN ROJO. Our misfortunes have prepared us to sacrifice our lives, so what are we waiting for? Our houses and vineyards have been burned down. They are tyrants and we must have our revenge.

(*Enter* LAURENCIA, *her hair disheveled.*)

LAURENCIA. Let me come in, for I sorely need the advice of men! Do you know me?

ESTEBAN. God in Heaven, is that my daughter?

JUAN ROJO. Don't you recognize your Laurencia?

LAURENCIA. Yes, I am Laurencia, but so changed that looking at me you still doubt it.

ESTEBAN. My daughter!

LAURENCIA. Don't call me your daughter!

ESTEBAN. Why not, my dear? Why not?

LAURENCIA. For many reasons!—chiefly because you let me be carried off by tyrants, by the traitors who rule over us, without attempting to avenge me. I was not yet Frondoso's wife, so you cannot say my husband should have defended me; this was my father's duty as long as the wedding had not been consummated; just as a nobleman about to purchase a jewel need not pay for it if it is lost while still in the merchant's keeping. From under your very eyes, Fernan Gómez dragged me to his house, and you let the wolf carry the sheep like the cowardly shepherd you are. Can you conceive what I suffered at his hands?—the daggers pointed at my breast, the flatteries, threats, insults, and lies used to make my chastity yield to his fierce desires? Does not my bruised and bleeding face, my disheveled hair tell you anything? Are you not good men?—not fathers and relatives? Do not your hearts sink to see me so grievously betrayed? . . . Oh, you are sheep; how well named the village of Fuente Ovejuna. Give me weapons and let me fight, since you are but things of stone or metal, since you are but tigers—no, not tigers, for tigers fiercely attack those who steal their offspring, killing the hunters before they can escape. You were born timid rabbits; you are infidels, not Spaniards. Chicken-hearted, you permit other men to abuse your women. Put knitting in your scabbards—what need have you of swords? By the living God, I swear that your women will avenge those tyrants and stone you all, you spinning girls, you sodomites, you effeminate cowards. Tomorrow deck yourselves in our bonnets and skirts, and beautify yourselves with our cosmetics. The Commander will hang Frondoso from a merlon[1] of the tower, without let or trial, and presently he will string you all up. And I shall be glad—you race of half-men—that this honorable town will be rid of effeminates, and the age of Amazons[2] will return, to the eternal amazement of the world.

ESTEBAN. Daughter, I will not stay to hear such names. I go now, even if I have to fight the whole world!

JUAN ROJO. I'll go with you, in spite of the enemy's power.

COUNCILMAN. We shall die together.

BARRILDO. Let us hang a cloth from a stick to fly in the wind, and death to the traitors.

JUAN ROJO. What are our orders?

MENGO. To kill the Commander without order. To rally the whole town around us: let's all agree to kill the tyrants.

ESTEBAN. Take swords, lances, crossbows, pikes, sticks!

MENGO. Long live the Kings, our only lords and masters!

ALL. Long live the Kings!

MENGO. Death to the traitor tyrants!

ALL. Death to the tyrants!

(*Exeunt all but* LAURENCIA.)

LAURENCIA. Go—God will be with you! Come, women of the town, your honor will be avenged—rally round me!

(*Enter* PASCUALA, JACINTA, *and other women.*)

---

1. **merlon:** the solid part between two openings in a battlement.
2. **Amazons:** a race of warrior women from Greek mythology.

PASCUALA. What's happening? What are you shouting about?

LAURENCIA. Can't you see how they're on their way to kill Fernan Gómez? Every man, boy, and child is rushing furiously to do his duty. Is it fair that the men alone should have the glory of a day like this, when we women have the greater grievances?

JACINTA. Tell us your plans then.

LAURENCIA. I propose that we all band together and perform a deed that will shake the world. Jacinta, your great injury will be our guide.

JACINTA. No more than yours.

LAURENCIA. Pascuala, you be our standard bearer.

PASCUALA. I'll be a good one. I'll put a cloth on a lance and we'll have a flag in the wind.

LAURENCIA. There's no time for that. We'll wave our caps for banners.

PASCUALA. Let's appoint a captain.

LAURENCIA. We don't need one.

PASCUALA. Why not?

LAURENCIA. Because when my courage is up, we don't need any Cids or Rodomontes.[3]

(*Exeunt all.*)

SCENE 2: *Hall in the castle of the* COMMANDER.

(*Enter* FRONDOSO, *his hands tied,* FLORES, CIMBRANOS, ORTUNO, *and the* COMMANDER.)

COMMANDER. I want him hung by the cord that binds his wrists, so that his punishment may be the more severe.

FRONDOSO. How this will add to your descendants' honor, my lord!

COMMANDER. Hang him from the highest merlon.

FRONDOSO. It was never my intention to kill you.

FLORES. Do you hear that noise outside?

(*Alarum.*)

---

3. Cids . . . Rodomontes: The Cid was a Spanish soldier (1040?–1099) who fought the Moors and became a national hero. Rodomonte was a brave but boastful Moorish hero in several Italian epic poems of the Renaissance.

COMMANDER. What can it be?

FLORES. It looks as if the villagers are planning to stay your sentence, my lord.

ORTUNO. They are breaking down the doors!

(*Alarum.*)

COMMANDER. The door of my house? The seat of the Commandry?

FRONDOSO. The whole town is here!

JUAN ROJO (*within*). Break them down, smash them in, burn, destroy!

ORTUNO. It's hard to stop a riot once it gets started.

COMMANDER. The town against me!

FLORES. And their fury has driven them to tear down all the doors.

COMMANDER. Untie him. And you, Frondoso, go and calm down the peasant mayor.

FRONDOSO. I'm going, sir—love has spurred them to action.

(*Exit* FRONDOSO.)

MENGO (*within*). Long live Ferdinand and Isabella, and down with the tyrants!

FLORES. In God's name, my lord, don't let them find you here.

COMMANDER. If they persist—why, this room is strong and well protected. They will soon turn back.

FLORES. When villages with a grievance decide to rise against their rulers they never turn back until they have shed blood and taken their revenge.

COMMANDER. We'll face this mob with our weapons, using this door as a portcullis.

FRONDOSO (*within*). Long live Fuente Ovejuna!

COMMANDER. What a leader! I'll take care of his bravery!

FLORES. My lord, I marvel at yours.

(*Enter* ESTEBAN *and the* PEASANTS.)

ESTEBAN. There's the tyrant and his accomplices! Long live Fuente Ovejuna, death to the tyrants!

COMMANDER. Wait, my people!

ALL. Wrongs never wait.

COMMANDER. Tell me your wrongs, and, on a knight's honor, I'll set them right.

ALL. Long live Fuente Ovejuna! Long live King Ferdinand! Death to bad Christians and traitors!

COMMANDER. Will you not hear me? It is I who address you, I, your lord.

ALL. Our lords are the Catholic Kings.

COMMANDER. Wait.

ALL. Long live Fuente Ovejuna, and death to Fernan Gómez!

(*Exeunt all. Enter* LAURENCIA, PASCUALA, JACINTA, *and other women, armed.*)

LAURENCIA. You brave soldiers, no longer women, wait here in this place of vantage.

PASCUALA. Only women know how to take revenge. We shall drink the enemy's blood.

JACINTA. Let us pierce his corpse with our lances.

PASCUALA. Agreed.

ESTEBAN (*within*). Die, treacherous Commander!

COMMANDER. I die. O God, in Thy clemency, have mercy on me!

BARRILDO (*within*). Here's Flores.

MENGO. Get that scoundrel! He's the one who gave me a thousand whippings.

FRONDOSO (*within*). I won't consider myself avenged until I've pulled out his soul.

LAURENCIA. There's no excuse for not going in.

PASCUALA. Calm yourself. We had better guard the door.

BARRILDO (*within*). I am not moved. Don't come to me with tears now, you fops.

LAURENCIA. Pascuala, I'm going in; I don't care to keep my sword in its scabbard.

(*Exit* LAURENCIA.)

BARRILDO (*within*). Here's Ortuno.

FRONDOSO (*within*). Slash his face!

(*Enter* FLORES, FLEEING, *pursued by* MENGO.)

FLORES. Pity, Mengo! I'm not to blame!

MENGO. Oh, no? Not for being a pimp, you scoundrel, not for having whipped me?

PASCUALA. Mengo, give him to us women, we'll . . . Hurry, Mengo!

MENGO. Fine, you can have him—no punishment could be worse!

PASCUALA. We'll avenge the whippings be gave you.

MENGO. That's fine!

JACINTA. Come on, death to the traitor!

FLORES. To die at the hands of women!

JACINTA. Don't you like it?

PASCUALA. Is that why you're weeping?

JACINTA. Die, you panderer to his pleasures!

PASCUALA. Die, you traitor!

FLORES. Pity, women, *pity!*

(*Enter* ORTUNO, *pursued by* LAURENCIA.)

ORTUNO. You know I have had nothing at all to do with it . . .

LAURENCIA. I know you! Come on, women, dye your conquering weapons in their vile blood.

PASCUALA. I'll die killing!

ALL. Long live Fuente Ovejuna! Long live King Ferdinand!

(*Exeunt all.*)

SCENE 3: *Room of the Catholic Kings, at Toro.*

(*Enter* KING FERDINAND, QUEEN ISABELLA, *and the* MASTER DON MANRIQUE.)

MANRIQUE. We planned our attack so well that we carried it out without any setback. There was little resistance—even if they had tried to organize any, it would have been weak. Cabra has remained there to guard the place in case of counterattack.

KING. That was a wise decision, and I am glad that he is in charge of operations. Now we can be sure that Alfonso, who is trying to seize power in Portugal, will not be able to harm us. It is fortunate that Cabra is stationed there and that he is making a good show, for in this way he protects us from any danger and, by acting as a loyal sentinel, works for the good of the kingdom.

(*Enter* FLORES, *wounded.*)

FLORES. Catholic King Ferdinand, upon whom Heaven has bestowed the Crown of Castile, excellent gentleman that you are—listen to the worst cruelty that a man could ever behold from sunrise to sunset.

KING. Calm yourself!

FLORES. Supreme Sovereign, my wounds forbid me to delay in reporting my sad case, for my life is ebbing away. I come from Fuente Ovejuna, where, with ruthless heart, the inhabitants of that village have deprived their lord and master of his life. Fernan Gómez has been murdered by his perfidious subjects, indignant vassals who dared attack him for but a trivial cause. The mob called him tyrant and inflamed by the power of the epithet, committed this despicable crime: they broke into his house and having no faith that he, a perfect gentleman, would right all their wrongs, would not listen to him, but with impatient fury pierced his chest which bore the cross of Calatrava with a thousand cruel wounds and threw him from the lofty windows onto the pikes and lances of the women in the street below. They carried him away, dead, and competed with one another in pulling his beard and hair, and recklessly slashing his face. In fact their constantly growing fury was so great, that some cuts went from ear to ear. They blotted out his coat-of-arms with their pikes and loudly proclaimed that they wanted to replace it with your royal coat-of-arms since those of the Commander offended them. They sacked his house as if it were the enemy's and joyfully divided the spoils among themselves. All this I witnessed from my hiding place, for my cruel fate did not grant me death at such a time. Thus I remained all day in hiding until nightfall, when I was able to slip away furtively to come to render you this account. Sire, since you are just, see that a just punishment is administered to the brutal culprits who have perpetrated such an outrage.

KING. You may rest assured that the culprits will not go without due punishment. The unfortunate event is of such magnitude that I am astonished; I will send a judge to investigate the case and punish the culprits as an example to all. A captain will accompany him for his protection, for such great offense requires exemplary punishment. In the meantime your wounds will be cared for.

(*Exeunt all.*)

SCENE 4: *The countryside.*

(*Enter* PEASANTS, *both men and women, with* FERNAN GÓMEZ'
head on a lance.)

MUSICIANS (*singing*).
Long live Isabella and Ferdinand
And death to the tyrants!

BARRILDO. Sing us a song, Frondoso.

FRONDOSO. Here goes, and if it limps let some critic fix it.
Long live fair Isabella
And Ferdinand of Aragon.
He is made for her
And she is meant for him.
May St. Michael guide them
To Heaven by the hand . . .
Long live Isabella and Ferdinand
And death to the tyrants!

LAURENCIA. Now it's your turn, Barrildo.

BARRILDO. Listen to this, for I've been working on it.

PASCUALA. If you say it with feeling, it's going to be good.

BARRILDO.
Long live the famous kings
For they are victorious.
They'll be our lords
Happy and glorious.
May they conquer always
All giants and dwarfs . . .
And death to the tyrants!

MUSICIANS (singing).
Long live Isabella and Ferdinand
And death to the tyrants!

LAURENCIA. Now it's your turn, Mengo.

FRONDOSO. Yes, Mengo.

MENGO. I'm a most gifted poet, you know.

PASCUALA. You mean a poet with a bruised backside.

MENGO.
I was whipped on a Sunday morning
My back still feels the pain
But the Christian Kings are coming
There'll be no tyrants here again.

MUSICIANS. Long live the Kings!

ESTEBAN. Take away that head!

MENGO. He has the face of one who has been hanged.

(JUAN ROJO *brings in a scutcheon with the royal arms.*)

COUNCILMAN. The scutcheon has arrived.

ESTEBAN. Let's see it.

JUAN ROJO. Where shall we place it?

COUNCILMAN. Here, in the Town Hall.

ESTEBAN. What a beautiful scutcheon!

BARRILDO. What joy!

FRONDOSO. A new day is dawning for us, and that's our sun.

ESTEBAN.
Long live Castile and Leon
And the bars of Aragon.
Down with tyranny!

People of Fuente Ovejuna, listen to the words of an old man whose life has been blameless. The Kings will want to investigate what has happened, and this they will do soon. So agree now among yourselves on what to say.

FRONDOSO. What is your advice?

ESTEBAN. To die saying Fuente Ovejuna and nothing else.

FRONDOSO. That's fine! Fuente Ovejuna did it!

ESTEBAN. Do you want to answer in that way?

ALL. Yes.

ESTEBAN. Well then, I'd like to play the role of questioner—let's rehearse! Mengo, pretend that you are the one being grilled.

MENGO. Can't you pick on someone else, someone more emaciated?

ESTEBAN. But this is all make believe.

MENGO. All right, go ahead!

ESTEBAN. Who killed the Commander?

MENGO. Fuente Ovejuna did it!

ESTEBAN. You dog, I'm going to torture you.

MENGO. I don't care—even if you kill me.

ESTEBAN. Confess, you scoundrel.

MENGO. I am ready to confess.

ESTEBAN. Well, then, who did it?

MENGO. Fuente Ovejuna.

ESTEBAN. Bind him tighter.

MENGO. That will make no difference.

ESTEBAN. To hell with the trial then.

(*Enter the* COUNCILMAN.)

COUNCILMAN. What are you doing here?

FRONDOSO. What has happened, Cuadrado?

COUNCILMAN. The questioner is here.

ESTEBAN. Send him in.

COUNCILMAN. A captain is with him.

ESTEBAN. Who cares? Let the devil himself come in: you know your answer.

COUNCILMAN. They are going around town arresting people.

ESTEBAN. There's nothing to fear. Who killed the Commander, Mengo?

MENGO. Who? Fuente Ovejuna.

(*Exeunt all.*)

SCENE 5: *Room of the* MASTER OF CALATRAVA, *at Almagro.*

(*Enter the* MASTER *and a* SOLDIER.)

MASTER. What a horrible thing to have happened! Melancholy was his end. I could murder you for bringing me such news.

SOLDIER. Sir, I'm but a messenger. I did not intend to annoy you.

MASTER. That a town should become so fierce and wrathful, that it would dare to do such a thing! It's incredible! I'll go there with a hundred men and raze the town to the ground, blotting out even the memory of its inhabitants.

SOLDIER. Calm yourself, sir. They have given themselves up to the King and the most important thing for you is not to enrage him.

MASTER. How can they give themselves up to the King? Are they not the vassals of the Commander?

SOLDIER. That, sir, you'll have to thrash out with the King.

MASTER. Thrash it out? No, for the King placed the land in his hands and it is the King's. He is the Sovereign Lord and as such I recognize him. The fact that they have given themselves up to the King soothes my anger. My wisest course is to see him, even if I am at fault. He will pardon me on account of my youth. I am ashamed to go—but my honor demands that I do so and I shall not forget my dignity.

(*Exeunt the* MASTER *and* SOLDIER.)

SCENE 6: Public square.

(*Enter* LAURENCIA.)

LAURENCIA.
Loving, to suspect one's love will suffer pain
Becomes an added suffering of love;
To fear that pain great harm to him may prove
Brings new torture to the heart again.

Devotion, watching eagerly, would fain
Give way to worry, worm of love;
For the heart is rare that does not bend or move
When fear his threat on the belov'd has lain.

I love my husband with a love that does not tire;
But now I live and move beneath
The fear that fate may take away his breath.
His good is all the end of my desire.

If he is present, certain is my grief;
If he is absent, certain is my death.

(*Enter* FRONDOSO.)

FRONDOSO. Laurencia!

LAURENCIA. My dear husband! How do you dare to come here?

FRONDOSO. Does my loving care for you give you such worries?

LAURENCIA. My love, take care of yourself. I am afraid something
may happen to you.

FRONDOSO. It would displease God, Laurencia, if I made you
unhappy.

LAURENCIA. You have seen what has happened to your friends and
the ferocious rage of that judge. Save yourself, and fly from
danger!

FRONDOSO. Would you expect cowardice from me? Do not advise
me to escape. It is inconceivable that in order to avoid harm I
should forgo seeing you and betray my friends and my own blood
at this tragic moment. (*Cries within.*) I hear cries. If I am not
mistaken, they are from someone put to the torture. Listen
carefully!

(*The* JUDGE *speaks within, and is answered.*)

JUDGE. Tell me the truth, old man.

FRONDOSO. Laurencia, they are torturing an old man!

LAURENCIA. What cruelty!

ESTEBAN. Let me go a moment.

JUDGE. Let him go. Now, tell me, who murdered Fernan?

ESTEBAN. Fuente Ovejuna killed him.

LAURENCIA. Father, I will make your name immortal!

FRONDOSO. What courage!

JUDGE. Take that boy. Pup, speak up! I know you know. What? You refuse? Tighten the screws.

BOY. Fuente Ovejuna, sir.

JUDGE. By the life of the King, I'll hang the lot of you, you peasants, with my own hands! Who killed the Commander?

FRONDOSO. They're racking the child, and he answers that way . . .

LAURENCIA. What a brave village!

FRONDOSO. Brave and strong.

JUDGE. Put that woman, over there, in the chair. Tighten it up!

LAURENCIA. He's blind with rage.

JUDGE. You see this chair, peasants, this means death to you all! Who killed the Commander?

PASCUALA. Fuente Ovejuna, sir.

JUDGE. Tighter!

FRONDOSO. I hadn't imagined . . .

LAURENCIA. Pascuala will not tell him, Frondoso.

FRONDOSO. Even the children deny it!

JUDGE. They seem to be delighted. Tighter!

PASCUALA. Merciful God!

JUDGE. Tighter, you bastard! Are you deaf?

PASCUALA. Fuente Ovejuna killed him.

JUDGE. Bring me someone a bit bigger—that fat one, half stripped already!

LAURENCIA. Poor Mengo! That must be Mengo!

FRONDOSO. I'm afraid he'll break down.

MENGO. Oh . . . Oh . . .

JUDGE. Give it to him!

MENGO. Oh . . .

JUDGE. Need any help?

MENGO. Oh . . . Oh . . .

JUDGE. Peasant, who killed the Commander?

MENGO. Oh . . . I'll tell, sir . . .

JUDGE. Release him a bit.

FRONDOSO. He's confessing!

JUDGE. Now, hard, on the back!

MENGO. Wait, I'll tell all . . .

JUDGE. Who killed him?

MENGO. Sir, Fuente Ovejuna.

JUDGE. Did you ever see such scoundrels? They make fun of pain. The ones I was surest of lie most emphatically. Dismiss them: I'm exhausted.

FRONDOSO. Oh, Mengo, God bless you! I was stiff with fear—but you have rid me of it.

(*Enter* MENGO, BARRILDO, *and the* COUNCILMAN.)

BARRILDO. Long live Mengo!

COUNCILMAN. Well he may . . .

BARRILDO. Mengo, bravo!

FRONDOSO. That's what I say.

MENGO. Oh . . . Oh . . .

BARRILDO. Drink and eat, my friend . . .

MENGO. Oh . . . Oh . . . What's that?

BARRILDO. Sweet cider.

MENGO. Oh . . . Oh . . .

FRONDOSO. Something for him to drink!

BARRILDO. Right away!

FRONDOSO. He quaffs it well! That's better, now.

LAURENCIA. Give him a little more.

MENGO. Oh . . . Oh . . .

BARRILDO. This glass, for me.

LAURENCIA. Solemnly he drinks it!

FRONDOSO. A good denial gets a good drink.

BARRILDO. Want another glass?

MENGO. Oh . . . Oh . . . Yes, yes.

FRONDOSO. Drink it down; you deserve it.

LAURENCIA. A drink for each turn of the rack.

FRONDOSO. Cover him up, he'll freeze to death.

BARRILDO. Want some more?

MENGO. Three more. Oh . . . Oh . . .

FRONDOSO. He's asking for the wine . . .

BARRILDO. Yes, there's a boy, drink deep. What's the matter now?

MENGO. It's a bit sour. Oh, I'm catching cold.

FRONDOSO. Here, drink this, it's better. Who killed the Commander?

MENGO. Fuente Ovejuna killed him . . .

(Exeunt MENGO, BARRILDO, and the COUNCILMAN.)

FRONDOSO. He deserves more than they can give him. But tell me, my love, who killed the Commander?

LAURENCIA. Little Fuente Ovejuna, my dear.

FRONDOSO. Who did?

LAURENCIA. You bully, you torturer! I say Fuente Ovejuna did it.

FRONDOSO. What about me? How do *I* kill *you*?

LAURENCIA. With love, sweet love, with lots of love.

SCENE 7: Room of the Kings, at Tordesillas.

(*Enter the* KING *and* QUEEN.)

ISABELLA. I did not expect to find you here, but my luck is good.

KING. The pleasure of seeing you lends new glory to my eyes. I was on my way to Portugal and I had to stop here.

ISABELLA. Your Majesty's plans are always wise.

KING. How did you leave Castile?

ISABELLA. Quiet and peaceful.

KING. No wonder, if you were the peacemaker.

(Enter DON MANRIQUE.)

MANRIQUE. The Master of Calatrava, who has just arrived, begs audience.

ISABELLA. I wanted very much to see him.

MANRIQUE. I swear, Madame, that although young in years, he is a most valiant soldier.

(Exit DON MANRIQUE, *and enter the* MASTER.)

MASTER. Rodrigo Téllez Girón, Master of Calatrava, who never tires of praising you, humbly kneels before you and asks your pardon. I admit that I have been deceived and that, ill-advised, I may have transgressed in my loyalty to you. Fernan's counsel deceived me and for that reason I humbly beg forgiveness. And if I am deserving of this royal favor, I pledge to serve you from now on; in the present campaign which you are undertaking against Granada, where you are now going, I promise to show the valor of my sword. No sooner will I unsheathe it, bringing fierce suffering to the enemy, than I will hoist my red crosses on the loftiest merlon of the battlements. In serving you I will employ five hundred soldiers, and I promise on my honor nevermore to displease you.

KING. Rise, Master. It is enough that you have come for me to welcome you royally.

MASTER. You are a consolation to a troubled soul.

ISABELLA. You speak with the same undaunted courage with which you act.

MASTER. You are a beautiful Esther, and you a divine Xerxes.[4]

(Enter MANRIQUE.)

MANRIQUE. Sire, the judge you sent to Fuente Ovejuna has returned and he asks to see you.

KING (*to the* MASTER.) Be the judge of these aggressors.

MASTER. If I were not in your presence, Sire, I'd certainly teach them how to kill Commanders.

KING. That is no longer necessary.

ISABELLA. God willing, I hope this power lies with you.

(Enter JUDGE.)

---

4. **Esther . . . Xerxes** (zẻrk´sēz): In the Old Testament, Esther is a Jewish maiden who, because of her beauty, becomes the bride and queen of Xerxes, King of Persia. By Esther's intercession, the Jewish people are saved from massacre.

JUDGE. I went to Fuente Ovejuna, as you commanded, and carried out my assignment with special care and diligence. After due investigation, I cannot produce a single written page of evidence, for to my question: "Who killed the Commander?" the people answered with one accord: "Fuente Ovejuna did it." Three hundred persons were put to torture, quite ruthlessly, and I assure you, Sire, that I could get no more out of them than this. Even children, only ten years old, were put to the rack, but to no avail—neither did flatteries nor deceits do the least good. And since it is so hopeless to reach any conclusion: either you must pardon them all or kill the entire village. And now the whole town has come to corroborate in person what they have told me. You will be able to find out from them.

KING. Let them come in.

> (*Enter the* TWO MAYORS, ESTEBAN *and* ALONZO, FRONDOSO, *and* PEASANTS, *men and women.*)

LAURENCIA. Are those the rulers?

FRONDOSO. Yes, they are the powerful sovereigns of Castile.

LAURENCIA. Upon my faith, they are beautiful! May Saint Anthony bless them!

ISABELLA. Are these the aggressors?

ESTEBAN. Fuente Ovejuna, Your Majesty, who humbly kneel before you, ready to serve you. We have suffered from the fierce tyranny and cruelty of the dead Commander, who showered insults upon us—and committed untold evil. He was bereft of all mercy, and did not hesitate to steal our property and rape our women.

FRONDOSO. He went so far as to take away from me this girl, whom Heaven has granted to me and who has made me so grateful that no human being can compete with me in joy. He snatched her away to his house on my wedding night, as if she were his property, and if she had not known how to protect herself, she, who is virtue personified, would have paid dearly, as you can well imagine.

MENGO. Is it not my turn to talk? If you grant me permission you will be astonished to learn how he treated me. Because I went to defend a girl whom his insolent servants were about to abuse, that perverse Nero handled me so roughly that he left my posterior like a slice of salmon. Three men beat my buttocks so relentlessly that I believe I still bear some wales. To heal my bruises I have had to use more powders and myrtleberries than my farm is worth.

ESTEBAN. Sire, we want to be your vassals. You are our King and in your defense we have borne arms. We trust in your clemency and hope that you believe in our innocence.

KING. Though the crime is grave, I am forced to pardon it since no indictment is set down. And since I am responsible for you, the village will remain under my jurisdiction until such time as a new Commander appears to inherit it.

FRONDOSO. Your Majesty speaks with great wisdom. And at this point, worthy audience, ends the play *Fuente Ovejuna*.

DISCUSSION QUESTIONS

1. Do you think the peasants were justified in killing the Commander? Were there any alternatives open to them?

2. What is the meaning of the name *Fuente Ovejuna*? In what way is this an appropriate name for the town?

3. Honor is the subject of almost all Spanish works written in the 1600s. How does the love story of Laurencia and Frondoso reinforce the theme of honor?

4. Shame, the opposite of honor, is something that the characters try to avoid at all costs. How does Laurencia shame the men into finally taking action against the Commander?

5. What impression do we get of King Ferdinand and Queen Isabella from this play? Why is Ferdinand ready to avenge his enemy, the Commander, against the rebellious inhabitants of Fuente Ovejuna?

6. Why do the peasants decide to answer all questions by saying, "Fuente Ovejuna did it"?

SUGGESTION FOR WRITING

Imagine that the king and queen of Spain have appointed you to be the judge of the peasant uprising in Fuente Ovejuna. You have heard the case, and now you must pronounce judgment. Will you let the townfolk go free, or will you inflict some kind of penalty or punishment? Write a letter to Ferdinand and Isabella explaining what you have decided to do and why you think it is the best course of action.

Literature of
the Americas

CIRO ALEGRÍA

(1909–1967)

Born and raised in a rural area of northern Peru, Alegría was well acquainted with Indian life, which became the constant focus of his literary and political work. He spent several years as a newspaper reporter and eventually joined a political movement dedicated to improving the life of oppressed Indians. As a result of his political activities, Alegría was imprisoned and later exiled to Chile. Penniless and ill, he began to write his first novel, *The Golden Serpent,* which won a prize for fiction in 1935. A few years later he gained an international reputation with the publication of *Broad and Alien Is the World,* a richly poetic novel about Indian ways. Several other novels and short stories followed, all of which were widely translated and enthusiastically received. Alegría lived and taught in New York, Puerto Rico, and Cuba until 1957 when, after 23 years of exile, he finally return to Peru, where he lived until his death. ∎

THE STONE AND THE CROSS

Translated by Zoila Nelken

The trees became smaller as the grade got steeper. The trail heaved, tracing violent curves between scrawny cacti, squat bushes, and angular rocks. The two horses were panting, and their riders had stopped talking. If a stone rolled off the path, it continued to bounce downhill sometimes dislodging others in its fall, and all were as grains of sand sliding down the grandeur of the Andes.

Suddenly, there were not even bushes or cacti. The rocks increased in size, expanding into slabs, gray and red, pointing toward the summit, standing vertically in dark boulders like immense stairsteps, or wrought into proud peaks that pierced the taut sky. Large rocks were scattered like huts in the distance, or stacked wall-like, forming a gigantic circle around the infinite. Where there was some earth, wild grass known as *ichu* grew tenaciously. The sun's brilliance formed pools in the yellow-gray grass.

The horses' and riders' breath began to freeze into fleeting, whitish puffs. The men felt the cold in their goose-pimpled skin, in spite of their thick woolen clothes and compact vicuña ponchos. The one in the lead turned his head as he halted his horse and said:

"Won't you feel *soroche,*[1] child?"

The boy he addressed answered, "I don't think so. I have climbed as high as the Manancancho with my father."

---

1. *soroche* (sō rō´chā): altitude sickness.

Then the one who had asked the question eyed the road that struggled upward, and spurred on. He was an old Indian, with an expressionless face. Beneath the rush hat whose shade somewhat concealed the coarseness of his face, his eyes sparkled like two black diamonds buried in stone. The boy following him was a white child about ten years old, still new to long trips in the bramble thickets of the craggy Andes, for which reason his father had assigned the Indian to him as a guide. The road to the village where the school was crossed a country whose reaches grew even lonelier and higher.

That the child was white could be easily seen, although the child knew very well through his mother's veins coursed a few drops of Indian blood. However, the child was considered white because of his color and also because he belonged to the landed class which had dominated the Indian village for more than four centuries.

The boy traveled behind the old man without any consideration for the fact that the latter was doing him a service. He was completely accustomed to having the Indians serve him. At that moment, the boy was thinking about his home and some of the events of his short life. It was certainly true that he had climbed with his father as far as Manancancho, the mountain on their hacienda that had attracted his attention because occasionally it was covered with snow. But the mountains he was climbing now were higher, and perhaps the *soroche*, the sickness of the high passes of the Andes, would attack him when he reached its frozen summit. And where might that famous cross be anyway?

On rounding the slope of the mountain, the riders ran into some men leading a string of tired mules that could hardly be seen under their immense loads. The packs smelled of cocoa and were covered by blankets that the muleteers would use at the inn. The vivid colors of the blankets were jubilant brushstrokes against the uniformly gray rocks and grass fields.

The guide and the child, with some difficulty, got through the slow-moving mules. On top of the two packs on one of the mules there was a large, beautifully blue, almost lustrous stone.

"The devotional stone," the guide remarked.

The two riders, going as fast as the steep trail allowed, still climbing, left the muleteers in the distance. From time to time, they would hear some fragment of the drivers' shouts: "Uuuuuuuuu!" . . . "Aaaaaaaaaa!" These would be multiplied by the echoes. It seemed as if several parties were driving mules among the rocks. But the immensity of the range soon became silent. Every now and then, the wind would whistle through the grass. When it ceased, the silence of the stones seemed to grow, its grandeur, born in darkened depths, rising impetuously toward the sky.

Below, the muleteers and their drove grew smaller, until they seemed a string of busy ants, carrying their burdens on their backs. The shadow of a cloud passed slowly over the slope of the mountain, tinting the grass fields a deeper hue. When it moved across the rushes, the shadow folded into airy waves.

The riders took the road that cut obliquely across a cliff. The rock had been worked with dynamite and pick. The eyes of the alert beasts were bright, and their breath more audible. The white child would not have known how to calculate the time it took them to get across the cliff riding over bare rock, at the edge of the precipice. Perhaps twenty minutes, or maybe an hour. The crossing ended when the trail, after curving and opening up like a door, led onto the plain. The old man mumbled:

"The very *jalca* itself!"

It was the Andean plateau. The wild grass grew short in the cold desolation of the plain. Behind the plain, another range of mountains rose. The wind was blowing tenaciously, running freely across the plain, ruffling the blades, howling. The route was marked through the *ichu* by a number of paths, ruts dug into the clay earth by travelers. Large bluish and reddish stones jutted up on either side like gigantic warts on the plain.

Medium sized stones were scarce, and there were even fewer small enough to be carried. The Indian dismounted suddenly, and walked straight to a stone he had spotted.

"Shall I get one for you, child?" he asked.

"No," was the boy's reply.

Even so, the old man looked for another, and returned with two. They filled both his large hands. Parsimoniously, looking at the white child out of the corner of his eye, he put them in the saddlebags behind the packsaddle, one on each side. He rode on then, and he said:

"One must carry the stones all the way from here. There are none farther on . . ."

The boy pointed with his finger, and said disdainfully:

"That muleteer carrying a stone is really more than silly. Imagine carrying it so far!"

"Perhaps he made some promise, child. Look at the cross . . ."

The old man pointed with his index finger to the top of the ridge. The boy did not see the cross in spite of his good eyesight, but he knew that the Indian, although he was very old, probably had better eyesight. The cross must be there.

The devout old man was referring to the great Cross on High (Cruz del Alto), known throughout that whole area to be miraculous and revered. It was situated at the spot where the trail crossed the top of the highest range. It was customary for all travelers who passed that way to leave a stone near its pedestal.

The boy also carried something concerning the cross, but he carried it inside himself, between his chest and back. On leaving home, his father had said to him:

"Don't place a stone at the cross. That's what Indians and cholos[2] do . . . that's for ignorant people."

---

2. cholos: people of mixed Spanish and Indian blood.

He remembered his exact words.

The boy knew that his father was not a believer but a rationalist, something he did not understand. But his mother was indeed a believer, and wore a small gold cross on her breast, and lit votive lamps before a niche in which she kept an image of the Virgin of Sorrows. The boy thought that maybe if he had time to ask his mother, she would have told him to place a stone before the cross. He was pondering all this when the Indian's voice sounded, daring to warn him:

"The stone is a form of devotion, little master. Everyone who goes by must place a stone."

"Even the masters?"

"The masters too. It is a devotion."

"I don't believe you. What about my father? . . ."

"Frankly, I never went with him past the Cross on High, but I swear to you that he must have done it . . ."

"That's not true. My father says that stuff is for ignorant people."

"May the Holy Cross forgive the master."

"A stone is a stone."

"Don't say that, little master. Remember that I saw Doctor Rivas, the judge in the village, man of letters that he is, man of much learning, place his stone. Why, he even shed a few tears . . ."

The wind increased, preventing them from talking. It raised their ponchos, and struck them in the face. The boy, in spite of being an Andean, began to feel really cold. Some pools of frozen water reflected the buffeted figures of the horses and riders. The fringes of their ponchos seemed like banners in the wind. When the wind subsided a little, the old man said once more:

"Place your stone, little master. Those who don't, run into evil . . . And I don't want anything evil to befall you, little master."

The boy did not answer him. He knew the old Indian very well as he had lived near the big house in a hut as old as himself. The old man called the boy "child" by habit, thus achieving his proper rank of old man, but when the Indian wanted the boy to do him a favor, he began calling him "little master," without thinking. "Little master, your father promised to get me a machete, and he has forgotten. Please remind him, little master." And now once more, the Indian tried the old refrain of "little master." He made still another attempt:

"Listen to me, little master. Years and years ago, a Christian by the name of Montuja or something like that, came up from the coast. Yes; that was his name. Well, this Montuja didn't want to place a stone at the Cross; he just laughed. And who could have foreseen then that as the man crossed these pampas, on this side of these very same lagoons, so the story goes, he was struck by lightning, and killed right where he was standing . . ."

"Aha!"

"It's true, little master. And it was clear that the bolt was meant for him. The man was riding with three others, who had placed their stones, and only Montuja was killed."

"It must have been a coincidence. Nothing has ever happened to my father, so you see."

The old man thought for a while and then said:

"May the Holy Cross forgive the master, but you, little master . . ."

The white child, feeling he should not go on arguing with an Indian, interrupted the old man to say,

"Shut up."

The Indian hushed.

Violent or calm, the wind did not stop blowing. Its persistence made it feel like an ice-cold bath. The boy's hands were stiff, and he felt that his legs were going to sleep. This might also be due to fatigue, and the altitude. Perhaps his blood was not circulating well. A slight humming had begun to sound in the depths of his ears. Making a swift decision, the boy dismounted, saying to his guide: "Pull my horse . . . Go on!"

Without another word they began to walk, the guide and the two horses in front. The boy slung his poncho over his back. He felt the tips of his toes stiff and cold, and his legs obeyed him badly. He could hardly breathe, as if he needed much more rarefied air, and his heart was pounding. After walking along for ten minutes, he became very tired, but in spite of everything, he stubbornly continued to walk. He had heard his father say that in the Andes, one must sometimes travel at altitudes of ten, twelve, fourteen thousand feet, and even higher. He did not know at what altitude he found himself at that moment, but undoubtedly, it must be very high. His father had also talked to him about how one should behave at these high altitudes, and that was what he was now doing. Only, it was difficult even to walk. To cross a flat area was fatiguing. The altitude robbed him of breath. The blowing wind had lashed his face as if it were a horsewhip. When he touched it, it burned. A salty taste grew stronger in his mouth. His lips were split and bleeding. The blood stained his fingers. He thought how his mother would have nursed him, and a deep anguish knotted his throat. His nostalgia for his mother made obstinate tears fill his eyes. He dried them rapidly, so as not to be seen crying by that Indian who stupidly was carrying two stones. Fortunately, his feet were beginning to warm up, and his legs felt less stiff.

Actually, the Indian had not stopped watching the boy in his own way, that is, on the sly. The Indian felt a certain admiration for the young white boy who was adequately facing his first taste of high altitude, observing him from the security of his own knowledge of the region and his Indian's traditional physical fortitude. Still, the Indian felt a certain uneasiness, even fear, at the boy's irreverence, in which he thought he saw something typical of all whites, that is, evil. No Indian would dare to talk like that. But he lacked the right words to make the boy understand, and after all, he had been ordered to keep quiet.

The boy, who was feeling better since even his hands had grown warm, shouted: "Hey! I'm going to mount."

The old man brought the horse closer, but said:

"Wait a little while yet."

The Indian dismounted, took out of one of the saddlebags a package wrapped in ochre-colored paper. It contained grease used to cure leather. He smeared the boy's face with it, saying as he did so:

"It is good for *puna* burns[3] . . . You have to cure yourself as I do, child . . . These high Andean plateaus will yet make you part Indian . . ."

The grease smelled bad, and the boy was being treated like leather, yet, without abandoning his arrogance, he smiled, although with a certain caution, because his split lips hurt when he stretched them.

Trotting on, the boy caught sight of the cross standing high in a hollow of the ridge. Atop a promontory, the cross extended its arms into space, under the immense sky.

A short distance away, they came to the ridge. The stones that formed it were gray-brown and blue, and not even grass was growing among them. The trail climbed, cutting zigzag paths among the rocks. The trail as well as the surrounding ground was practically clean of any stone of carrying size.

The child, returning to their conversation, said:

"And when did the devotion of placing stones begin?"

"There is no memory of it. My old father used to tell of it, and his old father before him."

"It is right to place votive lamps and to light candles before images of saints and crosses . . . But stones!"

"It is all the same, little master. And note that a stone is not to be disdained. What would the world be without stone? It would sink. Rocks uphold the earth."

"That is something else. My father says that the Indians are so ignorant, that they even worship stones. There are mounds of stones which they hold to be gods, and they take offerings of coca and *chicha*[4] to them. One of them is the Huara,[5] isn't it?"

"That's true, little master . . . It is a pile of stones. But why aren't you going to place a stone at the cross? The cross is the cross . . ."

Both were silent. Neither the old man nor the boy knew anything of the innumerable mythical stones in their ancestral history, yet, in some way, the discussion had disturbed them both. Beyond the reasons they had given each other, there were still others which they were unable to bring to the surface of their minds with words. The old man felt a confused sorrow for the boy, and thought of him as a mutilated being who shrank from a profound alliance with the earth and stones, the dark fountains of life. The child seemed to be outside existence, like a rootless tree, or as absurd as a tree with its roots in the air. To be white, after all, and up to a certain point, turned out to be a very sad thing.

---

3. *puna* burns: burns caused by a cold mountain wind in Peru.

4. coca . . . *chicha*: Coca is certain dried leaves that, when chewed, provide stimulation; *chicha* is a fermented beverage.

5. Huara: an Inca god.

The boy, on his part, would have liked to shake the old man's faith, but he found that the word ignorance meant very little; that in the last analysis, it lacked any meaning at all in the face of faith. It was evident that the old man had his own explanation of things, or, if he did not, it made no difference to him. Unable to go beyond these considerations, he accepted them as facts which might be explained later.

The road plunged into a gully, and coming out of it, in the deepest part of the curve circling the peaks, the riders found the revered Cross on High.

It stood about fifty feet from the road, to one side, its timber blackened by time. The quadrangular pedestal on which it stood was completely covered with stones piled there by the devout. The stones surrounding the cross covered a large area, perhaps two hundred meters around.

The Indian dismounted; and the white child did so too in order to have a better view of what was going on. The old man took the two stones out of the saddlebags, placing one on the ground, in full view, right on top of the saddlebags themselves. Holding the other in his hand, he walked over to the edge of the pile, and with his eyes chose an appropriate place. He removed his hat, and bowing low, in the attitude of prayer, he placed his own stone on top of the others. Then he looked at the cross. He did not move his lips, but he seemed to be praying. There was a quiet fervor in his eyes. Under his disheveled white hair, his wrinkled, citron-colored face reflected the nobility his untroubled faith gave him. There was something profoundly moving and at the same time dignified, about his whole attitude.

Not wishing to disturb him, the boy stepped a short distance away, and climbing up a small hill about halfway up the ridge, was able to see the widest panorama of peaks his eyes had ever seen.

At the horizon, the mountains were etched, blue and black, their sharp edges somewhat flattened, against the clouds that formed a white frame. Nearer to the boy, the hills took on different colors: purple, reddish, black, pale yellow, according to their contours, their height, and their distance, sometimes surging up from the banks of rivers that meandered like gray serpents. Tinted by trees and huts at their base, the mountains in their heights grew cleaner of earth, until their peaks, if not crowned by shimmering snow, ended in dramatic crescendos of bare rock. The rock sang its epic clamor of abyss, peak, ocean promontory, ridge, and all other types of sharp mountain top and ruffled summit, lofty rock heap, and angry peak, in an endless series whose grandeur was magnified by their air of eternity. Symbolically, perhaps, that whole world of stone was there at the foot of the cross, in the offerings of thousands of songs, of votive stones carried there throughout time, throughout countless years, by the people of that world of stone.

Silently, the white child walked up to the saddlebags, took the stone, and stepped forward to make his offering.

DISCUSSION QUESTIONS

1. If you had gone on this trip, what would you have advised the boy to do? Explain why.

2. Why do you think the two main characters in this story are never named?

3. What two value systems appear to be in conflict in "The Stone and the Cross"?

4. At one point the Indian mentally compares the boy to a "rootless tree." Explain why he regards the boy in this way.

5. When the Indian puts grease on the boy's face to protect him from *puna* burns, he remarks, "These high Andean plateaus will yet make you part Indian." Explain the double meaning of this remark.

6. What are some of the influences that help to account for the boy's last-minute decision to make the stone offering?

SUGGESTION FOR WRITING

Imagine that a travel agency has asked you to write a travel brochure for visitors who wish to make a trip to the Cruz del Alto (Cross on High) in the Andes. The brochure should describe the scenery and climate of the area, explain the customs associated with the cross, and provide some practical information about making the trip up the mountain. Since the brochure will be used for advertising purposes, you will want to make the area sound as inviting as possible.

JORGE CARRERA ANDRADE

(1902–1978)

Raised on a large country estate in Ecuador, Andrade developed a love of the countryside and rural folkways that would later figure into his poetry. He enrolled in law school at the University of Quito but found himself dedicating more time to poetry than to law. In 1922 he published his first volume of poetry, *The Ineffable Pool,* which is notable for its highly visual imagery. A few years later he published *Wreath of Silence,* another intriguing collection of poems.

Andrade's strong sense of social justice eventually drew him into politics. In 1928 he left Ecuador for Moscow to be a delegate to the Fifth International Congress. He soon left that position to study diplomacy at the University of Barcelona. Over the years he held diplomatic positions in France, the Netherlands, Peru, the United States, and Nicaragua. His wide-ranging experiences all left their mark on his poetry, which is contained in twenty volumes, all different and all highly original. Andrade spent his final years in Paris. ■

HANDBILL FOR GREEN

Translated by John Igo

Marine green, of greens the admiral.
Green of earth, companion to the peasant,
countless hints of happiness for all,
endless heaven of cattle grazing fresh eternities.

5   Submarine gleam of the grove,
where insects, plants, and birds teem prodigally
in the hushed love of a green god.
Green scent of the fleshy century plant
achieving in its vegetable magazine
10   a profound liquor
of mingled rain and shade.

Tropical plateau where green plumes steam
on the pineapple's tattooed head.
Shrubs of hunching green,
15   mean kinsmen of the hills.

Green music of insects ceaselessly seaming
a coarse cloth of pasture grass,

mosquitoes living in violins,
and the flutter of the frog's opaque, green tambourine.

20   The green spleen of the cactus,
and the patience of trees that receive in their green net
a miraculous gleaning of birds.

All the serening green of the world
drowning itself in the sea, mounting to heaven up the mountains,
25   and flowering with the river, unsheathing school,
and in the nostalgic lowing of the wind.

A MAN FROM ECUADOR
BENEATH THE EIFFEL TOWER

Translated by Thomas Merton

You turn into a plant on the coasts of time
With your goblet of round sky
Your opening for the tunnels of traffic
You are the biggest ceiba tree[1] on earth.

5   Up go the painter's eyes
By your scissor-stair, into the blue.

Over a flock of roofs
You stretch your neck, a llama of Peru.

Robed in folds of winds,
10   A comb of constellations in your hair
You show yourself
To the circus of horizons.

Mast of an adventure above time!

Pride of five hundred and thirty cubits.

15   Pole of the tent set up by men
In a corner of history
Your gaslit drawing in the night
Copies the milky way.

---

1. **ceiba tree:** a massive tropical tree having a large trunk with buttress-like ridges, also known as the kapok tree.

First letter of a cosmic alphabet
20   Pointing in the direction of heaven;
Hope standing on stilts;
Glorification of the skeleton.

Iron to brand the flock of clouds
Or dumb sentinel of the industrial age.
25   The tides of heaven
Silently undermine your pillar.

THE WEATHERCOCK OF THE CATHEDRAL OF QUITO[2]

Translated by Thomas Merton

The cock on the weathervane
Cannot flap his wings
Even though today is a feast.

The sun spreads his great yellow
5   Carpet in the courtyard
As Anna del Campo passes by.

Gold quilts on the balconies,
Diamonds on the roofs
Domes and towers.

10   Anna del Campo has come
With her nose in the air
A dew damsel.

The cock would like to crow
Poor tin Don Juan
15   Stuck on his belfry.

Clouds wheel round him
In his blue hen-yard,
The burning bird flashes.

Silver cock in the wind,
20   Sun-cock, paralyzed
In a desert of roofs.

---

2. **Quito:** capital of Ecuador.

Cathedral ascetic
He knows no other corn
Than the sky's kind: hail.

25   Anna del Campo goes by:
He flashes sun-signals
To his friend, the lightning rod.

Anna: take me to the door
Of your house of flowers
30   Where bliss never ends.

Give me your cool dew
For my throat of sand:
Give me your lily-field!

DISCUSSION QUESTIONS

1. In what way does the first poem resemble a handbill? What associations does the word *green* evoke in "Handbill for Green"?

2. Tourist attractions such as the Eiffel Tower and the Statue of Liberty are meant to inspire admiration. Have you ever visited a tourist site and found yourself experiencing something other than admiration? Describe your reaction.

3. In "A Man from Ecuador Beneath the Eiffel Tower," Andrade is obviously using images that reflect his own background. What comparisons with the tower does Andrade draw from South American culture? How do the last two lines affect the impact of the poem?

4. "The Weathercock of the Cathedral of Quito" is a humorous poem describing the burning love of the cock for Anna del Campo. What words and images express the overheated feelings of the cock? What images are associated with Anna del Campo? What is meant by the expressions "tin Don Juan" and "cathedral ascetic"?

SUGGESTION FOR WRITING

Select a color (besides green) or a common shape (circle, square, triangle) and write a poem that is a "handbill" demonstrating the importance of that color or shape in the world.

ARMANDO ARRIAZA

(20th century)

Arriaza began his literary career in 1925, writing under the pseudonym Hermes Nahuel. After a procession of short stories and novels, he was awarded the Blasco Ibáñez Prize for Literature in 1931. He maintained a successful teaching career along with his fiction writing and in 1933 was commissioned by the Chilean government to study the organization of teacher-preparatory schools in Argentina, Peru, and Bolivia. ∎

PILGRIMAGE

Translated by Alis De Sola

She opened her eyes in the darkness. It was heavy, it lay upon her temples like a palpable weight. She knew there was something she had to do, but for the moment she was aware only of that pressure on her brows and the thick silence of the countryside and a curious unlocalized anxiety. Then a sudden sense of shock jerked her upright in the bed, listening intently. She sighed and her shoulders sagged with relief. From the next room she could just make out the breathing, so shallow as to be almost imperceptible, of her sick son.

She got up and padded on bare feet to the small closed window, a vague rectangle in the gloom. Outside, a bluish brightness was spreading over space. Objects detached themselves mistily from the void around them, their outlines edged with a pallor like frost. The stillness was profound, the world lay as though dead. She turned away from the window and began to dress, quickly and noiselessly. When she was ready, she went back to the bed and leaned over her husband, who still slept there, oblivious, calling to him softly, "Juan . . . Juan . . ." feeling him stretch sluggishly at the sound, hearing his murmured response, "Ahhh . . . ?" that seemed to come from a distance, from the far reaches of his violated sleep. "It's time," she said in the same low tone. "It's almost dawn."

She entered the sick boy's room, slipping through the doorway like a shadow. Close to him, she listened again, painfully, to the slight breath with its faltering, imperfect rhythm like a rusted machine's. Her body curved over him in a yearning arc, but she did not touch him; her hands cupped themselves, without contact, around that loved, invisible face. It was as though she held his fading life in her hands, as though her strong peasant's will could guard him against dissolution.

He was her child, her only delight, and he was dying. His green young body, just approaching manhood, was blighted as a plant's might be, sickening on its stem. Nobody had been able to cure him nor even to arrest that fatal decay. There was no hope left outside of a miracle, the potent intercession of the saint. Today they would go to his shrine at Yumbel, on the other side of the mountains. It was a long journey, five or six hours of difficult traveling; the boy was feeble, the risk great. Yet it had to be taken, there was no other way. Perhaps the saint would be gracious on his feast day and give her back her son.

As she stood there, brooding, confidence swept over her like a wind, dispelling her bitter fears. She remembered the scene on the hillside, among the yellowing wheat fields, when the desperate hope had first come to her. She had been confiding her anxiety to the farmhand, Eusebio, when the latter's little granddaughter came near, bringing his midday meal. The child had listened solemnly, her wide blue eyes as unfathomable as the sky, and then she had spoken in a grave, wondering tone.

"Why don't you make an offering to Saint Sebastian[1] for him?"

The old man had stared at her, a superstitious awe in his face. "Did you hear that, Señora Mercedes? It's innocent ones like her that speak with the voice of our Lord."

She had thought about it for several days, her brain struggling with the problem, and at last the illumination had come. Not only would she make an offering to the saint, she would take her beloved child into his very presence, exposing him to that mystic and health-giving force . . . Now the feast day was here. In a little while they would start.

Her husband entered the room, another shadow, his bulk oddly diminished, reduced to flatness by the absence of light. "You'd better get him ready," he said, and, in the darkness, his deep masculine voice was freighted with mystery. "I'm going outside to see about the wagon."

"Let him rest just a bit longer," Mercedes whispered. "He's so tired." Juan nodded and went out. The sky was low, a solid gray mass, and the dawn wind felt damp on his skin. He walked over to where Eusebio was already yoking the oxen. "Looks like we might get rain," he said.

The older man glanced up from his work, scanning the thick curtain of cloud. "We might," he agreed, "but I don't think so. Anyway, we'll be in Yumbel by that time."

Together they adjusted the white tarpaulin over the wagon. When Juan looked toward the house again, the obscure rectangle of the window had become a bright yellow patch. "Mercy's got the boy up," he said. "We'll be starting in a minute." He went back and lifted his son in his arms, holding him gently so as not to bruise the frail flesh, averting his eyes from the hollowed waxy cheeks. Carrying him, he walked stiffly and carefully, Mercedes watchful at his side. They laid him on the straw pallet inside the wagon and covered him with thick woolen blankets. It was dark under the tarpaulin, and the boy closed his eyes again at once, as though grateful for the night.

---

1. **Saint Sebastian:** an early Christian martyr (died A.D. 288). He is the patron saint of archers, soldiers, and athletes but is also petitioned for protection against plagues.

"You've got the silver for the offering?" Mercedes asked, settling herself beside him, taking one of the thin hands in her own.

"Yes. It's all arranged." He pulled down the flap and fastened the knots securely, then climbed up on the front seat with Eusebio.

They rolled slowly through the sleeping countryside. The road wound among the foothills, always rising, so steeply sometimes that the wheels creaked loudly and the muscles of the oxen trembled under their yoke. Up and up to the bare blackish ridges where the air was high and thin and the heart hammered upon the chest and the lungs clogged. There, on the heights, the distant brightening horizon was visible, even a rosy cloud showed here and there, but all between was strange, an inchoate world still in the process of becoming, the shapes of things fluid and uncertain in the watery light. Rocks seemed to shift uneasily, trees had the semblance of half-formed giants, and a lime-whitened wall surged out of the mist like a wave.

The two men stared ahead without speaking, mile after mile. When the downgrade began, they slackened in their seats, breathing more easily, exchanging a casual remark now and then. The light grew sharper. The small villages which nestled in the folds of the hills became clearly distinguishable, their roofs no longer a blur but separate, individualized. A solitary horseman galloped past. Later, other riders appeared, both men and women, seeming to come from everywhere and nowhere, springing into being with the day.

"They're going to see the saint," Eusebio said.

From the inside of the wagon the woman's voice sounded, high and strained with emotion. "If our pilgrimage is successful, I shall dress myself in the habit of the Sebastians."

Juan compressed his lips. Many of the country women in these parts had adopted the habit, but he did not care for it, he shrank instinctively from the shapeless red gown with the yellow stripes along its hem. "You'd wear it on feast days, I suppose, Mercedes," he said tentatively, afraid of offending her.

"No, always . . . my whole life!" she cried out with fervor.

The hours passed. It was now full day. The sick boy's heavy lids parted slightly, then closed again. He was passive, uninterested, lying back wearily in his mother's arms, cushioned against the rough, jolting motion of the wagon by that staunch and tender embrace. Occasionally he moaned. At such times the woman's body would wince and stiffen as though a dagger's point touched her heart.

When they entered Yumbel around nine o'clock, the town was already swarming with people: people on foot, on horseback, in crude carts or in elegant carriages. Clouds of acrid dust rose from the streets and swirled around that mass of humanity which never stood still, but was swayed back and forth by some rhythmic compulsion like a field of grain in the wind. Here and there an individual face would detach itself for a moment from the throng: a shy girl with glowing eyes, a bearded hunter, or an old peasant woman with the impenetrable look, as though carved from dark wood, which native idols have.

On feast days, Yumbel took on a spurious cosmopolitan air, an animation not its own. For twenty-four hours it would vibrate with life borrowed from all the towns of the region, the lonely farms, and the distant mines. The people would come, make their offerings, and then, having discharged this devout duty, spend the rest of the holiday amusing themselves. The wretched little shops were full of customers and the taverns overflowed. Peddlers dodged in and out screaming their wares, selling as much in a day as they usually did in weeks. The raw colors of skirts and shawls, of blankets and ponchos, blended into gay and vivid patterns, as swiftly changing as a kaleidoscope's. And, above all, there was sound, continuous sound, of talk, of laughter, of music, the plucked delicate notes of a guitar suddenly clear among the coarser tones of the barrel organs.

The wagon with its burden rolled slowly through the town until it reached the big central square. Keeping to one side to avoid collision with faster-moving vehicles, it drew up finally by the tavern adjoining the church. The sick boy was taken out and put to bed. Mercedes would have liked to lead him immediately into the holy presence, but he looked so exhausted that she decided to wait. It would be better to conserve his slight strength for the afternoon's procession.

"Take good care of him," she said to the men. "I'm going to make my offering." And, shrouding herself in her black cloak, she returned to the street, mingling with the other pilgrims, happy to be among them, a pilgrim herself, sensing in that stir and tumult a mystical significance, a promise beyond reason or despair. To her wondering and uncomplicated mind the very number of the faithful was a reassurance, indicating as it did the power of the saint.

She reached the church. In the monastic courtyard, the throng was even thicker, the movement more incessant. She crossed it as in a dream, swept along without conscious volition by the crowd, a tiny atom in that huge fluctuating mass. After a while she found herself in a spacious vestibule where grave young priests, standing at intervals, accepted the offerings. It was a silent ceremony, the bills and small change piling up and then disappearing into the maw of the boxes provided for them. The pilgrims came and went, dumb, prayerful, receiving in return for their contributions a blessing and small gifts. Among them were melancholy faces, eyes faded and quenched from looking too long upon a vision of distant joy, bent pious shapes whose only mission it was to kneel.

Mercedes left the vestibule, her hands clutching the picture she had been given, the book, and the holy medals. She walked along a gallery which led past the great dormitories where pilgrims with no other place to stay found welcome sanctuary. Beyond them, in the kitchen, the big pots steamed and simmered with the meal which the saint gave freely to his guests.

A turn, another short gallery, and she was inside the church itself. On the altar at the right, surrounded by flowers and brilliant in the light of the candles, stood the gilded image of the saint. It was a poor little thing, rudely carved by some anonymous sculptor, with strained gesture and an archaic disproportion, but, at sight of it, her heart was shaken and her spirit lifted in utter adoration.

A murmur broke her trance, a murmur deep and tragic, yet somehow disembodied, like the very essence of grief. Down the center aisle a row of penitents was advancing, slowly and painfully, on their knees. They held tapers in their hands and all their faces were fixed in the same look of abstract and reticent sorrow.

Mercedes surrendered herself to ecstasy. "He, too," she whispered. "My son . . . He will come to you on his knees, a supplicant." And, bending her head before that mystic force, she prayed, confident now, serene, knowing the miracle would take place, and soon.

He was just able to walk, propped firmly on Juan's arm. His cheeks, angular, almost fleshless, were stained with a rosy flush. The flare, the luster of fever was in his eyes, burning like coals in their hollow sockets.

They went slowly to the square, hunting for a sheltered place from which to watch the procession.

"Are you tired?" Mercedes asked over and over.

"No, mama." The voice lacked resonance; it had the flat dull sound of a counterfeit coin.

They found room to stand in the doorway of the church. From this vantage point they could see the entire square. Barefoot penitents moved among the light-hearted holiday-makers, serious and intent upon the business of piety. A woman knelt in the dust, oblivious, another kissed the steps of the church. A white-haired man, naked except for a loincloth, stood with his legs together and his arms outstretched in the form of a cross, stark against the sky. And there were many others, each seeking some new and special gesture by which better to deserve the saint's grace.

Bells began to chime, the clear notes so alike that one seemed to echo the other. Traffic stopped and a sudden abstraction seized the congregated throng. There was a low persistent hum, the murmur of many prayers. Under a silken canopy, the ecclesiastical authorities moved forward sedately, followed by acolytes carrying lighted tapers. The procession had begun.

Mercedes had a feeling of tremendous excitement, the premonition of something superlative, a culmination of grace. The boy was at her side, Juan and Eusebio right behind her. She sensed them as part of herself, caught up with her in this extraordinary election, the raw material of a miracle. If only the saint would come! Her eyes were eager, her spirit wide to receive him. At last he appeared. Small and gilded and hung with white flowers, riding his platform like a bark on the waves, he seemed to float toward her, toward her alone, straight across the black sea of uncovered heads.

"Do you see him, boy?" she shouted in ecstasy to her son.

"I can't make him out very well. No, I can't make him out," he whispered, as though it were a secret he would have preferred to keep to himself.

"Ah, darling, you will! When he comes nearer, you'll see him!"

The boy's head drooped, the color faded from his cheeks.

And now the saint was passing directly in front of them. Stiff, archaic, shining, he was power, he was the whole substance of hope. "Look at him!" Mercedes screamed. "Beg him for health!"

The boy made an effort and raised his eyes. His lips moved. But the voice remained locked in his throat and his head bent like a broken flower's. The sagging body lurched against her side. "Tell him you must get well!" she cried desperately. "Tell him he must make you well! Beg it of the saint . . ."

But the boy did not respond, the procession did not pause. She saw the colored standards, the image fading in the distance, and something stirred and crumbled in her heart. And yet she kept on screaming, her eyes brilliant with frenzy, turned up accusingly to the low gray arc of the sky: "Beg it of the saint!"

In her arms her son's body grew heavier as though impatient to return to earth.

DISCUSSION QUESTIONS

1. As you were reading "Pilgrimage," did you expect that the boy would be healed by the saint? What clues led you to form these expectations?

2. The first paragraph does not tell the reader anything about the problems or plans of Mercedes, and yet it prepares the reader by creating an atmosphere of anxiety. How does Arriaza create this atmosphere?

3. Where does Mercedes get the idea of going to Yumbel to seek help from St. Sebastian?

4. Describe Mercedes' changing state of mind throughout the day. What various sights in the town of Yumbel influence her feelings and expectations?

SUGGESTION FOR WRITING

This entire story is told from the point of view of Mercedes, the boy's mother. However, there is also a father on the scene, Juan, whose feelings are not revealed to us. Imagine that you are Juan and that you have decided to write diary entries throughout the day expressing your feelings about the pilgrimage. (Before you begin writing, look through the story for clues about the thoughts and feelings of Juan.)

JORGE LUIS BORGES

(1899–1986)

The most influential writer of short fiction in the history of South America, Borges was born in Buenos Aires but traveled widely in Europe with his family. He learned several languages fluently and finished his education in Switzerland. When he returned to Argentina at the age of 21, he joined a group of experimental poets and dedicated himself to writing poetry for the next 15 years.

In 1938 Borges changed course and began writing fiction of a highly original and curious nature. Up to this time, most Spanish American fiction had concentrated on documenting reality, but Borges used fiction to invent new realities and to gain insight into mental processes. His two early collections of short stories, *Fictions* (1944) and *The Aleph* (1949), broke with tradition by focusing on the inner workings of the characters, presenting complex interpretations of reality, and expressing universal (rather than regional) themes. In 1955 Borges' eyesight suddenly deteriorated, and he spent the last 30 years of his life almost totally blind. He died in Geneva, Switzerland.

Borges is generally unsurpassed in turning philosophical topics into intriguing fiction, and his works have gained him a strong international reputation. Under his hand, a traditional form of fiction, such as the detective or spy story, often becomes a vehicle for exploring complex themes such as time, identity, and eternity. The story that appears below, "The Garden of Forking Paths," is a spy story that gradually acquires a much deeper significance. ■

THE GARDEN OF FORKING PATHS

Translated by Helen Temple and Ruthven Todd

In his *A History of the World War* (page 212), Captain Liddell Hart reports that a planned offensive by thirteen British divisions, supported by fourteen hundred artillery pieces, against the German line at Serre-Montauban, scheduled for July 24, 1916, had to be postponed until the morning of the 29th. He comments that torrential rain caused this delay—which lacked any special significance. The following deposition, dictated by, read over, and then signed by Dr. Yu Tsun, former teacher of English at the Tsingtao *Hochschule,*[1] casts unsuspected light upon this event. The first two pages are missing.

. . . and I hung up the phone. Immediately I recollected the voice that had spoken in German. It was that of Captain Richard Madden. Madden, in Viktor Runeberg's office, meant the end of all our work and—though

---

1. **Tsingtao *Hochschule*:** Tsingtao is a major Chinese port on the Yellow Sea. A hochschule is a German high school.

this seemed a secondary matter, *or should have seemed so to me*—of our lives also. His being there meant that Runeberg had been arrested or murdered.* Before the sun set on this same day, I ran the same risk. Madden was implacable. Rather, to be more accurate, he was obliged to be implacable. An Irishman in the service of England, a man suspected of equivocal feelings if not of actual treachery, how could he fail to welcome and seize upon this extraordinary piece of luck: the discovery, capture and perhaps the deaths of two agents of Imperial Germany?

I went up to my bedroom. Absurd though the gesture was, I closed and locked the door. I threw myself down on my narrow iron bed, and waited on my back. The never changing rooftops filled the window, and the hazy six o'clock sun hung in the sky. It seemed incredible that this day, a day without warnings or omens, might be that of my implacable death. In despite of my dead father, in despite of having been a child in one of the symmetrical gardens of Hai Feng, was I to die now?

Then I reflected that all things happen, happen to one, precisely *now*. Century follows century, and things happen only in the present. There are countless men in the air, on land and at sea, and all that really happens happens to me. . . . The almost unbearable memory of Madden's long horse face put an end to these wandering thoughts.

In the midst of my hatred and terror (now that it no longer matters to me to speak of terror, now that I have outwitted Richard Madden, now that my neck hankers for the hangman's noose), I knew that the fast-moving and doubtless happy soldier did not suspect that I possessed the Secret—the name of the exact site of the new British artillery park on the Ancre. A bird streaked across the misty sky and, absently, I turned it into an airplane and then that airplane into many in the skies of France, shattering the artillery park under a rain of bombs. If only my mouth, before it should be silenced by a bullet, could shout this name in such a way that it could be heard in Germany. . . . My voice, my human voice, was weak. How could it reach the ear of the Chief? The ear of that sick and hateful man who knew nothing of Runeberg or of me except that we were in Staffordshire. A man who, sitting in his arid Berlin office, leafed infinitely through newspapers, looking in vain for news from us. I said aloud, "I must flee."

I sat up on the bed, in senseless and perfect silence, as if Madden was already peering at me. Something—perhaps merely a desire to prove my total penury to myself—made me empty out my pockets. I found just what I knew I was going to find. The American watch, the nickel-plated chain and the square coin, the key ring with the useless but compromising keys to Runeberg's office, the notebook, a letter which I decided to destroy at once (and which I did not destroy), a five shilling piece, two

* A malicious and outlandish statement. In point of fact, Captain Richard Madden had been attacked by the Prussian spy Hans Rabener, alias Viktor Runeberg, who drew an automatic pistol when Madden appeared with orders for the spy's arrest. Madden, in self defense, had inflicted wounds of which the spy later died.—*Note by the manuscript editor.*

single shillings and some pennies, a red and blue pencil, a handkerchief—and a revolver with a single bullet. Absurdly I held it and weighed it in my hand, to give myself courage. Vaguely I thought that a pistol shot can be heard for a great distance.

In ten minutes I had developed my plan. The telephone directory gave me the name of the one person capable of passing on the information. He lived in a suburb of Fenton, less than half an hour away by train.

I am a timorous man. I can say it now, now that I have brought my incredibly risky plan to an end. It was not easy to bring about, and I know that its execution was terrible. I did not do it for Germany—no! Such a barbarous country is of no importance to me, particularly since it had degraded me by making me become a spy. Furthermore, I knew an Englishman—a modest man—who, for me, is as great as Goethe.[2] I did not speak with him for more than an hour, but during that time, he *was* Goethe.

I carried out my plan because I felt the Chief had some fear of those of my race, of those uncountable forebears whose culmination lies in me. I wished to prove to him that a yellow man could save his armies. Besides, I had to escape the Captain. His hands and voice could, at any moment, knock and beckon at my door.

Silently, I dressed, took leave of myself in the mirror, went down the stairs, sneaked a look at the quiet street, and went out. The station was not far from my house, but I thought it more prudent to take a cab. I told myself that I thus ran less chance of being recognized. The truth is that, in the deserted street, I felt infinitely visible and vulnerable. I recall that I told the driver to stop short of the main entrance. I got out with a painful and deliberate slowness.

I was going to the village of Ashgrove, but took a ticket for a station further on. The train would leave in a few minutes, at eight-fifty. I hurried, for the next would not go until half past nine. There was almost no one on the platform. I walked through the carriages. I remember some farmers, a woman dressed in mourning, a youth deep in Tacitus' *Annals*[3] and a wounded, happy soldier.

At last the train pulled out. A man I recognized ran furiously, but vainly, the length of the platform. It was Captain Richard Madden. Shattered, trembling, I huddled in the distant corner of the seat, as far as possible from the fearful window.

From utter terror I passed into a state of almost abject happiness. I told myself that the duel had already started and that I had won the first encounter by besting my adversary in his first attack—even if it was only for forty minutes—by an accident of fate. I argued that so small a victory

---

2. **Goethe:** Johann Wolfgang von Goethe (1749–1832), German dramatist and poet, was considered a universal genius.

3. **Tacitus' *Annals*:** Cornelius Tacitus (c. A.D. 55–120) was a Roman historian whose work titled Annals records the history of the Roman emperors from Tiberius to Nero.

prefigured a total victory. I argued that it was not so trivial, that were it not for the precious accident of the train schedule, I would be in prison or dead. I argued, with no less sophism,[4] that my timorous happiness was proof that I was man enough to bring this adventure to a successful conclusion. From my weakness I drew strength that never left me.

I foresee that man will resign himself each day to new abominations, that soon only soldiers and bandits will be left. To them I offer this advice:

Whosoever would undertake some atrocious enterprise should act as if it were already accomplished, should impose upon himself a future as irrevocable as the past.

Thus I proceeded, while with the eyes of a man already dead, I contemplated the fluctuations of the day which would probably be my last, and watched the diffuse coming of night.

The train crept along gently, amid ash trees. It slowed down and stopped, almost in the middle of a field. No one called the name of a station. "Ashgrove?" I asked some children on the platform. "Ashgrove," they replied. I got out.

A lamp lit the platform, but the children's faces remained in a shadow. One of them asked me: "Are you going to Dr. Stephen Albert's house?" Without waiting for my answer, another said: "The house is a good distance away but you won't get lost if you take the road to the left and bear to the left at every crossroad." I threw them a coin (my last), went down some stone steps and started along a deserted road. At a slight incline, the road ran downhill. It was a plain dirt way, and overhead the branches of trees intermingled, while a round moon hung low in the sky as if to keep me company.

For a moment I thought that Richard Madden might in some way have divined my desperate intent. At once I realized that this would be impossible. The advice about turning always to the left reminded me that such was the common formula for finding the central courtyard of certain labyrinths. I know something about labyrinths. Not for nothing am I the great-grandson of Ts'ui Pên.

He was Governor of Yunnan and gave up temporal power to write a novel with more characters than there are in the *Hung Lou Mêng*,[5] and to create a maze in which all men would lose themselves. He spent thirteen years on these oddly assorted tasks before he was assassinated by a stranger. His novel had no sense to it and nobody ever found his labyrinth.

Under the trees of England I meditated on this lost and perhaps mythical labyrinth. I imagined it untouched and perfect on the secret summit of some mountain; I imagined it drowned under rice paddies or beneath the sea; I imagined it infinite, made not only of eight-sided pavilions and

---

4. **sophism:** an argument that appears to be correct but is not valid.

5. *Hung Lou Mêng:* This Chinese novel, known for its numerous characters, details the decline of the Chia family while giving a vivid picture of the social life of the time.

of twisting paths but also of rivers, provinces and kingdoms. . . . I thought of a maze of mazes, of a sinuous, ever growing maze which would take in both past and future and would somehow involve the stars.

Lost in these imaginary illusions I forgot my destiny—that of the hunted. For an undetermined period of time I felt myself cut off from the world, an abstract spectator. The hazy and murmuring countryside, the moon, the decline of the evening, stirred within me. Going down the gently sloping road I could not feel fatigue. The evening was at once intimate and infinite.

The road kept descending and branching off, through meadows misty in the twilight. A high-pitched and almost syllabic music kept coming and going, moving with the breeze, blurred by the leaves and by distance.

I thought that a man might be an enemy of other men, of the differing moments of other men, but never an enemy of a country: not of fireflies, words, gardens, streams, or the West wind.

Meditating thus I arrived at a high, rusty iron gate. Through the railings I could see an avenue bordered with poplar trees and also a kind of summer house or pavilion. Two things dawned on me at once, the first trivial and the second almost incredible: the music came from the pavilion and that music was Chinese. That was why I had accepted it fully, without paying it any attention. I do not remember whether there was a bell, a push-button, or whether I attracted attention by clapping my hands. The stuttering sparks of the music kept on.

But from the end of the avenue, from the main house, a lantern approached; a lantern which alternately, from moment to moment, was crisscrossed or put out by the trunks of the trees; a paper lantern shaped like a drum and colored like the moon. A tall man carried it. I could not see his face for the light blinded me.

He opened the gate and spoke slowly in my language.

"I see that the worthy Hsi P'eng has troubled himself to see to relieving my solitude. No doubt you want to see the garden?"

Recognizing the name of one of our consuls, I replied, somewhat taken aback.

"The garden?"

"The garden of forking paths."

Something stirred in my memory and I said, with incomprehensible assurance:

"The garden of my ancestor, Ts'ui Pên."

"Your ancestor? Your illustrious ancestor? Come in."

The damp path zigzagged like those of my childhood. When we reached the house, we went into a library filled with books from both East and West. I recognized some large volumes bound in yellow silk—manuscripts of the Lost Encyclopedia which was edited by the Third Emperor of the Luminous Dynasty. They had never been printed. A phonograph record was spinning near a bronze phoenix. I remember also a rose-glazed jar and yet another, older by many centuries, of that blue color which our potters copied from the Persians. . . .

Stephen Albert was watching me with a smile on his face. He was, as I have said, remarkably tall. His face was deeply lined and he had gray eyes and a gray beard. There was about him something of the priest, and something of the sailor. Later, he told me he had been a missionary in Tientsin before he "had aspired to become a Sinologist."[6]

We sat down, I upon a large, low divan, he with his back to the window and to a large circular clock. I calculated that my pursuer, Richard Madden, could not arrive in less than an hour. My irrevocable decision could wait.

"A strange destiny," said Stephen Albert, "that of Ts'ui Pên—Governor of his native province, learned in astronomy, in astrology and tireless in the interpretation of the canonical books, a chess player, a famous poet and a calligrapher. Yet he abandoned all to make a book and a labyrinth. He gave up all the pleasures of oppression, justice, of a well-stocked bed, of banquets, and even of erudition, and shut himself up in the Pavilion of the Limpid Sun for thirteen years. At his death, his heirs found only a mess of manuscripts. The family, as you doubtless know, wished to consign them to the fire, but the executor of the estate—a Taoist or a Buddhist[7] monk—insisted on their publication."

"Those of the blood of Ts'ui Pên," I replied, "still curse the memory of that monk. Such a publication was madness. The book is a shapeless mass of contradictory rough drafts. I examined it once upon a time: the hero dies in the third chapter, while in the fourth he is alive. As for that other enterprise of Ts'ui Pên . . . his Labyrinth. . . ."

"Here is the Labyrinth," Albert said, pointing to a tall, lacquered writing cabinet.

"An ivory labyrinth?" I exclaimed. "A tiny labyrinth indeed . . . !"

"A symbolic labyrinth," he corrected me. "An invisible labyrinth of time. I, a barbarous Englishman, have been given the key to this transparent mystery. After more than a hundred years most of the details are irrecoverable, lost beyond all recall, but it isn't hard to image what must have happened. At one time, Ts'ui Pên must have said; 'I am going into seclusion to write a book,' and at another, 'I am retiring to construct a maze.' Everyone assumed these were separate activities. No one realized that the book and the labyrinth were one and the same. The Pavilion of the Limpid Sun was set in the middle of an intricate garden. This may have suggested the idea of a physical maze.

"Ts'ui Pên died. In all the vast lands which once belonged to your family, no one could find the labyrinth. The novel's confusion suggested that *it* was the labyrinth. Two circumstances showed me the direct solution to

---

6. **Sinologist:** a specialist in the study of Chinese language, history, and culture.

7. **Taoist or a Buddhist:** Taoism is a Chinese religion and philosophy founded in the 6th century B.C. Buddhism, founded by Siddhartha Gautama (563?-483? B.C.), is a religion and philosophy primarily of eastern and central Asia.

the problem. First, the curious legend that Ts'ui Pên had proposed to create an infinite maze; second, a fragment of a letter which I discovered."

Albert rose. For a few moments he turned his back to me. He opened the top drawer in the high black and gilded writing cabinet. He returned holding in his hand a piece of paper which had once been crimson but which had faded with the passage of time: it was rose-colored, tenuous, quadrangular. Ts'ui Pên's calligraphy was justly famous. Eagerly, but without understanding, I read the words which a man of my own blood had written with a small brush: "I leave to various future times, but not to all, my garden of forking paths."

I handed back the sheet of paper in silence. Albert went on:

"Before I discovered this letter, I kept asking myself how a book could be infinite. I could not imagine any other than a cyclic volume, circular. A volume whose last page would be the same as the first and so have the possibility of continuing indefinitely. I recalled, too, the night in the middle of *The Thousand and One Nights* when Queen Scheherezade,[8] through a magical mistake on the part of her copyist, started to tell the story of *The Thousand and One Nights,* with the risk of again arriving at the night upon which she will relate it, and thus on to infinity. I also imagined a Platonic hereditary work, passed on from father to son, to which each individual would add a new chapter or correct, with pious care, the work of his elders.

"These conjectures gave me amusement, but none seemed to have the remotest application to the contradictory chapters of Ts'ui Pên. At this point, I was sent from Oxford the manuscript you have just seen.

"Naturally, my attention was caught by the sentence, 'I leave to various future times, but not to all, my garden of forking paths.' I had no sooner read this, than I understood. *The Garden of Forking Paths* was the chaotic novel itself. The phrase 'to various future times, but not to all' suggested the image of bifurcating in time, not in space. Rereading the whole work confirmed this theory. In all fiction, when a man is faced with alternatives he chooses one at the expense of the others. In the almost unfathomable Ts'ui Pên, he chooses—simultaneously—all of them. He thus *creates* various futures, various times which start others that will in their turn branch out and bifurcate in other times. This is the cause of the contradictions in the novel.

"Fang, let us say, has a secret. A stranger knocks at his door. Fang makes up his mind to kill him. Naturally there are various possible outcomes. Fang can kill the intruder, the intruder can kill Fang, both can be saved, both can die and so on and so on. In Ts'ui Pên's work, all the possible solutions occur, each one being the point of departure for other bifurcations. Sometimes the pathways of this labyrinth converge. For

---

8. **Queen Scheherezade** (shə her ə zäd'): wife of King Shahriyar and narrator of a series of entertaining tales. The king, who intended to have her beheaded the morning after their wedding, allowed her to live in order to finish the first tale. The storytelling continued until he relented after 1,001 nights.

example, you come to this house; but in other possible pasts you are my enemy; in others my friend.

"If you will put up with my atrocious pronunciation, I would like to read you a few pages of your ancestor's work."

His countenance, in the bright circle of lamplight, was certainly that of an ancient, but it shone with something unyielding, even immortal.

With slow precision, he read two versions of the same epic chapter. In the first, an army marches into battle over a desolate mountain pass. The bleak and somber aspect of the rocky landscape made the soldiers feel that life itself was of little value, and so they won the battle easily. In the second, the same army passes through a palace where a banquet is in progress. The splendor of the feast remained a memory throughout the glorious battle, and so victory followed.

With proper veneration I listened to these old tales, although perhaps with less admiration for them in themselves than for the fact that they had been thought out by one of my own blood, and that a man of a distant empire had given them back to me, in the last stage of a desperate adventure, on a Western island. I remember the final words, repeated at the end of each version like a secret command: "Thus the heroes fought, with tranquil heart and bloody sword. They were resigned to killing and to dying."

At that moment I felt within me and around me something invisible and intangible pullulating.[9] It was not the pullulation of two divergent, parallel, and finally converging armies, but an agitation more inaccessible, more intimate, prefigured by them in some way. Stephen Albert continued:

"I do not think that your illustrious ancestor toyed idly with variations. I do not find it believable that he would waste thirteen years laboring over a never ending experiment in rhetoric. In your country the novel is an inferior genre; in Ts'ui Pên's period, it was a despised one. Ts'ui Pên was a fine novelist but he was also a man of letters who, doubtless, considered himself more than a mere novelist. The testimony of his contemporaries attests to this, and certainly the known facts of his life confirm his leanings toward the metaphysical and the mystical. Philosophical conjectures take up the greater part of his novel. I know that of all problems, none disquieted him more, and none concerned him more than the profound one of time. Now then, this is the *only* problem that does not figure in the pages of *The Garden*. He does not even use the word which means *time*. How can these voluntary omissions be explained?"

I proposed various solutions, all of them inadequate. We discussed them. Finally Stephen Albert said: "In a guessing game to which the answer is chess, which word is the only one prohibited?" I thought for a moment and then replied:

"The word is *chess*."

---

9. **pullulating:** swarming; teeming.

"Precisely," said Albert. "*The Garden of Forking Paths* is an enormous guessing game, or parable, in which the subject is time. The rules of the game forbid the use of the word itself. To eliminate a word completely, to refer to it by means of inept phrases and obvious paraphrases, is perhaps the best way of drawing attention to it. This, then, is the tortuous method of approach preferred by the oblique Ts'ui Pên in every meandering of his interminable novel. I have gone over hundreds of manuscripts, I have corrected errors introduced by careless copyists, I have worked out the plan from this chaos, I have restored, or believe I have restored, the original. I have translated the whole work. I can state categorically that not once has the word *time* been used in the whole book.

"The explanation is obvious. *The Garden of Forking Paths* is a picture, incomplete yet not false, of the universe such as Ts'ui Pên conceived it to be. Differing from Newton and Schopenhauer,[10] your ancestor did not think of time as absolute and uniform. He believed in an infinite series of times, in a dizzily growing, ever spreading network of diverging, converging and parallel times. This web of time—the strands of which approach one another, bifurcate, intersect or ignore each other through the centuries—embraces *every* possibility. We do not exist in most of them. In some you exist and not I, while in others I do, and you do not, and in yet others both of us exist. In this one, in which chance has favored me, you have come to my gate. In another, you, crossing the garden, have found me dead. In yet another, I say these very same words, but am an error, a phantom."

"In all of them," I enunciated, with a tremor in my voice, "I deeply appreciate and am grateful to you for the restoration of Ts'ui Pên's garden."

"Not in *all*," he murmured with a smile. "Time is forever dividing itself toward innumerable futures and in one of them I am your enemy."

Once again I sensed the pullulation of which I have already spoken. It seemed to me that the dew-damp garden surrounding the house was infinitely saturated with invisible people. All were Albert and myself, secretive, busy and multiform in other dimensions of time. I lifted my eyes and the short nightmare disappeared. In the black and yellow garden there was only a single man, but this man was as strong as a statue and this man was walking up the path and he was Captain Richard Madden.

"The future exists now," I replied. "But I am your friend. Can I take another look at the letter?"

Albert rose from his seat. He stood up tall as he opened the top drawer of the high writing cabinet. For a moment his back was again turned to me. I had the revolver ready. I fired with the utmost care: Albert fell without a murmur, at once. I swear that his death was instantaneous, as if he had been struck by lightning.

---

10. Newton . . . Schopenhauer: Isaac Newton (1642–1727) was an English scientist and
  mathematician; Arthur Schopenhauer (1788–1860) was a German philosopher.

What remains is unreal and unimportant. Madden broke in and arrested me. I have been condemned to hang. Abominably, I have yet triumphed! The secret name of the city to be attacked got through to Berlin. Yesterday it was bombed. I read the news in the same English newspapers which were trying to solve the riddle of the murder of the learned Sinologist Stephen Albert by the unknown Yu Tsun. The Chief, however, had already solved this mystery. He knew that my problem was to shout, with my feeble voice, above the tumult of war, the name of the city called Albert,[11] and that I had no other course open to me than to kill someone of that name. He does not know, for no one can, of my infinite penitence and sickness of the heart.

---

11. **Albert:** industrial town in northern France. An aircraft factory just outside the town actually was destroyed in World War I.

HENGEST CYNING

Translated by Norman Thomas di Giovanni

THE KING'S EPITAPH

Beneath this stone lies the body of Hengest[1]
Who founded in these islands the first kingdom
Of the royal house of Odin[2]
And glutted the screaming eagle's greed.

THE KING SPEAKS

I know not what runes will be scraped on the stone
But my words are these:
Beneath the heavens I was Hengest the mercenary.
My might and my courage I marketed to kings
Whose lands lay west over the water
Here at the edge of the sea
Called the Spear-Warrior;
But a man's might and his courage can
Not long bear being sold,
And so after cutting down all through the North
The foes of the Briton king,[3]

---

1. **Hengest:** legendary leader of the first Anglo-Saxon settlers in Britain. *Cyning* means "king" in Anglo-Saxon. Hengest is said to have reigned as king from 455 to 488. The historic kings of Kent traced their direct descent to him.

2. **Odin:** chief god of the ancient Scandinavians, also called Woden.

3. **Briton king:** According to legend, at the invitation of the British king Vortigern, Hengest came to help fight the Pict invaders from 446 to 454.

From him too I took light and life together.
I like this kingdom that I seized with my sword;
It has rivers for the net and the oar
And long seasons of sun
And soil for the plough and for husbandry
And Britons for working the farms
And cities of stone which we shall allow
To crumble to ruin,
Because there dwell the ghosts of the dead.
But behind my back I know
These Britons brand me traitor,
Yet I have been true to my deeds and my daring
And to other men's care never yielded my destiny
And no one dared ever betray me.

AFTERGLOW

Translated by Norman Thomas di Giovanni

Sunset is always disturbing
whether theatrical or muted,
but still more disturbing
is that last desperate glow
that turns the plain to rust
when on the horizon nothing is left
of the pomp and clamor of the setting sun.
How hard holding on to that light, so tautly drawn and different,
that hallucination which the human fear of the dark
imposes on space
and which ceases at once
the moment we realize its falsity,
the way a dream is broken
the moment the sleeper knows he is dreaming.

THE DAGGER

Translated by Norman Thomas di Giovanni

A dagger rests in a drawer.
It was forged in Toledo[4] at the end of the last century.
    Luis Melián Lafinur[5] gave it to my father, who brought it

---

4. **Toledo:** city in central Spain known for its fine steel.
5. **Luis Melián Lafinur:** Argentine writer (1850–1939).

from Uruguay. Evaristo Carriego[6] once held it in his hand.

Whoever lays eyes on it has to pick up the dagger and toy with it, as if he had always been on the lookout for it. The hand is quick to grip the waiting hilt, and the powerful obeying blade slides in and out of the sheath with a click.

This is not what the dagger wants.

It is more than a structure of metal; men conceived it and shaped it with a single end in mind. The dagger that last night knifed a man in Tacuarembó[7] and the daggers that rained on Caesar are in some eternal way the same dagger. The dagger wants to kill, it wants to shed sudden blood.

In a drawer of my writing table, among draft pages and old letters, the dagger dreams over and over its simple tiger's dream. On wielding it the hand comes alive because the metal comes alive, sensing itself, each time handled, in touch with the killer for whom it was forged.

At times I am sorry for it. Such power and single-mindedness, so impassive or innocent its pride, and the years slip by, unheeding.

---

6. **Evaristo Carriego:** Argentine poet (1883–1912).

7. **Tacuarembó:** town in north central Uruguay.

DISCUSSION QUESTIONS

1. Like many detective or spy stories, "The Garden of Forking Paths" presents a puzzle that is finally clarified at the end. In what way is this story different from other mystery or spy stories that you know?

2. What does Yu Tsun hope to accomplish murdering Dr. Albert? Why does he wait until Richard Madden's arrival before pulling the trigger? Is his mission successful?

3. Why does Borges begin his story with Liddell Hart's military history? Why is the story narrated as a flashback, starting from a point in time just before Yu Tsun's execution?

4. The labyrinth is a central image in several of Borges' fictional works. What do you think the labyrinth signifies in "The Garden of Forking Paths?"

5. The final scene pulls together all the threads of the story, clarifying both the murder mission and the riddle of the labyrinth. Explain the meaning of the following "threads," many of which may have been puzzling when you first encountered them:

- A man . . . leafed "infinitely through newspapers, looking in vain for news of us."
- "The telephone directory gave me the name of the one person capable of passing on the information."
- "The book is a shapeless mass of contradictory rough drafts . . . the hero dies in the third chapter, while in the fourth he is alive."
- "I leave to various future times, but not to all, my garden of forking paths."
- "It seemed that the dew-damp garden surrounding the house was infinitely saturated with invisible people. All were Albert and myself . . ."

6. What view of time, human identity, and the nature of reality is presented in this story?

7. What different glimpses of the king does the reader get from the two parts of "Hengest Cyning"? Which report do you think is more accurate—the one provided by Hengest or the one provided by the writer of the epitaph?

8. In "Afterglow" what is the "hallucination" that occurs with the setting of the sun? What eventually causes this hallucination to cease?

9. Why does the speaker in "The Dagger" express sympathy for the weapon? What does the poet mean when he says that "the hand comes alive because the metal comes alive, sensing itself"?

SUGGESTION FOR WRITING

In "The Garden of Forking Paths" Yu Tsun's murder mission could have been derailed by any number of possible events that, fortunately for him, did not occur. Below are a few of these unplayed possibilities. Select just *one* of them and construct a tree diagram with forking paths that demonstrates as many plausible outcomes as you can imagine, given this particular event.

- Richard Madden caught the same train as Yu Tsun.
- Dr. Albert was not home when Yu Tsun called.
- Yu Tsun missed when he shot at Dr. Albert.
- Richard Madden never arrived at Dr. Albert's house.

JESÚS del CORRAL
(1871–1931)

Like many Latin American writers of his time, Jesús del Corral led an active political life and served for a time as Colombia's Minister of Agriculture. His stories, published in reviews and periodicals, were often amusing tales of the clever "little man." These tales drew heavily on the Spanish *picaresque* tradition, a word derived from the Spanish word *picaro*, meaning "rogue" or "rascal." The picaresque tale, usually told as a first-person narrative, centers on a carefree character who lives by his wits, rather than by his labor, and who can wiggle out of any difficulty. The story that follows is a fine example of a picaresque tale. ■

CROSS OVER, SAWYER!

Translated by Harry Kurz

I was opening up a plantation on the banks of the river Cauca, between Antioquia and Sopetrán.[1] As superintendent I took along Simón Pérez, a prince of a fellow, now thirty years old, twenty of which he had lived in a constant and relentless fight with nature, without ever suffering any real defeat.

For him obstacles just didn't exist and whenever I proposed that he do something tough he had never tried before, his regular answer was the cheerful statement, "Sure, I'll tend to it."

One Saturday evening after we'd paid off the ranch hands, Simón and I lingered around chatting on the veranda and discussing plans for next week's undertakings. I remarked that we should need twenty boards to set up gutters in the drainage ditch but that we didn't have any sawyers on the job. Whereupon he replied, "Oh, I can saw those up for you one of these days."

"What?" was my answer. "Are you an expert at sawing lumber?"

"First class. I'm what you might call a sawyer with a diploma, and perhaps the highest paid lumberman who ever pulled a saw. Where did I learn? I'll tell you the story, it's quite funny."

And he told me the following tale which I consider truly amusing.

In the civil war of '85, I was drafted and stationed on the coast. Soon I decided to desert along with an Indian. One night when we were on duty as sentinels, we beat it, following a brook, and without bothering to leave our regards for the General.

---

1. **Antioquia . . . Sopetrán:** towns in northwest central Colombia in the Cauca River valley.

By the following day we were deep in the mountains ten leagues away from our illustrious ex-commander. For four days we kept on hoofing it in the forests, without food and our feet pretty well torn by the thorns, since we were really making our way through wild territory, breaking a trail like a pair of strayed cows.

I had heard about a mining outfit operated by Count de Nadal on the Nus River, and I resolved to head for that direction, groping our way and following along one side of a ravine which opened out on that river, according to reports I'd heard. And indeed, on the morning of our seventh day, the Indian and I finally emerged from our gully into the clear. We were overjoyed when we spied a workman, because we were almost dead of hunger and it was a sure thing that he would give us something to eat.

"Hey, friend," I shouted to him, "what's the name of this place? Is the Nus mine far from here?"

"This is it. I'm in charge of the rope bridge but my orders are not to send the basket over for any passengers because the mine doesn't need workers. The only labor we're accepting now is lumbermen and sawyers."

I didn't hesitate a moment with my reply. "That's what I'd heard and that's why I've come. I'm a lumberjack. Send the basket over this way."

"How about the other man?" he asked, pointing to my companion.

The big chump didn't hesitate either with his quick reply. "I don't know anything about that job. I'm just a worker."

He didn't give me a chance to prompt him, to tell him that the essential thing for us was to get some food at all costs, even if on the following day they kicked us out like stray dogs, or even to point out the danger of dying if he had to keep on tramping along and depending on chance, as settlements were widely scattered in these regions. There was also the risk, even if he did manage to strike some town before the end of a month, of being beaten up as a deserter. It was no use. He didn't give me the time to wink an eye at him, for he repeated his statement even though he wasn't asked a second time.

There wasn't a thing I could do. The man in charge of the rope bridge sent the basket to our side of the river after shouting, "Cross over, sawyer!"

I took leave of the poor Indian and was pulled over.

Ten minutes later I was in the presence of the Count with whom I had this conversation:

"What do you ask for your work?"

"What's the scale of pay around here?"

"I had two first-class lumberjacks, but two weeks ago one of them died. I paid them eight reals² a day."

"Well, Count, I can't work for less than twelve reals. That's what I've been getting at all the companies where I've been. Besides, the climate here is bad; here even the quinine gets the fever."

---

2. **reals:** former Spanish silver coins.

"That's fair enough, if you're a master sawyer. Besides we need you badly and a monkey will eat prickly pears if he has nothing else. So we'll take you on and we'll pay you your price. You had better report to the peon quarters and get something to eat. Monday, you start on the job."

God be praised! They were really going to give me something to eat! It was Saturday, and next day also I was going to get free grub, I, who could hardly speak without holding on to the wall. I was practically walking backwards through weakness from starvation.

I went into the kitchen and even gobbled up the peels of the bananas. The kitchen dog watched me in amazement, presumably saying to himself, "To the devil with this master craftsman; if he stays a week in this place, the cat and I will be dead of hunger!"

At seven o'clock that night I walked over to the Count's house, where he lived with his wife and two children.

A peon gave me some tobacco and lent me a guitar. I got busy puffing and singing a popular mountain ballad. The poor lady of the Count, who had been living there more bored than a monkey, was considerably cheered by my song, and she begged me to stay on the veranda that evening and entertain her and the children.

"Here's your chance, Simón," I softly whispered to myself. "We might as well win these nice people over to my side in case this business of sawing wood turns out badly."

So I sang to them all the ballads I knew. The fact was, I'll admit, I didn't know a thing about a lumberman's job but when it came to popular songs, I was an old hand at it.

The upshot of it was that the lady of the manor was delighted and invited me to come over in the morning to entertain the children, for she was at her wit's end to keep them interested on Sundays. And she gave me lots of crackers with ham and guava jelly!

The boys spent the next day with the renowned master sawyer. We went bathing in the river, ate prunes and drank red wines of the best European brands.

Monday came and the boys wouldn't let the sawman report for his work, because he had promised to take them to a guava-tree grove to catch orioles with snares. And the Count laughingly permitted his new lumberjack to earn his twelve reals in that most agreeable occupation.

Finally on Tuesday, I really began to tackle my job. I was introduced to the other sawyer so that we might plan our work together. I made up my mind to be high-handed with him from the start.

In the hearing of the Count who was standing nearby I said to him, "Friend, I like to do things in their proper order. First let's settle on what's needed most urgently—boards, planks or posts?"

"Well, we need five thousand laurel-wood boards for the irrigation ditches, three thousand planks for building jobs and about ten thousand posts."

I nearly fell over: here was work enough to last two years . . . and paid at twelve reals a day . . . and with good board and lodging . . . and no danger of being arrested as a deserter because the mine was considered "private territory" outside of military jurisdiction.

"Very well then, let's proceed according to some plan. The first thing we have to do is to concentrate on marking the laurel trees on the mountain that are fine and straight and thick enough to furnish us with plenty of boards. In that way we won't waste any time.

"After that we'll fell them and last of all, we'll start sawing them up. Everything according to plan, yes siree, if we don't do things in order, they won't come out right."

"That's the way I like it too," said the Count. "I can see you are a practical man. You go ahead and arrange the work as you think best."

That's how I became the master planner. The other fellow, a poor simple-minded chap, realized he would have to play second fiddle to this strutting, improvised lumberjack. And soon afterward we sallied out in the mountain to mark our trees. Just as we were about to enter into the timber tract, I said to my companion, "Let's not waste any time by walking along together. You work your way toward the top while I select trees down below in the ravine. Then in the afternoon we can meet here. But be very careful not to mark any crooked trees."

And so I dropped down into the ravine in search of the river. There, on its bank, I spent the whole day, smoking and washing the clothing that I had brought from the General's barracks.

In the afternoon, in the appointed place, I found my fellow lumberman and asked him, "Let's see now. How many trees did you mark?"

"Just two hundred and twenty, but they're good ones."

"You practically wasted your day; I marked three hundred and fifty, all first class."

I had to keep the upper hand on him.

That night the Count's lady sent for me and requested that I bring the guitar, as they had a meal all set out. The boys were most eager to have me tell them the tale of Sebastian de las Gracias, and then the one about Uncle Rabbit and Friend Armadillo, also the one about John the Fearless which is so exciting. This program was carried out exactly. Funny stories and songs, appropriate jokes, dinner on salmon because it was the eve of a fast day, cigars with a golden band on them, and a nip of brandy for the poor Count's jack who had worked so hard all that day and needed something comforting to keep up his energy. Ah, and I also put in some winks at a good looking servant girl who brought his chocolate to the master sawyer and who was enraptured when she heard him singing, "Like a lovesick turtledove whose plaintive coo is heard in the mountain . . ."

Boy, did I saw wood that evening! I even sawed the Count into little pieces, I was that good. And all this clowning was intermingled for me with the fear that the lumber business wouldn't turn out too well. I told the Count that I had noticed certain extravagances in the kitchen of the peons' quarters and quite a lot of confusion in the storeroom service. I mentioned to him a famous remedy for lameness (thought up by me, to be sure) and I promised to gather for him in the mountain a certain medicinal herb that worked wonders in curing disorders of the stomach. (I can still remember the gorgeous-like name I gave it: Life-Restorer.)

Yes, all of them, the man and his whole family, were enchanted with the master craftsman Simón. I spent the week in the mountains marking trees with my fellow workman, or to be more accurate, not with but far away from him since I always sent him off in a different direction from the one I chose for myself. But I must confess to you that since I didn't know what a laurel tree looked like, I had to first walk around and examine the trees that the real lumberjack had marked.

When we had selected about a thousand, we started to fell them with the aid of five laborers. On this job in which I played the role of supervisor, we spent more than two weeks.

And every evening I went to the Count's house and ate divinely. On Sundays I lunched and dined there because the boys had to be entertained—and the servant girl also.

I became the mainspring of the mine. My advice was the deciding factor and nothing was done without consulting me.

Everything was sailing along fine when the fearful day finally dawned on which the sawbuck was to be put in place. The platform for it was all set up. To be sure when we constructed it there were difficulties because my fellow craftsman asked me, "At what height do we set it up?"

"What's the usual practice around here?"

"Three meters."

"Give it three twenty, which is the generally accepted height among good sawyers." (If it works at three meters, what difference would twenty centimeters more make?)

Everything was now ready: the log athwart the platform and the markings on it made by my companion (for all I did was to give orders)—all was in place as the nuptial song relates:

"The lamp lit and the bridal veil at the altar."

The solemn moment came and one morning we sallied forth on our way to the trestle, our long sawing blades on our shoulders. This was the first time I had ever looked right into the face of one of those wood-devourers.

At the foot of the platform, the sawyer asked me, "Are you operating below or above?"

To settle such a serious matter I bent down, pretending to scratch an itch in my leg and quickly thought, "If I take the upper part, it is probable this fellow will send me flying into the air with that saw blade of his." So that when I straightened up, I answered, "I'll stay below; you go on up."

He climbed upon the platform, set the blade on the traced marking and . . . we began to saw wood.

Well, sir, the queerest thing was happening. A regular jet of sawdust kept spurting all over me, and I twisted from side to side without being able to get out of the way. It was getting into my nostrils, my ears, my eyes, ran down inside my shirt . . . Holy Mother! And I who had had a notion that pulling a gang saw was a simple matter.

"Friend," my companion shouted to me, "the saw is not cutting true on the line."

"Why, devil take it, man! That's why you're up there. Steady now and watch it as you should!"

The poor fellow couldn't keep us from sawing awry. How could he prevent a deflection when I was flopping all over the place like a fish caught on a hook!

I was suffocating in the midst of all those clouds of sawdust, and I shouted to my companion, "You come down, and I'll get up there to control the direction of the saw."

We swapped places. I took my post at the edge of the scaffold, seized the saw and cried out, "Up she goes: one . . . two . . ."

The man pulled the blade down to get set for the upstroke just when I was about to say "three," and I was pulled off my feet and landed right on top of my companion. We were both bowled over, he with his nose banged up and I with some teeth knocked out and one bruised eye looking like an eggplant.

The surprise of the lumberjack was far greater than the shock of the blow I gave him. He looked as stunned as if a meteorite had fallen at his feet.

"Why, master!" he exclaimed, "why, master!"

"Master craftsman my eye! Do you want to know the truth? This is the first time in my life that I have held the horn of one of those gang saws in my hand. And you pulled down with such force! See what you've done to me"—(and I showed him my injured eye).

"And see what a fix I'm in"—(and he showed me his banged-up nose).

Then followed the inevitable explanations in relating which I pulled a real Victor Hugo[3] stunt. I told him my story and I almost made him weep when I described the pangs I suffered in the mountain when I deserted. I finally ended up with this speech.

"Don't you say a word of what's happened because I'll have you fired from the mine. So keep a watch on your tongue and show me how to handle a saw. In return I promise to give you every day for three months two reals out of the twelve I earn. Light up this little cigar (I offered him one) and explain to me how to manage this mastodon of a saw."

As money talks, and he knew of my pull at our employers' house, he accepted my proposition and the sawing lessons started. You were supposed to take such a position when you were above, and like this when you were below; and to avoid the annoyance of the sawdust, you covered your nose with a handkerchief . . . a few insignificant hints which I learned in half an hour.

---

3. **Victor Hugo:** French novelist of the 1800s known for his heartbreaking stories.

And I kept on for a whole year working in that mine as head sawyer, at twelve reals daily, when the peons got barely four. The house I now own in Sopetrán I bought with money I earned up there. And the fifteen oxen I have here all branded with a sawmark, they too came out of my money earned as a sawyer. . . . And that young son of mine who is already helping me with the mule-driving is also the son of that servant girl of the Count and godson of the Countess. . . .

When Simón ended his tale, he blew out a mouthful of smoke, looked up at the ceiling, and then added, "And that poor Indian died of hunger . . . just because he didn't know enough to become a sawyer!"

DISCUSSION QUESTIONS

1. Would you like to have Simón Pérez working for you? Why or why not?

2. "Cross Over, Sawyer!" is narrated as a frame story, a story within a story. How does the use of the frame at the beginning and end enhance our understanding of the main character?

3. What strategies and attitudes contribute to Simón's success on the job?

4. What finally motivates Simón to tell the lumberjack that he is not really a sawyer? How does Simón ensure that the lumberjack will not reveal his secret?

SUGGESTION FOR WRITING

Imagine that you have been asked to write a letter of recommendation for Simón Pérez, who is seeking a job as head sawyer on a new project. Address your letter to the Manager of Human Resources and describe what you think Simón's particular strengths and weaknesses would be as an employee.

PABLO ANTONIO CUADRA

(born 1912)

One of Nicaragua's finest poets, Cuadra began his career as a cattle rancher but eventually moved into editing and poetry writing. His best-known collections of poetry are *The Jaguar and the Moon* (1959), *Talking Land* (1974), and *Seven Trees Against the Dusk* (1980). He taught poetry at several universities in the United States and in South America before dedicating himself to journalism. In 1978 he became the editor of *La Prensa,* Nicaragua's most important newspaper.

Cuadra's poetry highlights the land and people of Nicaragua, with special emphasis on its Indian heritage and its ancient mythology. Unromantic and unsentimental, his poems often reflect the toughness of the Indians' grim existence. ■

POEMS

Translated by Thomas Merton

THE BIRTH OF THE SUN

I have invented new worlds. I have dreamed
Nights built out of ineffable substances.
I have made burning stars, subtle lights
Next to half-dosed eyes.

5   Yet never
Can I recover that first day when our fathers
Emerged, with their tribes, from the humid jungle
And looked to the East. They listened to the roar
Of the jaguar, the song of birds; and they saw
10   Rise up a man with a burning face,
A youth with a resplendent face,
Whose looks, full of light, dried up the marshes,
A tall, burning youth whose face was aflame:
Whose face lit up the whole world!

THE JAGUAR MYTH

Rain, the earliest creature,
(Made even before the stars) said:
"Let there be moss that feels, and is alive."
And the jaguar's hide was made. But
5   Lightning struck its flint, saying:
"Let there be also his claw." Then came
The talon with cruelty sheathed in a caress.

"Let him move," said the wind
Upon its flutes, "with the rhythms of the breeze."
10   And he started off
Like harmony, like the measures
With which the gods foreshadowed our dances.

But fire saw this and stayed his advance:
And went to the place where "yes" and "no" were parted
15   (The place where the serpent's tongue received its division).
Fire said: "Let his coat be made of light and shadow."

So his kingdom was death, indistinct
And blind.
           But men mocked
20   The inexorable, calling it "mad,"
When it united accident and crime.
Now not necessity with its devouring law
(Not the moon eaten by the earth to fill her hungry nights
Nor the weak one feeding with his blood
25   The glory of the strong)
But mystery, presiding over destruction. Fortune,
Fate blindfolding Justice—gods—
The rebels cried: "We will read in the stars
The hidden laws of destiny."

30   Lightning in his sleepless pallor,
Heard their clamor. He said:
"Alas for man!"
And kindled in the jaguar's empty sockets
The deadly nearness of a star.

MEDITATION BEFORE AN ANCIENT POEM

The flower asked: "Will my scent,
Perhaps, survive me?"

The moon asked: "Shall I keep
Some light after perishing?"

5   But man said: "How is it that I end
And that my song remains among you?"

THE SECRET OF THE BURNING STARS

To him who fought for liberty
Was given a star next door
To the shining mother
Dead in giving dawn to life.

5   —"Was it great, your suffering?" asked
The warrior.
        —"Not so great as the joy
Of giving a new man to the world."
—"And your wound," she asked,
10   "Was it deep? Did it burn?"
        —"Not so much
As the joy of giving a new world to man."
—"And did you know your son?"
        —"Never."
15   —"And did you know the fruit of your battle?"
        —"I died too soon."
—"Do you sleep?" asked the warrior.
The mother replied: "I dream."

DISCUSSION QUESTIONS

1. How would you describe the subject matter of Cuadra's poems? In other words, what kinds of topics seem to appeal to him?

2. In "The Birth of the Sun" the first sunrise is more than just a beautiful sight. What special significance does it have for the primitive people who were there to witness it?

3. In "The Jaguar Myth" what different forces of nature give the jaguar its various parts? How is each of these gifts an appropriate reflection of the giver? How is the gift of the lightning different from all the other gifts?

4. In "Meditation Before an Ancient Poem" how is man shown to be different from the other creatures and objects of the natural world?

5. In "The Secret of the Burning Stars" what do the warrior and the mother have in common? Why would the mother (and probably the warrior) be more likely to dream than to sleep?

SUGGESTION FOR WRITING

Select a North American animal and invent a myth that explains the origins of its various traits. Describe the animal's creation, using either poetry or prose. Try to include personality characteristics as well as physical characteristics.

JUAN CARLOS DÁVALOS

(1887–1959)

A poet and short story writer, Juan Carlos Dávalos spent most of his life in the city of Salta, Argentina, where he divided his time between teaching, writing, and public service. His first volume of poetry, which celebrates his native town and surrounding area, bears the title *Salta*. His other important books of poetry include *Songs of the Mountain* and *Wild Songs*. Known primarily as a regional writer, Dávalos' poems and stories dramatize the rugged mountain areas of northern Argentina and its inhabitants. Many of his best short stories are collected in *Stories and Tales of Northern Argentina*. ■

THE WHITE WIND

Translated by Angel Flores

Antenor Sánchez called a halt. The herd, disciplined by six days and five nights of travel, stopped at the same time as the herders.

Including the boss, the men were four, a number sufficient to drove the one hundred head of which the herd consisted. The job of droving was fatiguing the first day, on leaving the Lerma Valley[1] after the branding. Then the steers were in the plenitude of their strength, fat and rebellious, spoiled as they were by the green alfalfa fields of the ranches, where some of them had lived for as long as six months. But once hemmed in along the Quebrada del Toro[2] they gradually got accustomed to plodding along slowly and quietly, and, the terrain being hard and stony, there was an end to attempted flights, clumsy rearings, helter-skelter lagging, for the pleasure of nibbling a mouthful of furze.

Now the voice of the boss brought the herd to a stop next to the meadows past Cauchari, in the territory of the Andes.

Slowly, economizing strength, sinking their hoofs in the burning dunes, their throats parched, their eyes tearful, their haunches taut, their heads lowered, step by step the steers veered off the trail in order to get

---

1. **Lerma Valley:** sub-Andean valley of Argentina, along the Toro River.
2. **Quebrada del Toro:** ravine of the Toro River, normally dry but filled with a torrent of water during a rain.

to the water. It was a sunny day at the end of June, a winter day in the Andean plateau. It was two o'clock in the afternoon. Only at this hour did the thawing of the meadows begin, and under the thick *iros* underbrush were little pools of crystalline water.

"Dandy place for a rest," said Sánchez, and he and his men dismounted.

Each one took down from his mount a little sack of provisions and untied the leather straps of his little canteen of fresh water; after unfastening the cinch straps, removing the bridles, and tying their mules, they sat down in a circle to prepare their lunch.

"What do you think, Loreto?" asked Sánchez. "Will the bay get as far as Catua?"

He brought out from his knapsack a few spoonfuls of sugar, put them in a jug, added water and parched flour, and stirred the mixture patiently.

"As for getting to Catua, it'll get there all right, even though it may be all fagged out."

These men spoke slowly, thinking over their questions, meditating their replies, as if the effort exacted of them by this sort of life made it necessary to preserve all the energy which the human organism generates; thus they were as sparing of gestures as they were sober of imagination and language.

While they were relishing their ration of *ulpada*,[3] the steers dispersed about the meadows. Some lapped the water from muddy pools, others sought a clean spot on which to lie down.

"A dandy mule when it comes to eating, boss," remarked one of the herders.

"It has made twelve trips with me. It manages somehow to get its feed," said Antenor, watching his mule kicking a stubble of *iro* to turn it around and eat it without pricking its mouth.

The air was clear, diaphanous, as it was in the best days of January. One realized that it was winter only by the yellowish hue of the *iros* on the nearby hills and by the snow, which, toward the east, covered the highest peaks of the cordillera.[4] A tenuous cold breeze blew from the summits down to the level of the dunes, warmed momentarily by the sun. It spread over the vast plains like a light sensation of shivering, so subtle that where a shrub cast its shade the frost did not melt, and where the sun beat, the air and the sand vibrated as if by the glow of a flame. In the almost absolute dryness of the atmosphere the fields exhaled a faint scent of jarillas and tolas.

They rested for more than an hour. Then the first steer got back onto the trail, a few more followed it, and little by little, with the shouting of the peons, the entire herd got on. They moved along in symmetrical files, plodding heavily with their coarsely muscled legs, keeping enough

---

3. *ulpada:* a drink made from corn meal dissolved in cold water, with or without sugar.

4. **cordillera:** chain of mountains.

distance not to interfere with one another's horns, regimented by the habit of walking thus, league[5] after league, one behind the other.

The men took up their customary positions: one at the head of the drove, two at the flanks, and the boss at the rear. At regular intervals the shouts "Gid-ap!" prolonged, sharp, stimulated the slow mass of passive and melancholy flesh. To the fore could be discerned, stretched out across the immense fields, the dark, straight line of the trail, a soft, ascending slope disappearing at length in a gorge, far away, amid flat and reddish hills.

From time to time they could glimpse, on the level of the horizon, those light clouds of dust raised by herds of fleeing savagely nervous vicuñas.[6]

On seeing them Antenor Sánchez recalled his hunting excursions during Holy Week in the mountains of the Incaña and the Chañe, when, accompanied at times by cronies from Salta,[7] he would spend the days trekking along from summit to summit, to descend later to his farm with twenty or thirty furs. At a thousand meters from a little herd of vicuñas running in those punas,[8] Antenor's bullet would hit whatever he aimed for. But when one is droving a herd of cattle it is not wise to waste time hunting nor even to carry along a gun. To march on, to march on always, to move along night and day, that is the constant anxiety of the herder, for with each league the herd loses weight, and it is necessary to get to Chile in exact accordance with the provisions of the contracts.

At nightfall they stopped in a dell. As it grew colder the men made a fire with cordillera roots—the so-called "goats' horns"—which they had brought along with them in their knapsacks. Their bodies cried out for something hot.

Fabián Martínez rounded the herd. Anastasio Cruz prepared in a small earthenware pot the soup of parched flour and dry meat called charqui. Antenor Sánchez, kneeling on the sand, guarded the fire with his poncho, his back to the wind. As for Loreto Peñaloza, he remained mounted, on the spot, holding the reins.

"What are you doing there like a ghost?" Sánchez inquired of him.

"The chills have got me," answered Loreto with tremulous voice.

The poor lad, his teeth chattering, shook all over, trembling with fever.

"Get down and rest a bit. Lie close to the fire."

"It's nothing, it'll go away soon . . . If I lie down it will be worse. Maybe you can give me something, if you have any . . ."

"Yes, here's some quinine."

Sánchez made him take a half-grain pill and began to boil a jug of wine with cinnamon. The sick lad swallowed down that concoction with one gulp, and then he dozed off in a fever coma, immobile on his mule.

---

5. league: a distance of approximately three miles.

6. vicuñas: an animal related to the alpaca and llama.

7. Salta: a province of northwest Argentina.

8. punas: treeless, windswept tablelands in the higher Andes.

The other men, reclining on the sand, took some soup and crackers and gulped down some wine and a pot of coffee. They ate in silence, staring absorbedly into the fire, warming their hands and crouching with their shinbones and loins and the soles of their feet close to the fire. After eating, they jammed into their mouths big gobs of coca,[9] rolled cigarettes, and began to smoke gravely, deeply tired and weighed down by the night.

Anastasio and Fabián sat together and went to sleep under their ponchos, like two dogs.

Antenor dozed off for a few minutes and then got up to make the rounds. At night, no matter how well he wrapped himself, his feet became cold and he could not sleep.

An hour later, Loreto Peñaloza, his back to the wind, was still hunched in his saddle. Antenor approached him. "How goes the body?"

"Much relieved, boss."

"Did the wine do any good?"

"Sure did, it made me sweat. I took a snooze."

"Want a *chilcán*?"[10]

"Don't bother, boss. I can make it myself."

"Well, man, I'm glad you feel better."

Antenor Sánchez made himself liked by his cattle drovers because, although he was their superior, he treated them as equals, with the affection of a friend. They respected him because he was more of a man than any of them, and admired him because he was capable of performing beautiful and generous actions. His entire person inspired frankness; his big, dark eyes expressed perspicacity and loyalty. He was a gentleman by birth and a gaucho by education and temperament.

Without losing the qualities of his caste he had assumed all the physical and spiritual aptitudes of the Indian; he was sober like an Indian, inured to war like an Indian, and he understood and loved, like an Indian, the ways and the life of the country.

Next day in the middle of the afternoon the herd arrived in Catua.

One of the herders remained guarding the steers in the meadows, while Sánchez and the other men trekked a short distance to a house so rustic it hardly differed in color and appearance from the nearby gullies, and so flat that it seemed to sink into the ground rather than rise from it. But the architecture was entirely suitable to the severity of the climate. The house stood near a well of drinking water and the hills protected it from snowdrifts and squalls.

Antenor entered the yard, his spurs jingling. Dense smoke and the appetizing smell of roasted meat floated out the tiny kitchen door.

After trekking some thirty leagues across the desolate puna without seeing a soul, it really was a comfort to reach the Catua meadows and see the simple, hospitable folk with their green lush pasture lands, sweet-

---

9. coca: dried leaves of a certain tropical shrub, used as a stimulant.

10. *chilcán*: a bread-like food similar to a tortilla.

smelling groundsel shrubs, and restless multicolored goats which, moving flowers that they are, brought gaiety to the naked hills.

"Hey there!" shouted Antenor, clapping his hands, "Isn't anybody around here?"

Immediately a door opened and, bending over on the dwarfish threshold, the robust figure of the master of the house appeared.

"Pot-bellied Calloja!" exclaimed Antenor.

"Yes, sir, and here's little Sánchez himself!"

"How goes it, Don Eriberto?"

With a clumsy gesture pot-bellied Calloja pulled his poncho over his neck and came forward to greet his visitor. The two friends, locked together in a cordial embrace, patted each other's backs in the gaucho manner.

Then they entered the storeroom, where, opposite the only door, stood a counter and some shelves.

On the shelves there were Chilean bridles and reins, woolen ropes, bales of barracan,[11] herders' boots, vicuña stockings and noseguards, cans of preserves and candies, boxes of matches, packs of cigarettes, a drum of coca, a string of garlic, and a bridal hat adorned with a pink veil. The floor and the corners were littered with saddles and harnesses, saddle blankets, salted skins, and fox and vicuña furs. On the earthen walls, hanging from poles, there were straps, cinches, a guitar, and some chinchilla and choschori rat furs. From this welter of objects clean and dirty, old and new, there emanated, in the dry weather, a composite smell that would scare away anybody who dared stick his nose in the place; anybody, that is, except a herder.

"It feels good here," remarked Antenor.

"It's the best-sheltered room in the house."

Calloja treated his guest to a few pisco[12] drinks from a bottle which he kept carefully hidden in a hole of the wall. He ordered his daughters to prepare some coffee, gave the herders some extra roasting meat to carry along with them, and rationed a feed bag of corn for his friend's mule.

In winter the people of Catua lived solely on roasted meat. Any steer that fell around those parts, whether because of the severity of the puna or the cold, was left for Calloja, and the herd moved on. In exchange for these valuable gifts which the herders were forced to make, the good man gave them a hand as guide.

For many years Calloja had been installed in Catua, inevitable post of travelers, smugglers, hunters, and miners; and since in those days the hunt was abundant and unrestricted, Calloja carried on a substantial trade in vicuña and chinchilla furs. From his numerous and lucrative expeditions he came to know the cordillera for twenty leagues around as well as his own hands.

---

11. **barracan:** waterproof wool.

12. **pisco:** a South American brandy.

He could predict unerringly all changes in the weather, and was the only one who could find his way when the snow obliterated every trail.

At Calloja's insistence, Sánchez lay down to sleep the siesta in his host's room. It was dusk when Eriberto awakened him to offer him some roast. They brought in a table and placed on it a platter of fine-smelling, sizzling, succulent roast and a loin of chops. All of which was devoured with a piquant sauce in the Tarija style and swallowed down with two or three jugs of excellent red wine.

When Sánchez ordered his men to get ready, Calloja tried to dissuade him.

"Stay here till tomorrow, Don Antenor."

"That's impossible, friend. By Monday I've got to be in San Pedro de Atacama."[13]

"But . . . haven't you taken a look at the cordillera?"

"It's fine weather."

"So it is, *now.* But tonight the moon changes. Another month is gone and it has not snowed yet."

"I know, but you can't fool around waiting on the weather!"

Already the herders were passing before the house with the herd and one could hear the clamor of the drive and the shouts:

"Aiooo . . . you, bastard, get on the trail!"

"Gid-ap, cow!"

"How's the bay mule?" asked Sánchez aloud on rejoining the herd.

"It was all in," a voice replied.

"We had its shoes changed and now it has no trouble."

"On the trail . . . on the trail . . . bull!"

And slowly they entered the somber desert again, while way up in the sky the stars twinkled, like snow flowers rainbow-hued with light.

They moved ahead the whole night long with only a few stops. At daybreak they halted at the foot of a slope, near a brook, where the cattle found good water and pasture in abundance. This was in the Huaitiquina dale,[14] a deep gully amid cliffs of gray slag.

Taking advantage of the shelter offered by the rocks, not far from the brook, the men went to sleep on their mounts. The steers scattered all about. Some ruminated, dozing off peacefully lying on the ground; others seemed to enjoy plunging their legs into the frost-covered puddles. Two heavy old bulls stared at one another in silent stubbornness. A corpulent Chaco ox, immobile in the middle of the trail, raised its slabbery mouth to the wind and let out a long, plaintive bellow: the cry of a wild soul homesick for its native meadows.

No ray of sun tinged the stream as yet, but up above a bright orange light was beginning to outline the peaks. The cooing of *quegües,* rhythmic and melancholy, could be heard in the distance.

An hour later the herd began laboriously to climb the mountainside.

---

13. **San Pedro de Atacama:** an oasis in the puna de Atacama, Chile.

14. **the Huaitiquina dale:** a pass in the Andes on the Argentina-Chile border.

Every now and then it would stop en masse, enveloped in the warm steam which their lungs exhaled, pumping like bellows in the rarefied air.

In their six-day journey on Chilean soil they were not going to find another drop of water, a blade of grass, or a place for shelter. Only the desolation of stony wasteland awaited them, the glacial forlornness of the bitter cordilleras, upon whose summits not even the condors alighted.

By noon they reached Lari, the loftiest point of the trail, one league above sea level.

A tepid wind struck them; then a cold blast blew from the Chilean side. And the four men suddenly felt their stout hearts contract.

"Eriberto Calloja was right," thought Sánchez, perceiving in the distance a dark cloud sailing over a hilltop. The blast became fiercer and more continuous. The hurricane hummed furiously in the rocks, tossing the sand. At times its violence was such that the herders could barely keep themselves on their mules. Their ponchos flapped and cracked in the wind like whiplashes. The mules lowered their ears and seemed to shrink.

Harassed by the cold, blinded by the sand, the herd huddled together confusedly bellowing, bereft of all direction.

"Get back on the trail!"

"On the tr-r-r-ail-l-l!" the men began to shout, and they advanced, bent over, face against the wind.

On the western horizon, bristling with volcanic cones, groups of clouds began to appear like black smoke from some gigantic eruption. It seemed as if all those craters, frozen forever, had begun to recall, in silent simulacre,[15] the incredible horror of their ancient convulsions.

On beginning the descent from Lari, Anastasio Cruz waited for Sánchez.

"Don't you think we had better turn back? There's still time! Catua is near!" he shouted so as to make himself heard.

The Indian had evil presentiments because the previous night, on leaving Catua, a fox had crossed his path, from right to left.

"I'm under contract and I can't back out," answered Antenor. "When one goes to a dance, one must dance!"

Anastasio lowered his head, resigned. He spurred the mule and went ahead to take his place alongside the herd.

"I also gave my word to Don Antenor," he thought, "and I must stick to him."

As it grew colder, the men had to bring out the coats which they kept in reserve. They substituted stockings and padded kneecaps for their boots, put on vicuña gloves, nose-guards, and dark glasses, and wrapped their necks in mufflers.

And then what they dreaded occurred. Hardly had they gone over the mountaintop when fog enveloped them and it began to snow. As the

---

15. **simulacre** (sim yə lā´ kər): likeness; representation.

wind had abated, the cold was less piercing, however, than it was on the summit.

A menacing silence, a dreamy twilight hung over Nature, bearing like a weight upon that taciturn herd which an audacious will was pushing onward across the awesome desert. Henceforth it was necessary to advance at all costs, to advance relentlessly, resting as little as possible so as to get out of the cordillera the sooner.

The fog shut off all signs of direction and the trail was obliterated by the snow. They had to guide themselves by the bones which in the course of many years of traffic had been scattered along the trail; heaps of ribs and vertebrae, big bones which the wolves had gnawed clean, horned skulls which still kept in the mummified hide of the snout the tortured grimace of brutal, solitary agony. Thus they trekked on the whole afternoon; thus they trekked on the whole night, crossing plains, climbing steeps, walking along the brink of defiles, always under the same canopy of silent, subtle, constant, endless snow. They trekked on until darkness, each moment thicker, anticipated nightfall. The herd on stopping melted the snow with the warmth of their bodies and remained as if enclosed in a fantastic corral. Then the work consisted in preventing the animals from lying down: they had to keep them moving by means of shouts and whiplashes.

Sánchez re-counted the cattle. Thanks to God not a head was missing. "It's pretty tough going," he said, "but perhaps it'll clear up by tonight."

He was soaking wet to the bone. He felt his lips growing still; his stinging ears seemed to be on fire; his fingers ached from holding the reins; and he had to keep knocking his frozen feet to make sure they were still in the stirrups, Frozen to his saddle, bent over, stiff with cold, sleepy, he came and went through the herd. From time to time he gulped down a mouthful of wine to warm himself a little. Night closed in and it went on snowing.

The men agreed to take turns: while one of them slept, the others would make the rounds. They rested and watched without thinking of dismounting, which they did only when it was time to ration a feeding bag to the mules. Who would have dared to walk around or to throw the saddles on the ground soaking with urine and full of dung?

"Steer!"

"S-s-s-teeeer!" the rounders shouted.

"One fell down here! Help!" Cruz yelled.

In the dark lay a huge black mass which moaned and snorted heavily.

Loreto came to the rescue. They whipped it violently, caught its tail and twisted it, then drove their spurs into its loins. To no avail. The heavy black mass remained immobile, silent.

The cattle, scenting death, began to bellow. At first they were heart-rending bellows, later a low, moaning, continuous clamor.

It was still snowing at dawn of the third day. And during that entire day it snowed and all the night of that day. The wall of snow was already as high as a bull.

Men and beasts wept. The beasts with their lugubrious lowings; the men with secret tears, haunted by the remembrance of their homes, far, far away in a beautiful benign land.

Antenor Sánchez, dumb from sheer exhaustion, felt on his conscience the responsibility for this mad adventure; he saw himself ruined through his own fault. He had insisted on going ahead more out of pigheadedness than necessity, for after all the contract provided for unavoidable delays.

Why had he brushed aside so lightly Calloja's warnings?

Why had Calloja hardly insisted and let him go on to face the storm?

Sánchez knew the cordillera perhaps better than the Indian. He had crossed it many times, even in winter; but to tell the truth, with his white man's optimism he had never considered it very dangerous. Now he recognized, too late, the implacable hostility of that natural force with which he had familiarized himself to the point of losing all fear of it.

He recalled Calloja's warnings. He considered the plight of the herders, loyal, passive fellows in whose rustic souls suffering was a heroic habit. They did not utter a word of complaint, but Sánchez had noticed them now and then concealing their anguish and sobbing secretly. Loreto, even more than the others, filled him with pity. As the poor lad was ill, he had lent him a poncho, and to prevent him from setting foot on the wet ground he had fed his mule on two occasions.

Sánchez was pondering over all this when a bull caught his attention. He noticed its sunken flanks, its wasted haunches, its arched spine. Its sharp, emaciated neck was curved in such a violent contraction that its horns almost touched its chine.[16] Its mouth hung open, showing its teeth and rigid tongue, and its eyes were turned toward the sky. The poor animal staggered, and falling on its knees turned on its side with a profound moan of defeat. This made five.

The men drove the herd onward. If some bullock lay down to rest, they forced it to rise.

About noon the atmosphere seemed to awaken from its somber lethargy and light, chilly gusts of wind began to reanimate the inert air. The snowfall gradually diminished and in a short while it ceased altogether. The clouds, rarefied, lifted themselves up above the mountaintops, and a glimmer from the sun's reverberation lighted up the vast extent of the bleak plateau. The steers began to bellow with all the strength of their lungs, as in the rodeos when they bellow in expectation of an answering echo. The mules, full of impatience, brayed and bit the reins nervously.

"Down there is the Lejía lagoon," said Cruz. "Yonder is the volcano. Look, boss!" and he pointed to the rugged mass with its craggy scarps.

They reckoned that they were near the shores of the lagoon, on a shoal where the snow, falling upon level ground, was deeper than on the slopes. Against the whiteness of clouds and mountainsides the dark summits loomed.

---

16. **chine:** spine; backbone.

"Down that slope!" exclaimed Antenor, having found his bearings. "There's the heap of stones left by the Indians as a landmark. We can get out near that spot."

"A trail goes down that way, but how are we going to get the herd to it?"

Antenor calculated the distance which separated them from the trail—a few thousand yards—and he figured a way out:

"We'll have to open up a ditch by shoveling off the snow with our saddle blankets. That'll be the only means of saving the herd . . . But since you fellows have already risked your lives on my account, I cannot ask you to do this. The wind may blow again and we'll find ourselves in a worse fix. Better leave the herd behind—it's all right with me—leave it and save your skins."

The men listened attentively, thought it over, and then Anastasio Cruz spoke: "Boss, you have suffered as much as we . . . Why do you think we would leave the herd behind? Let's try again. As for me, I'm with you!"

"So are we," affirmed the others.

"Thank you. In plights like this you always find out who are your friends," answered Antenor. "Thank you! But let's not waste time—unsaddle the mules!"

And they set to work, with hurried, feverish activity. Using their leather saddle blankets as shovels they began to dig a ditch through the snow straight to the slope. They felt neither the fatigue of the puna nor the increasingly penetrating cold. All afternoon they worked with desperate eagerness until they reached the foot of the slope, where they found on the hard ground the exit they knew was there.

Then they returned to the place where the herd was corralled; they saddled the mules and began to drive. The quieter steers moved on through the ditch, the others followed by dint of lashes. The herd was being saved.

But night was already coming over them and the cold wind of the early hours was gradually attaining the strength of a squall. Suddenly they heard in the distance the frightful crash of avalanches rushing downhill.

"The white wind!"

"The white wind!" the men shouted. And they saw the hurricane denuding the rocks, they saw the immense white sheet shifting, undulating, driving the pulverized snow down the defiles, in the twilight, like legions of maddened phantoms.

The blast closed up the ditch, suddenly burying the whole herd under the snow. Only the steers' snouts stood out here and there like black dots. Then their anguished bellowings died out without an echo, and in their dark pupils, dilated by fear, the light of innumerable stars was reflected.

Antenor Sánchez who, as always, had remained in the rear, was the last one to reach the hillock. The other men were waiting for him. He found them, like himself, all covered with snow. They were mute, immobile, crushed. Their teeth chattered and they hardly had the strength to shield their swollen faces with the brim of their hats.

"Fix the cinches!" he ordered.

Automatically they dismounted.

"Boss, I'm very cold," whimpered Loreto.

"I'll be back in a minute," Sánchez answered. Stiff to the bone, he could hardly move. He felt excruciating pains in hands and feet.

When he had finished girting his mule, he returned to the lad and saw him squatting on the ground, a little bit of a fellow all rolled up in a knot.

"Loreto!"

But Loreto uttered no answer, did not move.

"Come here, fellows, let's rub him down with snow."

He approached Loreto, tore off his nose-guard, touched his cheeks, and stared into his eyes.

"No use—it's all over . . . he's dead!"

They could not afford to waste time. They took off his poncho, laid him down on his mattress, crossed his hands over his chest, and the white wind covered his body like a shroud.

Fighting death hand to hand, the three men continued on their journey, lashed by the wind which froze their blood, goaded on by the instinctive urge to live . . .

DISCUSSION QUESTIONS

1. Do you consider Antenor Sánchez to be a good leader? Why or why not?

2. Dávalos never defines the term *white wind,* but its meaning can be inferred from the context. Explain the meaning of the term, as you understand it.

3. The author's characterization of the herders strongly suggests that they are used to fighting the elements. What personality traits mark them as men who have constantly endured hardship?

4. What details does the author supply to indicate how bitter the cold is?

5. Generally speaking, "The White Wind" is presented as a realistic narrative. Occasionally, however, there are poetic passages that move beyond realism, such as the following description of the cattle's eyes: " . . . in their dark pupils, dilated by fear, the light of innumerable stars was reflected." What is the effect of this description?

SUGGESTION FOR WRITING

Write a short narrative describing a test of endurance that you experienced. The challenge can be either physical or psychological. For example, you might select an athletic event, a dangerous encounter of some kind, a stage appearance, a high-pressure social situation, a job interview, or any other experience that tested your powers of endurance. Explain how you coped with the situation. Did you succeed?

GASTON FIGUEIRA
(20th century)

The son of a famous educator, Figueira is the author of over 30 volumes of poetry. His first book of poems, *Sweet Visions*, was published when he was only 14 years old. Figueira served as a literary spokesman for brotherhood and peace throughout his writing career and is widely respected for a book entitled *For the Children of America*, which contains verses in Spanish, English, and Portuguese dedicated to all the children living in the New World. "The Pineapple," which is included in this section, is from this children's book. In 1928 he began writing a 20-volume series called *Marvelous America*, an ambitious work that features poems for every country in North and South America. ■

POEMS
Translated by Willis Knapp Jones

BALLAD OF LIFE

Life said to me: "Come, now! Your dreams surrender."
To life my dreams I tender.

Life said to me: "Give me your gaiety."
I did, immediately.

Life said to me: "And all your tears I need."
Now am I poor indeed.

Return again!—I'm tired of strife.
And ask for one thing more: my life.

THE PINEAPPLE

With my green, feathered plume
And my pock-marked face, all browned,
I'm an Indian in ambush
On the ground.

DISCUSSION QUESTIONS

1. Could you have guessed that these two poems were written by the same author? What characteristics do they have in common?

2. How does the last stanza of "Ballad of Life" show a change in the speaker's feelings and style of expression?

3. "Ballad of Life" begins and ends with the word *life,* but this word has an entirely different meaning in each of these two instances. Explain the difference.

SUGGESTION FOR WRITING

Select a common object from the natural world. Then, using "The Pineapple" as a model, write a short, light-hearted poem in which you compare this object to something that might entertain children.

CARLOS FUENTES

(born 1928)

The son of a Mexican diplomat, Fuentes lived in several Latin American countries before studying international law in Switzerland. After graduating from college, he began a long career in foreign affairs. His works usually blend fiction and history into brilliant narratives that examine his country's roots. Often these works are historical nightmares that present dark and delirious visions of humanity's tragic struggle for justice. Fuentes' first novel, *Where the Air Is Clear* (1958), is a frank portrayal of social and political inequity in Mexico City. Other important novels include *The Death of Artemio Cruz* (1962), a dramatization of corruption in present-day Mexico, *Terra Nostra* (1975), a cruel and penetrating vision of Spanish conquest in the New World, and *Christopher Unborn* (1987), a novel about the economic and environmental crises afflicting Mexico. The story that follows takes place during the Mexican Revolution. ■

THE LIFE LINE

Translated by Lysander Kemp

It was a March night in 1913. The moonlit air tasted of dust as Enrique Cepeda, Governor of the Federal District, arrived at the Belén prison. Thirty armed men climbed out of the cars, wiping their noses on their sleeves, lighting ragged cigarettes, polishing their leather boots against their trouser legs. Islas shouted to the prison guard, "Here comes the District Governor!" and Cepeda swaggered up to the first official and belched: "Here comes the District Governor . . ."

Gabriel Hernández was asleep in a cell. His bleared eyes opened and his obsidian mask cracked into a scowl at the kick of a black boot.

"Come on, you, get dressed!"

Hernández stood up, and from the corner of his eye he saw the guards posted outside his cell. "Take him to the patio," the Subwarden ordered.

The purple air, the gray walls of Belén . . . the great riddled wall of the patio with its gunpowder blossoms. . . . Cepeda, Islas and Casa Eguía offered each other cigarettes, roaring with laughter at their complicity. The guards approached the patio wall with General Hernández in their midst.

"If I'd had a gun you wouldn't be able to murder me."

Cepeda's fat hand struck him in the face.

The five guards fired, among the echoes of the Governor's laughter. He stopped laughing with the last shot and pointed to the ground. "Burn him right here," he said, and leaned against the wall.

While the fire was consuming the General's body, while the smoke from his charred flesh was blackening Cepeda's features, Gervasio Pola and three other prisoners escaped from Belén by hiding in the garbage wagon.

During the trip from Belén to the dump, Pola thought that this was how a dead man must feel, wanting to shout to the burial party that he was still alive, had not died at all, had merely suffered a fainting spell; that they should not nail shut the coffin, should not heap dirt on him. The four men, face down under the load of garbage, pressed their nostrils to the cracks in the wooden floor, breathing the loose dust of the streets. One of them punctuated his hoarse gasping with deep sighs, and Pola would have liked to steal that lost air. His lungs were clogging up with the odors of rotten garbage when the wagon finally stopped. He nudged the man next to him and they all waited for the doors to open, for the crew to begin shoveling the refuse onto the dump.

Then they were out in the fields near San Bartolo. The two garbage men had not put up any resistance, and now they were tied to the wheels of their wagon. The mounds of gray filth, swarming with flies, spread from the road to the foot of the nearest mountain. Pola felt discouraged when he glanced at the smeared faces and wet clothing of his companions.

One of them said, "We have to reach the nearest Zapata[1] camp by morning."

Pola looked down at the man's bare feet. Then, still looking down, he stared at the feeble naked legs of the second, the oozing fetter-sores on the ankles of the third. The mountain wind began to stir the heaps of rubbish. They had to decide on their route, on which way to flee among the rocks and thorns.

Gervasio began the march, heading toward the mountain, and the others fell in behind him Indian file. At first, as they crossed the field, their feet sank in the mud and deep weeds; later they were scratched and bloody from the daggers of the dry scrub. Gervasio slackened his pace at the foot of the sierra. A cold wind creaked in the bushes.

"We'll have to separate," he murmured without raising his eyes. "We'll keep together until just outside Tres Marías. Then Pedro and I will turn off . . . we'll take the easier route, but we'll have to dodge the Federal outpost. You and Sindulfo turn off to the left, Froilán, because you know the way to Morelos[2] better than we do. If we don't find the camp before dark, we'll separate again, each man on his own, and hide until daybreak or hope that a Zapata detachment goes by so we can join it. If this doesn't work out . . . well, we'll see each other in Belén."

---

1. **Zapata:** Emiliano Zapata (1883–1919), rebel leader during the Mexican Revolution (1910–1920). He opposed the dictatorial governments of presidents Díaz, Madero, Huerta, and Carranza. His principal object was land redistribution to benefit the lower classes and Indian peasants.

2. **Morelos:** Mexican state directly south of Mexico City.

"But Sindulfo can't make it with his bad leg," Froilán Reyero said, "and the road to the left is the hardest. It would be better for Sindulfo to go with you, Gervasio, and Pedro with me."

"It would be better to keep together," Sindulfo said, "no matter what happens."

Pola raised his eyes. "You heard the plan. At least one of us can save his hide. It's better for one to escape alone than for all of us to die together. We'll follow the plan."

The cold wind that rises before dawn whipped their tired bodies, and Gervasio led the way along the path that wound up the cliffs.

Sometimes the immensities of nature do not make one feel small. Gervasio felt that his little band was a heroic army, and that their bleeding feet would sound like the marching of a throng, would ring like metal hoofs, until they had conquered the grandeur of the sierra and made it a slave to their triumph. The dawning sun revealed the dark pines along their ascent. They climbed slowly, without speaking.

Then Pola said, "Look, Froilán, who could have told you that you'd feel even lonelier up here than you did in Belén, and even more like a prisoner? I remember the first night I heard the cries. There were so many first nights, and first mornings . . . all of them the same, and all new. Like the first morning I heard the drums and the shots in the patio. But I was never the first, or the next, or the last. It was never time for me to get up and tell them I was ready and wasn't afraid, they didn't have to blindfold me. I wanted them to get mad at me, so I could show them who I was. But they never did. You know how some died weeping and thrashing and begging for mercy. They didn't know I was there in solitary waiting for the chance to spit their mercy in their faces. Every one that went to the wall left me waiting there, wanting to go in his place with my head held up. I could have taken the place of any one of them on the march to the patio. They never let me."

"I don't care what happens," Pedro said, "as long as you don't leave me alone out here. We're better off together. They caught us together and they'll catch us again and shoot the four of us at once. But I don't want to be left alone out here on the mountain."

Sindulfo said nothing, merely reached down with his arms, trying to touch his festering ankles without stopping walking.

They halted at noon among the highest peaks, where they were to separate, and sat down in the shadow of a pine.

"There isn't any water here to wash Sindulfo's sores," Froilán Reyero said.

"Don't think about water," Sindulfo said.

"Or about food," Gervasio said with a laugh.

"Food," Pedro murmured.

"I said, don't think about it."

"We're getting near Tres Marías."

"I know. It's time to split up."

"I don't like it, Gervasio."

"You know the country better than any of us. Don't complain. I'm the one who's going to have a hard time."

"I don't want to be alone."

"There was an old man back home in the village who wanted to die all alone, He'd thought about death for a long time, so that it wouldn't take him by surprise. When he thought it was near he told everybody to get out of the house and let him meet it by himself. He wanted to enjoy it alone because he'd waited for it for so long. That night, when he knew it was almost time, he got out to the door somehow, with his eyes staring, and tried to tell the others what dying was like. I saw the whole thing because I'd sneaked into the yard to steal oranges. I was grateful I could see him die."

Pedro was silent.

"But there won't be anybody to say anything to . . . before. The moment before."

"You can tell it to the one of the Federals."

"They don't give you time. If you're alone, that's the end. If you're with others, you can exchange a look with your friends before you die."

"And there won't be anybody to pardon you," Pedro said.

Gervasio thought that the vultures pardon us, the earth pardons us, even the worms pardon us at the end of their feast. He stood up under the tree and looked out across the valley. Suddenly he knew that some-where, far away, far from the wounds of his companions, from the sorrow of this land in chains, from the ruined mountainsides and the sound of murders, somewhere on the shore of Mexico's vast and indifferent world, there would be room for the salvation of a man like himself, a man stained with filth and weariness, forgotten by the rest of Mexico, but faithful, and most faithful to Mexico when he was most faithful to himself. *I must save myself now, to save others later. They want me to die with them: it would be a comfort to my men to know we are dying together. They would even prefer to have me die first, to make their own deaths easier. I want to save them if they will let me. But first I must save myself.*

"You know how they shot General Hernández," Froilán was saying. "And then they burned his body. He was all alone. That's what'll happen to us if they capture us again. We're better off here in the sierra, the four of us together."

"I don't want to die alone here," Sindulfo said. "Or in the prison either."

Pola hit him across the shoulders with a dry branch. The dawn light from the valley softened the anger in his eyes. "You fool! Why do you have to blubber? You've given us enough trouble already, hauling you along with that damned foot of yours. Why can't you keep your mouth shut?"

"All right, boss, all right . . ."

Froilán grasped Pola's arm. "Don't hit him again, Gervasio." Spirals of smoke were rising from the forest below them, smelling of burnt leaves and dry pine boughs.

"Let's go, then. They're cooking down there, look at the smoke. It can mean friends or enemies. If you just think about how hungry you are, and walk straight in to the first . . ."

They separated at Tres Marías, Froilán holding up Sindulfo, clutching him around the waist, and Gervasio with Pedro behind him, rubbing his arms against the chill mountain mist. They had to avoid the Federal outpost with its numbed soldiers, its smell of fried beans, that stood between them and the first Zapata camp. Gervasio led him through the damp firs and rocks. The earth felt cold and dead under their feet. At sunset Pedro grasped his stomach with both hands and fell to his knees. Then he began to vomit. The shadows of twilight spread through the dark tangle of the forest. Pedro looked at Gervasio, his mouth twitching, and silently begged a rest, a moment to breathe.

"It's almost dark, Pedro. We've got to keep on for a while longer, then we'll separate. Come on, get up."

"Like General Hernández, the way Froilán said. First shot and then burned. That's what's ahead of us, Gervasio. It's better to stay here in the mountains and die alone, with God. Where are we going? Tell me, Gervasio, where are we going?"

"Don't talk. Give me your hand and get up."

"Yes, you're the boss, the strong man, you know we have to keep walking and walking. What you don't know is where. If we join up with Zapata, then what?"

"You don't think in a war, Pedro. You fight."

"But what's the use of fighting if you don't know what's going to come out of it? Do you think it makes any difference if we fight or not? Here we are all alone, where nobody will find us, and I've got this fever, so stop and think. What can we do, the two of us? What difference does it make what we do or say? Whatever's going to happen will happen anyway. We've done enough already. Let's go away, Gervasio, let's get out of it as fast as we can. It won't make any difference."

"What do you want to do?"

"Let's go to Cuautla[3] and see if we can find some decent clothes or some money. Then each one to his own home."

"They'll hunt you down, they'll catch you, Pedro. You can't get out of it now. Besides, there's no place to go. Mexico doesn't have any hiding places. It's the same for everybody."

"And afterwards?"

"Then we go home."

"To the same as before?"

"Don't ask questions. When you get into a revolution you stop asking questions. You just do what you have to do, that's all."

"But seriously, who's going to win? Have you ever thought about that?"

"We don't know who's going to win. Everyone'll win, Pedro. Everyone who stays alive. We're still alive. Come on, stand up."

---

3. **Cuautla:** town in the state of Morelos.

"It's that fever, Gervasio. As if I had rats eating in my stomach."

"Let's go. It's almost night."

"We ought to sleep here. I can't go any farther."

The air was loud with the whir of the cicadas, and a cold wind came up the slope. Pedro was still on his knees, rubbing his arms again. It grew darker.

"Don't leave me, Gervasio, don't leave me . . . . You're the only one who knows where we should go. . . . Don't leave me, for the love of God . . ."

He reached down and clawed the earth. "Please come up close . . . I'm cold . . . we can warm each other . . ." He pitched forward with his face in the dust. "Talk to me, Gervasio. Don't bury me here all alone . . ." He wanted to look at his hands, to see if he was still alive, but the night was black now, and full of terrors. "Take me away," he shouted, "take me away, Gervasio. Let's go back to prison. I'm afraid of this mountain. I don't want to be free, I want my fetters back. I want them back on, Gervasio. Gervasio! . . ."

Pedro clasped his ankles and for a moment he felt that he was a prisoner again. *But I want to be in the real prison, not a prisoner of the cold and the darkness. Dear God, tell them to put my fetters back on. I don't want to be free. I wasn't born free . . .*

"Gervasio! Don't leave me alone. You're the boss, Gervasio, take me away. . . . Gervasio . . ."

His words echoed among the rocks. Gervasio Pola was running down the mountainside, toward the yellow bonfire in the valley of Morelos.

General Inés Llanos wiped his fingers on his stomach and sat down near the fire. The broad, pale sombreros of the soldiers, and their Indian eyes, shone in the firelight.

"Speak up, don't be afraid. You say you escaped from Belén?"

"Yes, sir. I escaped by myself and crossed the mountain in one day." He blew on his chilled hands. "Now I want to join Zapata and keep on fighting."

The General laughed and took another tortilla from the brazier. "You're so stupid I almost pity you. Don't you know how to read? What does the *Plan de Ayala* say? It says that Madero was too weak. And who kicked him out? General Victoriano Huerta,[4] our new boss . . ."

"But Zapata?"

"To hell with Zapata. You're talking to Inés Llanos, your humble servant. I represent the legitimate government and tomorrow you'll be back in Belén. So eat a few tortillas, because it's a long hard trip."

---

4. *Plan de Ayala* . . . **Madero** . . . **Huerta:** Zapata's *Plan de Ayala,* formulated in 1911 while Francisco Madero was president, was a plan for land reform. Madero thought it was too radical. In February 1913 General Huerta and a group of army rebels compelled Madero to resign. Huerta then assumed the presidency and four days later allegedly had Madero shot. Huerta's rule was a military dictatorship.

Gervasio Pola entered the gray walls of Belén for the second time. The black splotch in the patio showed where the body of General Hernández had been burned. Pola walked across the ashes, and his knees trembled. In solitary he wanted to sleep, but two officials came into his cell.

"I don't need to tell you," the blond Captain said, "that we're going to take you out to the wall." He stared at the ceiling. "But first you're going to tell us where to find the prisoners that escaped with you. Pedro Ríos, Froilán Reyero, and Sindulfo Mazotl."

"You'll catch them anyhow . . ."

"Of course. But we want to shoot the four of you together, as an example. So tell us where or tomorrow you'll stand against the wall all alone."

The cell door creaked shut, and Gervasio heard their footsteps fading away on the stones of the long gallery. A cold wind blew in through the bars. Gervasio lay down on the stone floor. *Tomorrow . . . against the wall. Alone. Tomorrow. And my knees trembled when I walked across those ashes. . . . We're going to be a bridge of ashes: Pedro will cross mine, and Sindulfo will cross Pedro's, and Froilán will cross Sindulfo's. We won't be able to say good-bye to each other except with our footsteps. Against the wall, alone. Trying to forget what I know, and remember what I've forgotten. We were going to be heroes, but what does it feel like when a bullet hits you in the guts . . . and then another one . . . and then another one? . . . You won't see the blood running out of you. There won't be time. You won't see the Captain either, he'll come up to you with his pistol to shoot you again, right between the eyes, to make sure you're dead, but you won't be able to speak to him, to beg him to have pity on you. I'm afraid. Dear God, I'm afraid, I'm afraid . . . and You aren't going to die with me. I'm going to die alone. I can't tell You about it, You wouldn't understand, You aren't going to die tomorrow. But my friends would understand. We could talk about it, about dying, and then stop talking at the right moment, and then die together. . . . Together, together . . .*

Gervasio stood up and shouted to the guard, "Tell the Captain to come back . . ."

(Pedro stopped in the mountains beyond Tres Marías, just beyond the Federal outpost. He was sick, he would still be there. Froilán and Sindulfo went left and the trail was bad and Sindulfo was a cripple, they could not have gone very far. Besides, they had not eaten for days, and with the cold weather . . .)

On a Sunday morning, before the church bells had begun to ring, Gervasio walked sleepily down the hollow gallery of Belén. He felt of his shoulders, his face, his stomach: they had a better right to live than he did, but they were going to die. He wanted to remember everything that had ever happened to him, but all he could remember was a bird wetting its wings in a river down in the lowlands. He tried to think of other things, of women, of his parents, but he could only see that wet bird. The guards halted and Froilán, Pedro, and Sindulfo came out of another cell. He didn't see their faces but he knew they were his friends. They were going to die together, then, all four of them. The dawning sun bathed his face. He felt as he had felt in the mountains, not small but great, a hero. They marched up the wall and gave a half-turn, so as to face the firing squad.

"We'll go to heaven together," Gervasio murmured to his companions.

"What a bitch of a way to die," Sindulfo said.

Gervasio filled his lungs with air. "We'll fall together. Give me your hand. Tell the others to join hands."

Then he saw the eyes of his companions, and felt that death would appear to them first. He closed his own eyes so that life would not leave him before it was time. The bird, torn to pieces, fell into the river, and the Captain stepped forward to give the *coup de grâce* to the four men writhing in the dust.

"Next time, see if you can't kill them yourselves," he said to the firing squad. Then he walked away, looking at the lines on the palm of his hand.

DISCUSSION QUESTIONS

1. Do you think it was wrong for Gervasio to tell the prison guards where to find his comrades? Why or why not?

2. Why do you think the brutal execution of Gabriel Hernández is included in this story?

3. What are some of the implications of the title "The Life Line"?

4. At first it appears that the four prisoners want freedom more than anything, but eventually it becomes clear that they are seeking something else. What do they really want? How do you know?

5. Just before his execution Gervasio's feelings are described in this way: "He felt as he had felt in the mountains, not small but great, a hero." Why would a man who had been captured and who is about to be killed feel like a hero?

6. As Gervasio is being led to execution, the dominant image in his mind is that of a bird wetting its wings. What is the significance of this image?

SUGGESTION FOR WRITING

Imagine that you are Gervasio and that you have been given the opportunity to write a letter to your family on the night before your execution. Explain to them how you feel about your recent escape and forthcoming death.

MONTEIRO LOBATO
(1883–1948)

Lobato was a lawyer who disliked his profession and decided to try running a coffee plantation instead. One day a forest fire, caused by the slash-and-burn agricultural technique practiced in Brazil, damaged his crops. He submitted a letter of protest to the leading newspaper in Brazil, a letter so original that the editor asked him to submit more of his writings. The subsequent articles he sent won him a host of admirers, and his writing career was launched.

In time Lobato turned from nonfiction articles to fiction and began to write realistic stories of Brazil's countryfolk. Full of local color and charming details, many of these stories were simple, humorous tales designed to entertain. Other stories, such as the famous collection of rural sketches called Urupês, were serious and pathetic portrayals of the poor and chronically abused masses. Their underlying purpose was to arouse compassion and to initiate social reform. The story that follows is one of his humorous tales. ■

THE FARM MAGNATE

A worse farm than the Corn Stalk estate didn't exist. It had already ruined three owners, so that malicious gossip whispered: "It's a stalk, all right." Its latest proprietor, a certain David Moreira de Souza, had acquired it on the installment plan, convinced that it was a bonanza; but there he was, too, dragging along under the burden of debt, scratching his head in despair.

The coffee trees would be bare as sticks, year in, year out, either lashed by the hail or blighted by terrible frosts, and their yield never filled a good-sized basket.

The pasture grounds, sterile, and pasture indeed to all manner of plagues, were the camping ground of destructive ants who shared the field with deadly weeds, swarming with lice. Any beast that set foot there was soon a framework of ribs covered with vermin, a most pitiful sight to see.

The underbrush which here replaced the native forests revealed through the sparsity of the wild cane, the most exhausted of dry soil. On such soil as this the manioc[1] waved thin little knotty branches, the sugar-cane grew no thicker than a reed, producing cane so wizened that they passed whole through the mill.

---

1. **manioc:** a tropical plant with starchy roots used in making tapioca.

The horses were covered with lice. The pigs that escaped the pest competed in thinness with the cows of Pharaoh's dreams.[2]

On every side the cutting ant, day and night, mowed down the grass of the pasture lands, so that in October the sky was clouded by winged ants at their aerial love-making.

The roads were left half laid, fences on the ground, farmhands' quarters with shaky, leaky roofs—the prophecy of ugly rooms beneath. Even upon the manor house the general decay had laid its hand, loosening sections of plaster, rotting the floors. Windows without panes, loose-jointed furniture, cracked walls. . . . It is doubtful that there was anything whole in the place.

Within this crumbling frame the owner, rendered prematurely old by his successive disappointments, and gnawed, moreover, by the voracious cankerworm of the recurring payments, would scratch the top of his gray head a hundred times a day.

His wife, poor Donna Izaura, with the strength of her maturity gone, had accumulated in her face all the spots and crow's feet that are the product of years of hard toil.

Zico, their eldest, had turned out a good-for-nothing, fond of rising at ten, primping until eleven, and spending the rest of the day in unsuccessful love affairs.

In addition to this idler they had Zilda, then about eighteen—a nice enough girl, but sentimental beyond all reason and parental peace of mind. All she did was read love stories and build castles in the air.

The one way out of this situation was to sell the accursed farm. It was difficult, however, to get hold of a big enough fool. Several prospective purchasers had already been decoyed there, by artful advertisements; but they all turned up their noses scornfully and had not deigned to make an offer.

"I wouldn't have it as a gift," they grumbled to themselves.

Moreira's dizzy brain, after so much diligent scratching, suggested a wily plan: to set plants from the rich neighboring soil in the fringes of the thickets and one or two of the other places where visitors might look.

The rascal did even more. In a certain hollow he stuck a stick of garlic imported from red earth. And he manured the coffee trees along the road enough to cover up the decrepitude of the others. Wherever a sunbeam plainly betrayed the sterility of the soil, there the old man would conceal the barrenness under a screen of rich sifted earth.

One day he received a letter from his agent announcing a new prospect. "Play up to this fellow," was the agent's advice, "for he'll fall. His name is Pedro Trancoso, and he's very rich, very young, very talkative, and wants to run a farm for the fun of it. Everything depends on how well you can take him in."

---

2. **Pharaoh's dreams:** Egypt's pharaoh dreamed of seven lean cows eating seven fat cows and yet remaining as gaunt as before. The dream forecast seven years of plenty followed by seven years of famine. (Genesis 4:1)

Moreira got ready for the job. First of all he notified all his hands to be at their posts and know what to say. He trained them to answer with consummate skill all the questions that visitors put, in such a way that the barren tracts were transformed into marvels of fertility. Prospective purchasers, inasmuch as they suspect the information furnished them by the proprietor, are in the habit of secretly questioning the help. Here, if this happened, and it always did happen, dialogues of this sort would take place:

"Does it ever freeze here?"

"A mite, and that only in bad years."

"Peas pretty good?"

"Holy Virgin! Only this year I planted five quarts and I gathered fifty bushels. You just ought to see them!"

"Are the cattle troubled with ticks?"

"Bah! One now and then. But there's no better place for breeding. No bad weeds in the pastures. It's a pity the poor owner hasn't the strength he needs, for this would be a model estate!"

The supernumeraries having been trained in their parts, at night, the family discussed the preparations for receiving their guest. The revival of their dying hopes filled everybody with happiness.

"Something tells me that this time the deal will go through," said the good-for-nothing son. And then he announced that he was going to need three *contos de reis*[3] to set himself up in business.

"What business?" asked his father, astonished.

"A store, in Volta Redonda."

"Volta Redonda! I wondered how any sensible idea could find lodging in your windy garret. What are you going to do? Sell Tudinha's people on trust?"

The youth did not blush, but he said nothing; he had his reasons.

The wife wanted a house in the city; for a long time she had had an eye on one, on a certain street—a nice house for people in comfortable circumstances.

Zilda asked for a piano, and crates and more crates of novels.

That night they went to bed happy and early the next day they sent to the city for some delicacies for their guests—butter, cheese, cookies. There was some hesitancy about the butter.

"It's really not worth the trouble," grumbled the wife. "It means three thousand *reis*. I'd rather buy the piece of goods that I need so much with that money."

"We've got to do it, old girl. Sometimes a mere trifle will clinch a bargain. Butter is grease and grease oils the wheels."

The butter won out.

While they were waiting for these things, Donna Izaura got busy with the house, sweeping, dusting and arranging the guest room. She killed the

---

3. **three *contos de reis*:** three million reis. The reis is a former monetary unit of Portugal and Brazil.

fattest of the bony chickens and a lame little suckling pig. She was making dough for pastry when:

"Here he comes!" shouted Moreira from the window, where he had been posted since early morning, as nervous as he could be, sweeping the road with an old pair of binoculars. Without leaving his observation post he kept transmitting to his busied wife the details that he could make out.

"He's young. . . . Well dressed. . . . Panama hat. . . . He looks like Chico Canhambora. . . ."

At last the guest arrived, dismounted and presented his card. Pedro Trancoso de Carvalhaes Fagundes. Fine appearance. The air of one who has plenty of money. Younger and far more refined than any that had thus far visited the estate.

He told a number of tales with the ease of one who is absolutely at home in the world; he related his trip, the incidents on the way,—a tiny, long-tailed marmoset that he had seen hanging from a branch.

After the two men had gone into the sitting room, Zico, unable to restrain his curiosity, put his ear against the keyhole, from which strategic point he whispered to the women who were busy arranging the table whatever he managed to catch of the conversation. All at once, making a suggestive grimace, he called to his sister in a stage whisper:

"He's a bachelor, Zilda!"

Without any pretense whatsoever the girl dropped her knives and forks and disappeared. A half an hour later she returned, wearing her best dress, and with two round red spots on her cheeks. Anybody who had gone into the farm chapel then would have noticed the absence of several petals from the red silk paper roses that adorned Saint Anthony, and a lighted candle at the feet of the image.

In the country, rouge and marriages spring alike from the oratory. . . .

Trancoso was going on at great length about various agricultural questions.

"Our native hogs? Pff! A backward stock, and wild to boot. I'm for Poland Chinas. Large Black isn't so bad, either. But the Polands beat them all!"

Moreira, who was innocent of all knowledge in the matter, and familiar with only his own famished pigs, who had neither name nor breed, unconsciously opened his mouth wide with astonishment.

"As far as cattle are concerned," continued Trancoso, "it's my opinion that all of the authorities, from Barreto to Prado, are dead wrong. I don't believe in either selection or cross-breeding. I'd like to see the finest breeds introduced at once—the Polled Angus, or Red Lincoln. We haven't any pastures, you say? Then let's make them. Let's plant alfalfa. Let's build silos. Assis Brasil once confessed to me . . ."

Assis Brasil! This fellow rubbed elbows with the authorities in agriculture! He was an intimate friend of them all—Prado, Barreto, Contrim. . . . And of ministers, as well! "I've already talked this over with Bezerra. . . ."

Never had the estate been honored by so distinguished a gentleman— so high up in society and so widely traveled.

He spoke of Argentina and of Chicago as if he had returned from there but yesterday.

Moreira's mouth opened wider and wider until it reached the maximum degree of aperture permitted by the maxillary muscles. At this juncture a timid, feminine voice announced that lunch was ready.

Introductions followed.

Zilda was the recipient of compliments such as she had never dreamed of, and they set her heart fluttering. Like praise was meted out to the chicken stew, the *tu'tu*,[4] the pie and even the drinking water.

"Such pure, crystal-clear, absolutely drinkable water, Senhor Moreira, is worth the best of wines. Happy those who may quaff of it!"

The family exchanged glances. Never had it occurred to them that they had anything so precious in the house, and each one unwittingly sipped his liquid as though he were tasting the nectar for the first time. Zico even smacked his lips.

Donna Izaura was beside herself with joy. The eulogy of her cooking had won her heart. That praise more than compensated her for all her trouble.

"There, Zico," she whispered to her son, "see what an education means. That's what you call refinement!"

After the coffee, which was greeted with a "Delicious!" Senhor Moreira invited the young man for a ride on horseback.

"Impossible, my dear man. I never go riding right after eating. It gives me cephalalgia."

Zilda blushed. Zilda always blushed when she did not understand a word.

"We'll go out in the afternoon. I'm in no hurry. I'd prefer a nice walk through the apple orchard; it's good for the digestion."

As the two men sauntered off toward the orchard, Zilda and Zico made a dash for the dictionary.

"It isn't in the S's," said the boy.

"Try C," advised the girl.

After some difficulty they found the word.

"Headache—well, what do you think of that! Such a simple thing!"

That afternoon, on their horseback ride, Trancoso admired everything that he laid eyes on, to the great amazement of the farmer, who heard his property praised for the first time.

Prospective purchasers, as a rule, ran down everything and had eyes only for the defects; in front of a hollow they exclaimed upon the dangers of sliding soil; they found the water either bad or insufficient; all they saw when they looked at an ox were the ticks. Not so Trancoso. He praised things to the skies. When they reached the camouflaged spots, and Moreira pointed with a trembling finger to the plants, the youth went into ecstasies.

---

4. *tu'tu*: a Brazilian dish of beans with manioc starch.

"The deuce! This is extraordinary!"

It was before the garlic that his amazement reached its climax.

"This is simply marvelous! Never did I imagine that I should find in these parts even the sign of such a plant!" he declared, plucking off a leaf which he put in his notebook as a souvenir.

In the house he took Donna Izaura into his confidence.

"Really, madam, the quality of this land far exceeds my expectations. Even garlic! That's positively astounding!"

Donna Izaura lowered her eyes.

The next scene took place on the veranda.

It was night. A night filled with the chirping of the crickets, the croaking of the frogs, the heavens star-studded and peace lying over all earth.

Trancoso, comfortably ensconced in a rocking chair, transformed his after-dinner drowsiness into poetic languor.

"This chirping of the crickets—how enchanting! I adore these starry nights, and this bucolic, rustic life—so healthy and happy!"

"But it's very sad," ventured Zilda.

"Do you think so, really? Would you rather have the strident song of the locust in the glaring sunlight?" he asked, mellowing his voice. "It must be that some little cloud casts its shadow over your heart. . . ."

Moreira, seeing that the situation was becoming sentimental, and well aware that it might lead to matrimonial consequences, clapped his hand to his forehead and roared: "The devil! I've forgotten all about . . ." He did not say just what he had forgotten, nor was it necessary. He hurried off, leaving the two alone.

The dialogue continued, with more honey and roses than before.

"You are a poet!" exclaimed Zilda, at one of his tenderest remarks.

"Who is not a poet beneath the stars of heaven and beside a star of the earth?"

"Ah me!" sighed the quivering lass.

Trancoso's bosom, too, heaved a sigh. His eyes rose to a cloud that resembled the Milky Way, and his lips murmured, as if to himself, one of those commonplaces that conquer maidens:

"Love! . . . The Milky Way of Life! The perfume of roses, the mists of dawn! . . . To love, to listen to the stars. . . . Love ye, for only those who love understand the message of the stars!"

This was mere smugglers' slop. Nevertheless, to the inexperienced palate of the maiden, it tasted like Lachrymæ Christi.[5] She felt the fumes rise to her head. She was eager to reciprocate. She rummaged among the rhetorical figures of her memory.

"What a pretty thing to put on a post card!"

Coffee and cakes came to interrupt the budding idyll.

What a night was that! One would have said that the angel of happiness had spread his glittering wings over that sad household. Zilda beheld before her very eyes the realization of all the passionate novels she had ever

5. **Lachrymæ Christi:** "tears of Christ," a kind of rich, sweet, Italian wine.

devoured. Donna Izaura had visions of marrying her off to a wealthy magnate. Moreira dreamed that his debts were all paid and that a handsome surplus jingled in his pockets. And Zico, picturing himself transformed into a merchant, spent the entire night in dreamland, selling goods on trust to Tudinha's people, until the man, won over by such magnanimity, conceded him his daughter.

Only Trancoso slept like a rock, unvisited by dream or nightmare. It's great to be rich!

The next day he visited the rest of the estate—the coffee plantation and the pastures; he informed himself about the methods of breeding and the modern improvements. And as the enthusiasm of the excellent young man continued, Moreira, who had decided the previous evening to ask forty *contos* for the "Corn Stalk," thought it would be a good idea to raise the price. After the scene of the garlic shoot, he made up his mind to ask forty-five, at the end of the examination of the cattle he had raised the figure to fifty; on the way back from the coffee plantation he went up to sixty. When at last the great question arrived, the old fellow replied in a firm voice:

"Seventy-five," and he awaited the answer, ready for a storm of objection.

To his surprise, however, Trancoso found the price reasonable.

"Why, that's not bad at all," he replied. "It's a lower figure than I had expected."

The old codger bit his lip and tried to remedy his error.

"Seventy-five, yes, but . . . not including the cattle."

"Oh, certainly," responded Trapcoso.

". . . nor the pigs, either."

"Of course."

". . . nor the furniture."

"Quite natural."

The farmer gasped; there was nothing more to exclude. He called himself a stupid ass. Why hadn't he asked eighty?

His wife, apprised of the situation, called him an idiot.

"But, woman, even forty would have been a fortune!"

"Then eighty would have been twice as good. Don't make excuses. I never yet saw a Moreira who wasn't a blockhead. It's in the blood. You're not to blame."

For a moment they were both sullen, but the cloud of their ill-humor was dispelled by their eagerness to build castles in their air with this unexpected windfall.

Zico took advantage of the favorable gale to clinch the promise of the three *contos* that he needed for establishing his business. Donna Izaura changed her mind about their new home. She had thought of another one now—on the street through which all the religious processions passed; Eusebio Leite's house.

"But that costs twelve *contos*," protested the husband.

"Yes, but it's much better than that other hovel. Well laid out. The only thing I don't like about it is the bedroom, so close to the roof. Too dark."

"We can put in a skylight."

"Then the garden needs repairs. Instead of the poultry yard . . ."

Into the wee small hours, they were busy restoring the house, painting it, transforming it into the most delightful of city residences. As they were drowsily putting the finishing touches to the job, Zico knocked at the door.

"Three *contos* won't be enough, father; I must have five. I forgot to count the taxes, and the rent and other little things. . . ." The father, between two yawns, generously conceded six.

And Zilda? She was sailing the high seas of a fairy-tale.

Let her sail on.

The day when the genial prospective purchaser had to leave came at last. Trancoso said his farewells. He was indeed sorry that he could not prolong so delightful a stay, but important matters demanded his presence elsewhere. The life of a capitalist is not so ideal as it seems. . . . The proposition was as good as settled; he would give his definite answer within a week.

So he left, taking with him a package of eggs—he liked the breed of hens they raised there very much. And a little sack of *carás*[6]—a tidbit of which he was gluttonously fond.

He took, in addition, an excellent souvenir: Rosilho, Moreira's roan, the best horse on the farm. He had praised the animal so highly during their rides that the proprietor had felt in honor bound to refuse to sell; instead he presented the horse to him.

"You see," said Moreira, summing up the general opinion, "a very wealthy young man; upright, as learned as a university graduate, and yet amiable, well-bred, not turning up his nose like the trash that has been coming here. Breeding will show!"

The old lady was most pleased by his lack of formality. To take eggs and *carás* away with him! How democratic!

They all agreed upon the fellow's merits, each praising him after his own fashion. And thus, even after he had left, the wealthy young man filled the thoughts of the household for a whole week.

But the week passed without bringing the eagerly awaited reply. Then another. And still another. Moreira, a little worried, wrote to him. No reply. He recalled a friend who lived in the same city, and sent him a letter requesting him to ask the capitalist for his definite decision. As for the price, he would come down a trifle. He would let the farm go at fifty-five, at fifty, even forty, including the cattle and the furniture.

His friend replied without delay. As the envelope was torn open, the four hearts beat violently; that paper contained their common fate.

The letter read:

"Dear Moreira:

"Either I am much mistaken or you have been taken in. There isn't any capitalist hereabouts by the name of Trancoso Carvalhaes. There is a Trancosinho, the son of Mrs. Veva, better known as Sacatrapos. He's a

---

6. *carás*: yams.

scamp who lives by his wits and deceives folks who don't know him. Not long ago he traveled through the state of Minas, from one farm to another, under various pretexts. At times he's a prospective purchaser, he spends a week at the home of the owner, wearing him out with walks and rides looking over the property. He eats and drinks of the very best, makes love to the servants, the daughter of the house, or whomever else he finds—he's a rare article!—and then, when everything is just about settled, he skips out. He's done this a hundred times, always changing the scene of his activities. The rascal likes a change of diet. As this is the only Trancoso around here, I won't bother transmitting your offer. Imagine that good-for-nothing buying a farm!"

Moreira collapsed into a chair, utterly crushed, the letter dropping from his fingers. Then the blood rushed to his face and his eyes blazed.

"The dirty dog!"

The four hopes of the household came tumbling down with a crash, amidst the tears of the daughter, the fury of the mother and the rage of the two men. Zico declared that he would set out at once in search of the rascal and smash his face for him.

"Patience, my boy. The world goes round. One fine day I'll come across the thief, and then I'll square accounts."

Poor air castles! The beautiful châteaux of Spain, reared during a month of miraculous wealth were transformed into gloomy, abandoned ruins. Donna Izaura mourned her cakes, her butter, her pullets. As for Zilda, the disaster was like a hurricane roaring through a flourishing garden. She took to bed with a fever. Her face grew thin. All the tragic passages of the novels she had devoured passed before her mind's eye; in every instance she was the victim. There were days when she thought of suicide. In the end she became accustomed to the idea and she continued to live. She thus had the opportunity of discovering that this business of dying for love occurs only in romantic fiction.

This is the end of the tale—for the parquet;[7] for the gallery there is a little more. Orchestra patrons are accustomed to be content with a few clever, amusing touches in good taste. They come into the theater after the play has begun, and leave before the epilogue. The gallery, however, wants the show complete, so that they may get their money's worth down to the last cent. In novels and tales they demand the definite solution of the plot. They want to know, and rightly, too, whether So-and-so died, whether the girl got married and lived happily ever after, whether the man sold the estate at last, and for how much.

A sound, human curiosity, worthy of all respect.

Did poor Moreira sell his farm?

It hurts me to confess that he didn't. And his failure to sell it came about in the most inconceivable manner that the devil ever concocted.

---

7. **parquet:** main floor of a theater.

The devil, of course. For who else is capable of snarling the thread of the skein with so many loops and blind knots just when the knitting is approaching its happy completion?

Fortune willed that that rascal, Trancosinho, should win fifty *contos* in the lottery. Don't laugh. Why shouldn't it have been Trancoso, since Luck is blind—and he had the right number in his pocket? He won the fifty *contos*—a sum which was the height of affluence for a pauper like him.

It took him weeks to get over his stupefaction. Then he decided to become a landed proprietor. He would stop gossip by realizing a project chat had never occurred to him in the wildest flights of his imagination: he would buy a farm.

He ran mentally over the list of all he had visited during the years of his wanderings, and finally settled upon the Corn Stalk. The determining factor was, above all, the recollection of the girl and the old lady's cakes. He planned to entrust the management to his father-in-law, and live a life of ease, lulled by Zilda's love and his mother-in-law's culinary accomplishments.

So he wrote to Moreira announcing his return for the purpose of closing the deal.

When that letter reached the Corn Stalk, there were roars of rage mingled with howls of vengeance.

"The day of reckoning has come!" cried the old man. "The scoundrel liked the feast and is coming back for more. But this time I'll spoil his appetite, see if I don't!" he concluded, rubbing his palms in foretaste of vengeance.

A flash of hope passed over Zilda's worn heart. The dark night in her soul was lighted by the moonbeam of a "Who can tell?" But she did not dare say a word for fear of her father and brother, who were plotting a terrible settlement. She hoped for a miracle. She lighted another candle to Saint Anthony.

The great day arrived. Trancoso burst in upon the estate mounted upon Rosilho, whom he set a-prancing. Moreira came out to welcome him, his arms behind his back. Before dropping his reins the amiable rogue burst into effusive greetings:

"My dear, dear Moreira! At last the day has come. I am ready to take over your estate at once."

Moreira was all a-quiver. He waited for the knave to dismount. No sooner had Trancoso released the reins and come toward him, all smiles, with open arms, than the old man drew from under his coat a cat-o'-nine-tails and fell upon him with ungodly zeal.

"So you want a farm, do you? Here, here's your farm. Thief!" and slash, slash fell the whip tails.

The poor young man, dazed by this unexpected attack, rushed to his horse and threw himself blindly on it, while Zico sailed into him with all the vigorous resentment of a brother-in-law-that-might-have-been.

Donna Izaura set the dogs upon him:

"Dig your teeth into him, Brinquinho! Chew him up, Joli!"

The ill-fated farm magnate, cornered like a fox, dug the spurs into his horse and fled beneath a shower of insults—and stones. As he cleared the gateway, he could make out, amidst the shouting, the shrieking taunts of the old lady:

"Cake-gobbler! Butter-glutton! You're welcome to them. This is your last trick, egg-robber, yam thief!"

And Zilda?

Behind the window, her eyes burned out with weeping, the sad lass saw the gallant cavalier of her golden dream disappear forever in clouds of dust.

And thus the unlucky Moreira lost the one good stroke of business that Fortune was ever to offer him: The double riddance of his daughter and of the Corn Stalk.

DISCUSSION QUESTIONS

1. Do you sympathize with Moreira at the end of this story, or do you think he got what he deserved? Explain your reaction.

2. What tactics does Moreira use to convince Trancoso that the farm is productive? What tactics does Trancoso use to convince Moreira that he is knowledgeable and wealthy?

3. The author gives this story two endings—one for orchestra patrons (those with high-priced seats) and one for the audience in the gallery (those with cheap seats). In what way is the first ending "classier" than the second? Do you think the story would have been better without the second ending?

4. Lobato writes that the last twist in this story is so ironic that it must have been concocted by the devil, for "who else is capable of snarling the thread of the skein with so many loops and blind knots just when the knitting is approaching its happy completion?" Explain the final irony of the story.

SUGGESTION FOR WRITING

Efforts at falsifying appearances in order to impress someone often backfire, as they did for the family at the Corn Stalk farm. Think of a situation when you or someone you know tried to create a good impression and the plan turned out badly. Write a light-hearted story explaining what happened. Narrate the story from the point of view of the person(s) trying to make the good impression. (The story will be more interesting if you provide some dialogue along with the narration.)

GABRIEL GARCÍA MÁRQUEZ

(born 1928)

The most renowned novelist in Latin America, Márquez was born in a small coastal town in Colombia, where he lived with his grandparents for the first eight years of his life. They spent a great deal of time recounting to their grandson the myths and legends of this remote area and instilled in him a love of storytelling. Eventually he began a career in journalism, traveling extensively in South America, Europe, and the United States. During the 1960s he moved to Mexico, where he wrote film scripts and published a novel called *No One Writes to the Colonel.*

In 1967 Márquez' most famous book, *One Hundred Years of Solitude,* brought him international recognition. This novel follows six generations of descendants in a small, backward town called Macondo, which is a microcosm of the world as it moves from Eden to Apocalypse. *The Autumn of the Patriarch* and *Love in the Time of Cholera,* which appeared later, were also well received and widely translated. Márquez is famous for his skillful use of "magic realism," a technique that weaves fantastic myth-like occurrences with everyday realism. In 1982 he received the Nobel Prize for Literature. ■

TUESDAY SIESTA

Translated by J. S. Bernstein

The train emerged from the quivering tunnel of sandy rocks, began to cross the symmetrical, interminable banana plantations, and the air became humid and they couldn't feel the sea breeze any more. A stifling blast of smoke came in the car window. On the narrow road parallel to the railway there were oxcarts loaded with green bunches of bananas. Beyond the road, in uncultivated spaces set at odd intervals there were offices with electric fans, red-brick buildings, and residences with chairs and little white tables on the terraces among dusty palm trees and rosebushes. It was eleven in the morning, and the heat had not yet begun.

"You'd better close the window," the woman said. "Your hair will get full of soot."

The girl tried to, but the shade wouldn't move because of the rust.

They were the only passengers in the lone third-class car. Since the smoke of the locomotive kept coming through the window, the girl left her seat and put down the only things they had with them: a plastic sack with some things to eat and a bouquet of flowers wrapped in newspaper.

She sat on the opposite seat, away from the window, facing her mother. They were both in severe and poor mourning clothes.

The girl was twelve years old, and it was the first time she'd ever been on a train. The woman seemed too old to be her mother, because of the blue veins on her eyelids and her small, soft, and shapeless body, in a dress cut like a cassock. She was riding with her spinal column braced firmly against the back of the seat, and held a peeling patent leather handbag in her lap with both hands. She bore the conscientious serenity of someone accustomed to poverty.

By twelve the heat had begun. The train stopped for ten minutes to take on water at a station where there was no town. Outside, in the mysterious silence of the plantations, the shadows seemed clean. But the still air inside the car smelled like untanned leather.

The train did not pick up speed. It stopped at two identical towns with wooden houses painted bright colors. The woman's head nodded and she sank into sleep. The girl took off her shoes. Then she went to the washroom to put the bouquet of flowers in some water.

When she came back to her seat, her mother was waiting to eat. She gave her a piece of cheese, half a cornmeal pancake, and a cookie, and took an equal portion out of the plastic sack for herself. While they ate, the train crossed an iron bridge very slowly and passed a town just like the ones before, except that in this one there was a crowd in the plaza. A band was playing a lively tune under the oppressive sun. At the other side of town the plantations ended in a plain which was cracked from the drought.

The woman stopped eating.

"Put on your shoes," she said.

The girl looked outside. She saw nothing but the deserted plain, where the train began to pick up speed again, but she put the last piece of cookie into the sack and quickly put on her shoes. The woman gave her a comb.

"Comb your hair," she said.

The train whistle began to blow while the girl was combing her hair. The woman dried the sweat from her neck and wiped the oil from her face with her fingers. When the girl stopped combing, the train was passing the outlying houses of a town larger but sadder than the earlier ones.

"If you feel like doing anything, do it now," said the woman. "Later, don't take a drink anywhere even if you're dying of thirst. Above all, no crying."

The girl nodded her head. A dry, burning wind came in the window, together with the locomotive's whistle and the clatter of the old cars. The woman folded the plastic bag with the rest of the food and put it in the handbag. For a moment a complete picture of the town, on that bright August Tuesday, shone in the window. The girl wrapped the flowers in the soaking-wet newspapers, moved a little farther away from the window, and stared at her mother. She received a pleasant expression in return. The train began to whistle and slowed down. A moment later it stopped.

There was no one at the station. On the other side of the street, on the sidewalk shaded by the almond trees, only the pool hall was open. The town was floating in the heat. The woman and the girl got off the train and crossed the abandoned station—the tiles split apart by the grass growing up between—and over to the shady side of the street.

It was almost two. At that hour, weighted down by drowsiness, the town was taking a siesta. The stores, the town offices, the public school were closed at eleven, and didn't reopen until a little before four, when the train went back. Only the hotel across from the station, with its bar and pool hall, and the telegraph office at one side of the plaza stayed open.

The houses, most of them built on the banana company's model, had their doors locked from inside and their blinds drawn. In some of them it was so hot that the residents ate lunch in the patio. Others leaned a chair against the wall, in the shade of the almond trees, and took their siesta right out in the street.

Keeping to the protective shade of the almond trees, the woman and the girl entered the town without disturbing the siesta. They went directly to the parish house. The woman scratched the metal grating on the door with her fingernail, waited a moment, and scratched again. An electric fan was humming inside. They did not hear the steps. They hardly heard the slight creaking of a door, and immediately a cautious voice, right next to the metal grating: "Who is it?" The woman tried to see through the grating.

"I need the priest," she said.

"He's sleeping now."

"It's an emergency," the woman insisted.

Her voice showed a calm determination.

The door was opened a little way, noiselessly, and a plump, older woman appeared, with very pale skin and hair the color of iron. Her eyes seemed too small behind her thick eyeglasses.

"Come in," she said, and opened the door all the way.

They entered a room permeated with an old smell of flowers. The woman of the house led them to a wooden bench and signaled them to sit down. The girl did so, but her mother remained standing, absent-mindedly, with both hands clutching the handbag. No noise could be heard above the electric fan.

The woman of the house reappeared at the door at the far end of the room. "He says you should come back after three," she said in a very low voice. "He just lay down five minutes ago."

"The train leaves at three-thirty," said the woman.

It was a brief and self-assured reply, but her voice remained pleasant, full of undertones. The woman of the house smiled for the first time.

"All right," she said.

When the far door closed again, the woman sat down next to her daughter. The narrow waiting room was poor, neat, and clean. On the other side of the wooden railing which divided the room, there was a worktable, a plain one with an oilcloth cover, and on top of the table a primitive typewriter next to a vase of flowers. The parish records were beyond. You could see that it was an office kept in order by a spinster.

The far door opened and this time the priest appeared, cleaning his glasses with a handkerchief. Only when he put them on was it evident that he was the brother of the woman who had opened the door.

"How can I help you?" he asked.

"The keys to the cemetery," said the woman.

The girl was seated with the flowers in her lap and her feet crossed under the bench. The priest looked at her, then looked at the woman, and then through the wire mesh of the window at the bright, cloudless sky.

"In this heat," he said. "You could have waited until the sun went down."

The woman moved her head silently. The priest crossed to the other side of the railing, took out of the cabinet a notebook covered in oilcloth, a wooden penholder, and an inkwell, and sat down at the table. There was more than enough hair on his hands to account for what was missing on his head.

"Which grave are you going to visit?" he asked.

"Carlos Centeno's," said the woman.

"Who?"

"Carlos Centeno," the woman repeated.

The priest still did not understand.

"He's the thief who was killed here last week," said the woman in the same tone of voice. "I am his mother."

The priest scrutinized her. She stared at him with quiet self-control, and the Father blushed. He lowered his head and began to write. As he filled the page, he asked the woman to identify herself, and she replied unhesitatingly, with precise details, as if she were reading them. The Father began to sweat. The girl unhooked the buckle of her left shoe, slipped her heel out of it, and rested it on the bench rail. She did the same with the right one.

It had all started the Monday of the previous week, at three in the morning, a few blocks from there. Rebecca, a lonely widow who lived in a house full of odds and ends, heard above the sound of the drizzling rain someone trying to force the front door from outside. She got up, rummaged around in her closet for an ancient revolver that no one had fired since the days of Colonel Aureliano Buendía, and went into the living room without turning on the lights. Orienting herself not so much by the noise at the lock as by a terror developed in her by twenty-eight years of loneliness, she fixed in her imagination not only the spot where the door was but also the exact height of the lock. She clutched the weapon with both hands, closed her eyes, and squeezed the trigger. It was the first time in her life that she had fired a gun. Immediately after the explosion, she could hear nothing except the murmur of the drizzle on the galvanized roof. Then she heard a little metallic bump on the cement porch, and a very low voice, pleasant but terribly exhausted: "Ah, Mother." The man they found dead in front of the house in the morning, his nose blown to bits, wore a flannel shirt with colored stripes, everyday pants with a rope for a belt, and was barefoot. No one in town knew him.

"So his name was Carlos Centeno," murmured the Father when he finished writing.

"Centeno Ayala,"[1] said the woman. "He was my only boy."

The priest went back to the cabinet. Two big rusty keys hung on the inside of the door; the girl imagined, as her mother had when she was a girl and as the priest himself must have imagined at some time, that they were Saint Peter's keys. He took them down, put them on the open notebook on the railing, and pointed with his forefinger to a place on the page he had just written, looking at the woman.

"Sign here."

The woman scribbled her name, holding the handbag under her arm. The girl picked up the flowers, came to the railing shuffling her feet, and watched her mother attentively.

The priest sighed.

"Didn't you ever try to get him on the right track?"

The woman answered when she finished signing.

"He was a very good man."

The priest looked first at the woman and then at the girl, and realized with a kind of pious amazement that they were not about to cry. The woman continued in the same tone:

"I told him never to steal anything that anyone needed to eat, and he minded me. On the other hand, before, when he used to box, he used to spend three days in bed, exhausted from being punched."

"All his teeth had to be pulled out," interrupted the girl.

"That's right," the woman agreed. "Every mouthful I ate those days tasted of the beatings my son got on Saturday nights."

"God's will is inscrutable," said the Father.

But he said it without much conviction, partly because experience had made him a little skeptical and partly because of the heat. He suggested that they cover their heads to guard against sunstroke. Yawning, and now almost completely asleep, he gave them instructions about how to find Carlos Centeno's grave. When they came back, they didn't have to knock. They should put the key under the door; and in the same place, if they could, they should put an offering for the Church. The woman listened to his directions with great attention, but thanked him without smiling.

The Father had noticed that there was someone looking inside, his nose pressed against the metal grating, even before he opened the door to the street. Outside was a group of children. When the door was opened wide, the children scattered. Ordinarily, at that hour there was no one in the street. Now there were not only children. There were groups of people under the almond trees. The Father scanned the street swimming in the heat and then he understood. Softly, he closed the door again.

"Wait a moment," he said without looking at the woman.

---

1. **Centeno Ayala:** In South America a person's first name and surname are customarily followed by his mother's maiden name. Thus, his full name was Carlos Centeno Ayala.

His sister appeared at the far door with a black jacket over her nightshirt and her hair down over her shoulders. She looked silently at the Father.

"What was it?" he asked.

"The people have noticed," murmured his sister.

"You'd better go out by the door to the patio," said the Father.

"It's the same there," said his sister. "Everybody is at the windows."

The woman seemed not to have understood until then. She tried to look into the street through the metal grating. Then she took the bouquet of flowers from the girl and began to move toward the door. The girl followed her.

"Wait until the sun goes down," said the Father.

"You'll melt," said his sister, motionless at the back of the room. "Wait and I'll lend you a parasol."

"Thank you," replied the woman. "We're all right this way."

She took the girl by the hand and went into the street.

DISCUSSION QUESTIONS

1. Judging from the woman's actions so far, how would you expect her to respond to the hostile curiosity of the crowd waiting outside for her? How would you expect her to act when she reaches the cemetery?

2. Think of the title of the story, "Tuesday Siesta." Why do you think the woman chose to arrive in town during the siesta?

3. In this story the author gradually reveals the mission of the woman and her daughter by supplying tiny details that finally add up to an explanation. Trace the clues that contribute to our understanding of their purpose.

4. What feelings does the mother project when she speaks of her son? Does she seem to be ashamed of his criminal act, or does she excuse him?

SUGGESTION FOR WRITING

Imagine that you have been asked to deliver a memorial speech for Carlos Centeno. It will be delivered in the cemetery on the day the headstone is placed on the grave. Your speech should present the deceased in a positive light and should try to engender compassion in the audience. Write the speech that you would like to deliver.

GABRIELA MISTRAL

(1889–1957)

Chilean writer Gabriela Mistral (pen name of Lucila Godoy de Alcayaga) was the first Latin American woman to be awarded the Nobel Prize for Literature (1945). She spent many years as a schoolteacher, occasionally publishing poems in periodicals. Her first book of poetry was *Sonnets of Death,* published in 1914. She gained widespread recognition for her 1922 collection of poems entitled *Desolation.* Soon afterward, she became active as an educational reformer and later received many diplomatic and political assignments, which took her all over the world. In her later years, she served as a professor of Spanish literature at several colleges and universities in the United States.

In spite of her success in public affairs, her personal life was often unhappy. The suicide of her lover when she was 20 years old made a lasting impression, as did the later deaths of a nephew and a close friend. Among her most common poetic subjects are childhood, love, sorrow, and recovery. ■

POEMS
Translated by Doris Dana

ROCKING

The sea rocks her thousands of waves.
The sea is divine.
Hearing the loving sea
I rock my son.

5   The wind wandering by night
rocks the wheat.
Hearing the loving wind
I rock my son.

God, the Father, soundlessly rocks
10   His thousands of worlds.
Feeling His hand in the shadow
I rock my son.

IF YOU'LL ONLY GO TO SLEEP

The crimson rose
plucked yesterday,
the fire and cinnamon
of the carnation,

5   the bread I baked
with anise seed and honey,
and the goldfish
flaming in its bowl.

All these are yours,
10   baby born of woman,
if you'll only
go to sleep.

A rose, I say!
And a carnation!
15   Fruit, I say!
And honey!

And a sequined goldfish,
and still more I'll give you
if you'll only sleep
20   till morning.

THE SAD MOTHER

Sleep, sleep, my infant lord,
without fear or trembling at my breast,
though my soul may never slumber,
though my soul may never rest.

5   Sleep, sleep, and in the night
sleep more silently
than a single blade of grass,
a silken strand of fleece.

In you, my fear, my trembling,
10   let my body sleep.
Let my eyes close on you,
in you my heart find rest!

FEAR

I don't want them to turn
my little girl into a swallow.
She would fly far away into the sky
and never fly again to my straw bed,
5   or she would nest in the eaves
where I could not comb her hair.
I don't want them to turn
my little girl into a swallow.

I don't want them to make
10   my little girl a princess.
In tiny golden slippers
how could she play on the meadow?
And when night came, no longer
would she sleep at my side.
15   I don't want them to make
my little girl a princess.

And even less do I want them
one day to make her queen.
They would put her on a throne
20   where I could not go to see her.
And when nighttime came
I could never rock her . . .
I don't want them to make
my little girl a queen!

DISCUSSION QUESTIONS

1. All of these poems deal with the subject of motherhood in some way. Would you like to have the writer as a mother? What kind of a parent would she seem to be? Illustrate your answer with specific examples.

2. What is the author's attitude toward the natural world and the universe as presented in "Rocking?" Do you find this view unusual?

3. In the poem "If You'll Only Go to Sleep," what does the mother promise the baby? How would you describe the mother's mood at this moment?

4. In "The Sad Mother," what conflicting feelings are aroused in the speaker by her child?

5. In the poem "Fear," what is the poet afraid of? Why?

SUGGESTION FOR WRITING

All of these poems are written from the mother's point of view. Select one of the four poems and rewrite it so that it is told from the child's point of view. Try to use the same poetic form used by Mistral. (If you select "Rocking," for example, you will write in four-line stanzas in which the last line repeats.)

PABLO NERUDA

(1904–1973)

One of the major poets of the twentieth century, Neruda studied to be a teacher but wrote poetry on the side. He experimented with many poetic styles over the years, moving from symbolism to surrealism and finally to a simple, down-to-earth form of expression. In 1924 a collection of his poems entitled *Twenty Love Poems and a Song of Despair* became a best seller, making him one of South America's most famous poets. Some of his other poetry collections include *Residence on Earth, Elementary Odes,* and *Canto General.*

Over the years Neruda became increasingly involved in politics and wrote many poems advocating social reform. His concern for oppressed people led to his being labeled "the poet of enslaved humanity." He became a prominent member of the Chilean Communist Party, serving in the Senate until 1948. In that year the Communist Party was outlawed in Chile, and Neruda was forced to go into exile. He wrote and traveled in Russia, Europe, and Mexico during his exile, finally returning to Chile in 1970. During the next two years Neruda served as Chile's ambassador to France. In 1971 he was awarded the Nobel Prize for Literature. ■

ODE TO MY SOCKS

Translated by Robert Bly

> Maru Mori brought me
> a pair
> of socks
> which she knitted herself
> 5   with her sheep-herder's hands,
> two socks as soft
> as rabbits.
> I slipped my feet
> into them
> 10   as though into
> two
> cases
> knitted
> with threads of
> 15   twilight
> and goatskin.
> Violent socks,
> my feet were
> two fish made

20   of wool,
      two long sharks
      seablue, shot
      through
      by one golden thread,
25   two immense blackbirds,
      two cannons,
      my feet
      were honored
      in this way
30   by
      these
      heavenly
      socks.
      They were
35   so handsome
      for the first time
      my feet seemed to me
      unacceptable
      like two decrepit
40   firemen, firemen
      unworthy
      of that woven
      fire,
      of those glowing
45   socks.

      Nevertheless
      I resisted
      the sharp temptation
      to save them somewhere
50   as schoolboys
      keep
      fireflies,
      as learned men
      collect
55   sacred texts,
      I resisted
      the mad impulse
      to put them
      in a golden
60   cage
      and each day give them
      birdseed
      and pieces of pink melon.
      Like explorers
65   in the jungle who hand

over the very rare
green deer
to the spit
and eat it
70   with remorse,
I stretched out
my feet
and pulled on
the magnificent
75   socks
and then my shoes.

The moral
of my ode is this:
beauty is twice
80   beauty
and what is good is doubly
good
when it is a matter of two socks
made of wool
85   in winter.

This is the second of a group of eleven poems that picture Latin America before the Europeans arrived. In other poems plants, trees, birds, rivers, minerals, and Aztec priests and temples are described.

SOME BEASTS

Translated by James Wright

It was the twilight of the iguana.
From the rainbow-arch of the battlements,
his long tongue like a lance
sank down in the green leaves,
5   and a swarm of ants, monks with feet chanting,
crawled off into the jungle,
the guanaco, thin as oxygen
in the wide peaks of cloud,
went along, wearing his shoes of gold,
10   while the llama opened his honest eyes
on the breakable neatness
of a world full of dew.

The monkeys braided a sexual
thread that went on and on
15   along the shores of the dawn,

demolishing walls of pollen
and startling the butterflies of Muzo
into flying violets.
It was the night of the alligators,
20   the pure night, crawling
with snouts emerging from ooze,
and out of the sleepy marshes
the confused noise of scaly plates
returned to the ground where they began.

25   The jaguar brushed the leaves
with a luminous absence,
the puma runs through the branches
like a forest fire,
while the jungle's drunken eyes
30   burn from inside him.
The badgers scratch the river's
feet, scenting the nest
whose throbbing delicacy
they attack with red teeth.

35   And deep in the huge waters
the enormous anaconda lies
like the circle around the earth,
covered with ceremonies of mud,
devouring, religious.

CRISTOBAL MIRANDA

Translated by Robert Bly

Shoveler at Tocopilla[1]

I met you on the broad barges
in the bay, Cristobal, while the sodium nitrate
was coming down, wrapped in a burning
November day, to the sea.
5   I remember the ecstatic nimbleness,
the hills of metal, the motionless water.
And only the bargemen, soaked
with sweat, moving snow.
Snow of the nitrates, poured
10   over painful shoulders, dropping
into the blind stomach of the ships.

---

1. Tocopilla: seaport in northern Chile. Neruda met Cristobal Miranda, a shoveler, in the nitrate
works there.

Shovelers there, heroes of a sunrise
eaten away by acids, and bound
to the destinies of death, standing firm,
15 taking in the floods of nitrate.
Cristobal, this memento is for you,
for the others shoveling with you,
whose chests are penetrated by the acids
and the lethal gases,
20 making the heart swell up
like crushed eagles, until the man drops,
rolls toward the streets of town,
toward the broken crosses out in the field,
Enough of that, Cristobal, today
25 this bit of paper remembers you, each of you,
the bargemen of the bay, the man
turned black in the boats, my eyes
are moving with yours in this daily work
and my soul is a shovel which lifts
30 loading and unloading blood and snow
next to you, creatures of the desert.

THE UNITED FRUIT CO.

Translated by Robert Bly

When the trumpet sounded, it was
all prepared on the earth,
the Jehovah parceled out the earth
to Coca Cola, Inc., Anaconda,
5 Ford Motors, and other entities:
The Fruit Company, Inc.
reserved for itself the most succulent,
the central coast of my own land,
the delicate waist of America.
10 It rechristened its territories
as the "Banana Republics"
and over the sleeping dead,
over the restless heroes
who brought about the greatness,
15 the liberty and the flags,
it established the comic opera:
abolished the independencies,
presented crowns of Caesar,
unsheathed envy, attracted
20 the dictatorship of the flies,
Trujillo flies, Tacho flies,

Carias flies, Martinez flies,
Ubico flies,[2] damp flies
of modest blood and marmalade,
25   drunken flies who zoom
over the ordinary graves,
circus flies, wise flies
well trained in tyranny.

Among the blood-thirsty flies
30   the Fruit Company lands its ships,
taking off the coffee and the fruit;
the treasure of our submerged
territories flow as though
on plates into the ships.

35   Meanwhile Indians are falling
into the sugared chasms
of the harbors, wrapped
for burial in the mist of the dawn:
a body rolls, a thing
40   that has no name, a fallen cipher,
a cluster of dead fruit
thrown down on the dump.

---

2. Trujillo flies . . . Ubico flies: A derogatory reference to former political leaders and dictators of various South American countries.

Toussaint L'Ouverture (tü san´ lü vèr tyr´), *a Negro slave born in Haiti in 1743, rose to become a powerful military leader who drove English, French, and Spanish influences from Haiti. In 1801 Napoleon Bonaparte sent troops to reconquer the part of Haiti formerly under French power. Early in 1802 the Haitian troops surrendered. Toussaint L'Ouverture, accused of conspiracy against the French, was sent to a prison in France, where he died in 1803.*

TOUSSAINT L'OUVERTURE

Translated by James Wright

Out of its own tangled sweetness
Haiti raises mournful petals,
and elaborate gardens, magnificent
structures, and rocks the sea
5   as a dark grandfather rocks
his ancient dignity of skin and space.

Toussaint L'Ouverture knit together
the vegetable kingdom,
the majesty chained,
10   the monotonous voice of the drums
and attacks, cuts off retreats, rises,
orders, expels, defies
like a natural monarch,
until he falls into the shadowy net
15   and they carry him over the seas,
dragged along and trampled down
like the return of his race,
thrown into the secret death
of the ship-holds and the cellars.
20   But on the island the boulders burn,
the hidden branches speak,
hopes are passed on,
the walls of the fortress rise.
Liberty is your own forest,
25   dark brother, don't lose
the memory of your sufferings,
may the ancestral heroes
have your magic sea-foam in their keeping.

PASTORAL

Translated by Ben Belitt

I go copying mountains and rivers and clouds:
I shake out my fountain pen, remark
on a bird flying upward
or a spider alive in his workshop of floss,
5   with no thought in my head; I am air,
I am limitless air where the wheat tosses,
and am moved by an impulse to fly, the uncertain
direction of leaves, the round
eye of the motionless fish in the cove,
10   statues that soar through the clouds,
the rain's multiplications.
I see only a summer's
transparency, I sing nothing but wind,
while history creaks on its carnival floats
15   hoarding medals and shrouds
and passes me by, and I stand by myself
in the spring, knowing nothing but rivers.

Shepherd-boy, shepherd-boy, don't you know
that they wait for you?

20 I know and I know it: but there by the water
in the crackle and flare of cicadas,
I must wait for myself, as they wait for me there:
I also would see myself coming
and know in the end how it feels to me
25 when I come to the place where I wait for my coming
and turn back to my sleep and die laughing.

A PINECONE, A TOY SHEEP . . .

Translated by Ben Belitt

The poet's heart, like all other hearts, is an interminable artichoke . . .

1

My great-great grandparents came to the *pampas* of Parral[1] and planted their vines. Their acres were scant and their offspring prodigious. Time passed and the family multiplied: indoors and out, they kept coming. The wine-making went on as before—a strong and acidulous wine, undistilled, in the hogshead. Little by little things worsened, my grandparents abandoned their homestead, moved off, and came back to die in the dust bowls midway in Chile.

My father died in Temuco:[2] he was made for a kindlier climate. He lies buried in one of the rainiest graveyards of the world. He was a nondescript farmer, a mediocre laborer assigned to the Talcahuano dike,[3] but a first-class railroader. Railroading, with my father, was a passion. My mother could pick out in the dark, among all the other trains, precisely the train that was bringing my father into the station house at Temuco, or taking him away.

Few people today know about gravel trains. In the north, in the typhoon country, the rains would wash away the rails, if there were not men on hand all hours around the clock to pack down the cross ties with gravel. They had to carry the slabs from the quarries in baskets and empty the cobble into flatcars. Forty years ago, a crew of that sort must have been something to reckon with. They had no choice but to live alone at isolated points, slashing away at the flint. Company salaries were menial.

---

1. **Parral:** town in south central Chile. The *pampas* are the wide grasslands of southern South America.

2. **Temuco:** capital city of the Cautín province, south central Chile.

3. **Talcahuano dike:** a dike in Talcahuano, one of Chile's major ports.

References were not required of those who signed up to work on the gravel trains. Teams were recruited from the gigantic and muscular peons: from the fields, from the suburbs, from the prison cells. My father was a train conductor, used to giving orders and obeying them. Sometimes, when my teachers put me in a rage, I signed for a stint on the gravel trains too. We hacked stone in Boroa, in the wilderness heart of the frontier, the scene of those bloody encounters between Spaniards and Araucanian Indians.

Nature went to my head like whisky. I was ten, or thereabouts, already a poet. The rhymes did not come; but the beetles and birds and partridge eggs of the *pampas* enchanted me. Coming on them by chance in the gorges—blue-tinted, shadowy, glowing, colored like the barrel of a shot-gun—was a miracle. I was stunned by the perfection of the insect world. I went looking for "snake-mothers"—that was our extravagant name for the largest coleopter[4] of all, black, burnished, and powerful, the Titan of Chilean insects. It thrilled me to see them there, all at once, on the gin-ger-tree trunks, or the wild apple, or the boughs of the *coigue* trees:[5] I knew I could throw the weight of my feet on them, without cracking their shells. . . .

My forays attracted the curiosity of the workers: they began to interest themselves in my discoveries. Heedless of even my father, they took off for the virgin timber, and with greater agility, stamina, and cunning than I could ever muster, returned with incredible prizes for me. There was one fellow, Monge by name, whom my father regarded as a dangerous knife slinger. Two long gashes scored the swarthiness of his face: one, the verti-cal scar of a knife slash, the other, a horizontal white grin full of guile and good fellowship. It was Monge who brought me white *copihues,*[6] great, shaggy spiders and sucking pigeons; and once he tracked down the most dazzling prize of them all: "snake-mothers," moon-beetles. . . . I saw only one in my lifetime—a lightning flash disguised as a rainbow. His capari-son glowed yellow and violet and crimson and green, and then he was gone from my hands like a bolt and lost in the timber. Soon Monge him-self was not there to hunt me another. . . . My father told me how he died. He fell from a freight car and bowled down a precipice . . . father said, Monge was nothing but a sack of bones. I mourned for a week.

2

It is hard to give a true picture of the house that we lived in—the typical frontiersman's home of forty years ago. All the family dwellings inter-communicated. In the well of the patios,[7] the Reyes, the Ortegas, the

---

4. **coleopter:** a member of the insect group coleoptera, which includes beetles.

5 **coigue trees:** Chilean evergreen trees.

6. *copihues:* climbing plants with flowers of striking beauty.

7. **well of the patios:** The well refers to the open space surrounded by the cluster of homes of relatives. This architectural feature is common in Spain and South America.

Candias, and the Massons exchanged hardware or books, birthday cakes and rubbing unguents, tables and chairs and umbrellas. All the hamlet's activities were rooted in the homestead. There, Don Carlos Masson, looking like Emerson—North American, with a mane of white hair—was the reigning patriarch of the communal household. His sons, the young Massons, were Creole[8] to the core. A first founder rather than an empire builder, Don Carlos lived by the Law and the Writ. Out of that clan, without whom we all would have been destitute, came the hotels and the slaughterhouses and the printing presses. Some of the Massons were newspaper editors, others worked for a wage in the printing house. All fell away with the passing of time and poverty was general, as before. Only the Germans, in the typical pattern of the frontier, preserved the cache of their worldly goods irreducibly intact.

All the houses had the air of a bivouac encampment or an explorer's safari. One saw, upon entering, great sixty-gallon casks, farm implements, saddle gear, and other indescribable objects. They remained "temporary" to the end, with abortive stairs going nowhere. All my life, there was talk of bringing things to completion. Parents began to think of sending their sons to the University.

In the house of Don Carlos Masson the great feast days were celebrated.

Nameday solemnities[9] always concentrated on turkey with celery, roast lamb on skewers, with snowy milk for dessert. . . . Heading the interminable table sat the white-headed patriarch with his wife, Doña Micaela Candia. Behind was the huge flag of Chile, to which a diminutive North American pennant had been pinned, as if to indicate the ratio of blood. The lone star of Chile predominated.

One room of the Masson house we youngsters entered only very rarely. The color of the furniture is unknown to me to this day, since all was hidden from sight under white sheaths, until fire carried them away. There, also, the album of family photographs was kept, with finer and more delicate images than the dreadful tinted enlargements that later invaded the frontier.

Among them was a portrait of my mother, dead in Parral not long after I was born: a lady slenderly built and bemused, dressed in black. She wrote verses once, I am told, but all I ever saw of her was the lovely family portrait. My father had taken a second wife, Doña Trinidad Candia, my stepmother. It is strange now to have to invoke that tutelary angel of my childhood in such terms. She was diligent and lovable, with a countrywoman's sense of humor and indefatigable gusto for kindness. Like all the women of that day and that region, she turned into an amenable and undeviating phantom, once my father appeared on the scene.

In that room I saw the dancers go by in quadrilles and mazurkas.

---

8. **Creole:** in Spanish America, a person born in the region but of European ancestry.

9. **Nameday solemnities:** In South America, the feast day of the saint after whom a person is named is celebrated rather than the person's birthday.

In my house was a trunkful of fascinating keepsakes. From its depths, a fabulous parrot glittered on a calendar. One day, when my mother was rifling that magical casket, I plunged in to salvage the parrot. Later on, as I grew older, I plundered it secretly: there were precious, impalpable fans.

The trunk had other associations: the first love story to inflame my imagination. In it were hundreds of post cards, all signed in one hand—was it Enrique or Umberto?—and addressed to a Maria Thielman. Each was a marvel: all the era's great actresses set into little embossed transparencies, sometimes cemented with patches of real hair. There were castles and cities and exotic perspectives. At first, I had eyes for only the figures; but as I grew older, I turned to the messages of love set down in a perfect calligraphy. I imagined the lover: a gallant in a slouch hat, with a walking stick and a diamond in his cravat. His words were words of unmitigated passion, mailed from all points of the compass by a man on the move, full of glittering turns of phrase and incandescent audacity. I, too, began to yearn for Maria Thielman of the letters: I evoked her in the guise of a pitiless prima donna, with pearls in her hair. How did those letters end up in the trunk of my mother? I never learned the answer.

3

The boys in the public school neither acknowledged nor reverenced my status as poet. The frontier still retained its "Far Western" stamp of a country without prejudice. My classmates were the Schnakes, the Schelers, the Hausers, the Smiths, the Taitos, the Scranis. All was equal between us: Aracenas, Ramirez, and Reyes. Basque names were absent, but Sephardic Albalas and Francos mingled freely with Irish McGintys and Polish Yanichewskys. Araucanian Indian names—Melivilus, Catrileos—glowed with a shadowy brilliance, smelling of timber and water.

We battled together in a great, barnlike barrack, with holm oak acorns: only those who have stopped one can judge of their sting. Before coming to school, which was close to the river bank, we all primed our pockets with artillery. I had little physical endurance, no strength to speak of, and limited cunning. I always came off badly in those sallies. While I gaped at the cut of a holm acorn, green, with a high polish, in its rugged, gray frieze-cap, or tried languidly to carve out of its cup one of those pipes that enchanted me so, I went down under a hail of acorns aimed at my head. It occurred to me, in my second year, to protect myself with a waterproof hat, bright green in color. It was my father's hat, originally, charged with the same fascination as his *manta de castilla*[10] and his red and green signal lanterns—which I could hardly hope to carry off with me to dazzle my classmates. . . .

Little by little, I armed myself with verses.

In the schoolhouse, the cold was glacial. Forty years ago, I sat quaking with cold, just as the boys in the new Liceo de Temuca do to this day. They

---

10. **manta de castilla:** cape from Castile, Spain.

have built a grand modern structure with large windows, and no heating facilities: that's life for you, out on the frontier! We made men of ourselves in my day. There was plenty of reason to. Southern houses are all ramshackle, hastily clapped together out of freshly cut boards, with zinc roofing. Incessant great rainfalls made music on the roofs. Then, one fine morning, a house facing the front would awake to find itself roofless: wind had carried it off two hundred meters. The streets were great quagmires; everywhere wagons fouled on the road. On the footpaths, picking our way from boulder to boulder, we dogged toward the schoolhouse in the rain and the cold. Our umbrellas spun away on the wind. Raincoats were costly, shoes were soon water-logged; gloves I despised. I shall never forget all the drenched stockings close to the braziers, the multitude of shoes sending up steam like small locomotives. Later, the floods came, sweeping away whole settlements—the most wretched of all, those who lived closest to the river. The earth rocked with temblors. Sometimes on the highest ranges of all a plume of terrible light stood up: the Llaima volcano was active again.

And worst of all, fires. In 1906 or '07, I don't recall which, all Temuco went up in a holocaust. Houses blazed like matchboxes; twenty-two street blocks were razed to the ground; nothing was left. But if there is one thing Southerners know how to build in a hurry, it is houses. They don't build for the ages; but they build. A man who has lived in the South all his life must expect to live through three or four holocausts. I remember myself first as a child planted on blankets in front of our house, watching it blaze for the second or third time.

But the saws sang. Timber was piled in the stations again; there was a tang of fresh boards in the villages. Some of my verses are still scrawled on the walls there: the paper-smooth boards, grained with mysterious veins, always tempted me. Since then, wood has been—not an obsession with me, for I admit to none—but a staple of my natural life:

> Oh, whatever it is that I know
> or invoke again
> among all of the things of the world,
> it is wood that abides
> as my playfellow,
> I take through the world
> in my flesh and my clothing
> the smell
> of the sawyer;
> the reek of red boards;
> my breast and my senses
> soaked up
> in my childhood the bulk
> of felled trees coming down,
> great stands in the forest, crammed
> with coming constructions;
> I smelled in the whiplash

the gigantic length of the larch tree
and the laurel branch, forty yards high.

4

People who live in plank houses have different habits of thinking and feeling from the folk of Central Chile. In some ways, they are like the people of the great North country and the desolate wastelands. Being born in a house of mud bricks is not the same thing as being born in a house just hewn from the forest. In those houses, birth happens for the first time. The graveyards are still fresh.

For that reason, too, one finds neither religious ceremony nor written poetry. My mother used to lead me to church by the hand. The courts of the Church of the Heart of Mary were planted with lilacs, and at the novena,[11] all was drenched in their powerful aroma.

The church itself was always empty. At twelve, I was almost the only young male in the temple. Mother let me do as I pleased in the temple. Not being religious by nature, I never troubled my head about ritual and remained erect on my feet almost always, while the others were chanting and genuflecting. I never learned how to cross myself; but no one in the Church of Temuco ever called attention to the young infidel at large in their midst, upright on his feet. Perhaps that is why I have entered all churches with respect ever since. In that very same parish, my first romance flourished. The name might have been Maria; I can never be sure. But I well remember the whole of that baffling first love, or whatever it was; it was splendid and woeful, full of tremors and torments, soaked through and through with the reek of conventual lilies.

Most of the city folk were agnostics. My father, my uncles, my innumerable in-laws and godparents gathered around the big dining-room table, were of no mind to say grace. Instead, they swapped tales of *el huaso Rios:* how he crossed the bridge at Malleco on horseback, and lassoed Saint Joseph.[12]

Everywhere there were hammers and handsaws—men working in wood and sowing spring wheat. Pioneers, it appears, require little of their god. Blanca Hauser—a Temucan with a house on the Manzano Plaza, on whose benches I wrote seas of bad verse—tells the story of an old codger and his wife who came running up in the midst of an earthquake. The old lady was beating her breast and crying loud cries: "Lord have mercy on, us! *Misericordia!*"[13] The old fellow overtook her and asked: "What's that you say? What's that you say?" "*Misericordia,* imbecile!" the old lady told him. And the old man, finding that too much to manage, came trotting after her, thumping his chest at odd moments and repeating: "It's just what she says it is! It's just what she says it is!"

---

11. **novena:** in the Roman Catholic church, devotional prayers or services on nine consecutive days.

12. **tales . . . Saint Joseph:** probably a local legend concerning a cowboy (huaso) named Ríos.

13. *Misericordia:* Have mercy! [Latin].

5

From time to time my uncle summoned me to the great rite of roast lamb. Eston Masson, as I have said, had North American blood in his veins, but the Massons were true Creoles. The tough virgin soil had soaked into its humors all the Nordic and Mediterranean strain, leaving only the Araucanian. Wine flowed under the willows and sometimes the guitar could be heard through the week. A salad of green peas was prepared in great washing troughs. Each morning I heard the terrible shriek of stuck pigs, but the most frightful of all was the preparation of the *ñachi*. They slit the throat of the lamb and the blood gushed into washbowls seasoned with strong spices. My uncles asked me to drink down the blood.

I went clad in the garb of a poet, as in deep mourning: I mourned for the rain, for the grief of the world, for no one at all. And the barbarous ones raised their goblet of blood.

I overcame my compunctions and drank with the others. One must learn how to live like a man.

The centaurs held festival, a true revel of centaurs: a jousting bout. Wherever two foals made a name for themselves—just as the prowess of two men might win them a local notoriety—first the talk, and then, little by little, the plans for the tourney began to take shape. The contest of the Thunderbolt and the Condor was already legendary: two colts of colossal proportions, one black and one gray. Came the day of the pike-thrust!

The men had already come down from the mountains—horsemen from all parts of the country: from Cholchol and Curacautin, from Pitrufquen and Gorbea, from Lanchoche and Lautaro, from Quepa, from Quitratue, from Labranza, from Boroa and from Carahue. There the two centaurs, might matched to might, tried to sweep all before them, or make the first pass with the pike. The colts quivered from their hooves to their froth-clabbered nostrils. The moments when nobody budged were deathly to live through; then the Thunderbolt or the Condor was victorious and we saw the hero pace by with his great flashing spurs on a soaked horse. The great feast followed, with its hundreds of trenchermen. The wits of the South put it this way:

With an olive's brine
and a lake of wine
and the sweet of the roast
till the belly burst.

Out of this violent fellowship came the Romantic who exercised a powerful influence on my life: Orlando Masson. He was the first man I ever knew to enlist in the social struggle. He founded a newspaper and printed my first verses: I drank in the odor of newsprint, rubbed elbows with compositors and dyed my fingers with printer's ink. He launched passionate campaigns at the abuses of the powerful; for with progress had come exploitation. On the pretext of liquidating the bandits, land was ceded to "colonizers," and Indians exterminated like rabbits. Araucanians are not timid or taciturn or crackbrained by nature: they became so under the shock of excruciating experience. After the Independence, after 1810, the good people of Chile took up the slaughter of Indians with the exaltation of Spanish conquistadors. Temuco was the last refuge of the Araucanian.

Against all these excesses Orlando made voluble protest. It was good, in a barbarous and violent land, to see his newspaper plead the cause of the just against the cruel, the weak against the all-powerful. The last fire I remember in Temuco was the newspaper plant of Orlando Masson. . . .

He was a jovial man, full of battles.

6

The summers of Cautín are searing. The wheat and the sky burn. Earth struggles to throw off its lethargy. The houses are as little prepared for the summer as for the winter. I head toward the open country, looking for poems. I walk and I walk: on the Nielal summit, I get lost. I am alone, with a pocketful of beetles and a great, hairy spider, in a box, newly caught. I can no longer see the sky over my head. In the eternal damp of the jungle I slither unsteadily, a bird cries out suddenly, the hallucinated cry of the *chucao*. It wells from below like a sinister warning. The *copihues* glimmer faintly, like blood drops. I walk very small under gargantuan ferns. Close to my mouth darts a wild pigeon, with a dry thrashing of feathers. Higher up, other birds mock me with a jarring sound of laughter. The going is hard; it grows late.

Father is not home yet: he is due at three or four in the morning. I go up to my cubicle. I open a page of Salgari.[14] The rain smashes down like a cataract: in a moment, night and the rain have covered the world. Alone there, I write verses in my arithmetic notebook. I am up early the next morning. The plums are all green. I vault over fences, carrying my little packet of salt. I clamber up a tree, make myself comfortable, nibble a plum circumspectly; I bite and I spit out a morsel; I douse it with salt; I eat it. I bolt down a hundred—far too many, I think now.

Our old house has burnt down, and the new one seems strange to me. I stand on a fence post and look all around. Nobody. I turn up some old timber: a few, miserable spiders insignificant in size—nothing at all. In the rear, the latrine; near it, the trees teem with caterpillars. The almond trees show me their fruits sheathed in white plush. I know how to catch horseflies with a handkerchief—that way no harm comes to them. I keep them caged for a few days, holding them up to my ears. What a glorious humming!

Solitude; a child-poet dressed in black, on the spacious and terrible frontier. Little by little my life and my books trace the harrowing signs of a mystery, uncertainly.

I call to mind what I read the night before: how the breadfruit saved Sandokan and his friends in far-off Malasia. I have no love for the Indian-

---

14. **Salgari:** Emilio Salgari (1863–1911), Italian novelist whose works highlight the exploits of pirates in the Malay seas.

killer, Buffalo Bill—but what a terror on horseback! The meadows are lovely to me and the conical tents of the redskins. I begin to read voraciously—leaping from Jules Verne to Vargas Vila, to Strindberg, to Gorki, to Felipe Trigo, and Diderot. The pages of *Les Misérables* leave me sick with pity and misery and I blubber my love into Bernardin de Saint-Pierre.

Human wisdom has split wide for me like a grain bag and scattered its seed in the night of Temuco . . .

7

In the recesses of the world, knowledge waits for us. For some, revelation comes in a geometrical treatise, for others, in the lines of a poem. For me, books were a jungle in which I could lose myself, press further and further away from myself. They were another world of sumptuous flowers, another steep and crepuscular foliage, a mysterious silence, voices out of the sky; but also they were lives on the other side of the mountain peaks, on the other side of the ferns, beyond the rain.

There came to Temuco a tall lady in flat heels and voluminous draperies, dressed in sand-color. She was the Principal of the Liceo; she came from a southerly city, from the snows of Magellan.[15] Her name was Gabriela Mistral.[16]

I saw her only rarely, because I shrank from the contact of outlanders. I had little to say. I lived mournfully, mutely, and avidly.

Gabriela had an ample, white smile in a tawny face flayed by blood and the weathers. I remembered that face from before: except for the absence of scars, it was the face of the pile driver, Monge! There was the very same smile, half-friendly, half-wary, the same knotting of eyebrows stung by snow or the glare of the *pampas*. She took books from the folds of her clerical robes and delivered them into my hands; it never seemed strange to me; I devoured them. It was she who first urged on me the great Russian masters who influenced me so. Then she went North. I wasted no tears on her; my friends now were legion, the agonized lives of my books. I knew where to find them. . . .

8

I'll tell you a story about birds. On Lake Budi some years ago, they were hunting down the swans without mercy. The procedure was to approach them stealthily in little boats and then rapidly—very rapidly—row into their midst. Swans like albatrosses have difficulty in flying; they must skim the surface of the water at a run. In the first phase of their flight they raise their big wings with great effort. It is then that they can be seized; a few blows with a bludgeon finish them off.

---

15. snows of Magellan: Snow-capped peaks line the majestic, fjord-like course of the Straits of Magellan.

16. Gabriela Mistral: famous Chilean poet. See page 183.

Someone made me a present of a swan: more dead than alive. It was of a marvelous species I have never seen since anywhere else in the world: a black-throated swan—a snow boat with a neck packed, as it were, into a tight stocking of black silk. Orange-beaked, red-eyed.

This happened near the sea, in Puerto Saavedra, Imperial del Sur.

They brought it to me half-dead. I bathed its wounds and pressed little pellets of bread and fish into its throat; but nothing stayed down. Nevertheless the wounds slowly healed, and the swan came to regard me as a friend. At the same time, it was apparent to me that the bird was wasting away with nostalgia. So, cradling the heavy burden in my arms through the streets, I carried it down to the river. It paddled a few strokes, very close to me. I had hoped it might learn how to fish for itself, and pointed to some pebbles far below, where they flashed in the sand like the silvery fish of the South. The swan looked at them remotely, sad-eyed.

For the next twenty days or more, day after day, I carried the bird to the river and toiled back with it to my house. It was almost as large as I was. One afternoon it seemed more abstracted than usual, swimming very close and ignoring the lure of the insects with which I tried vainly to tempt it to fish again. It became very quiet; so I lifted it into my arms to carry it home again. It was breast high, when I suddenly felt a great ribbon unfurl, like a black arm encircling my face: it was the big coil of the neck, dropping down.

It was then that I learned swans do not sing at their death, if they die of grief.

I have said little about my poems. I know very little about such things, really. I prefer instead to move among the evocations of my childhood. Perhaps, out of these plants and these solitudes and this violent life come the truths and the secret things—the profoundest *Poetics* of all, unknown because no one has written them down. We come upon poetry a step at a time, among the beings and things of this world: nothing is taken away without adding to the sum of all that exists in a blind extension of love.

Once, looking for little trophies and creaturely things of my world in the back of our house in Temuco, I came on a knothole in a neighboring fence post. I peered through the opening and saw a plot very like our own, all wilderness and waste. I withdrew a few steps, with the vague sense of portents to come. Suddenly a hand appeared—the tiny hand of a child just my age. I came closer, and the hand disappeared; in its place was a lovely white sheep—a toy sheep of nondescript wool. The wheels had fallen away—but that only made it more lifelike. I have never seen a more ravishing animal. I peered through the knothole, but the child was nowhere in sight. I went back to the house and returned with a prize of my own which I left in the very same spot: a pine-cone I treasured above all things, half-open, balsamic, sweet-smelling. I left it there and I went away with the little toy sheep . . .

DISCUSSION QUESTIONS

1. What expectations did you bring to the poem entitled "Ode to My Socks"? Were those expectations confirmed, or were you surprised?

2. What is the basic conflict in "Ode to My Socks"? What does the author mean when he says of the socks that he "resisted / the mad impulse / to put them / in a golden / cage"?

3. In "Some Beasts" what specific words and phrases convey the idea that something is coming to an end? What exactly is ending? What is the "enormous anaconda" that lies in wait?

4. What is Neruda's attitude toward the shoveler named Cristobal Miranda? What does the figure of Christobal represent in this poem?

5. What are some of the implications of the sounding trumpet in the first line of "The United Fruit Co."? In what way is the Indian worker viewed simply as "a cluster of dead fruit"?

6. In "Toussaint L'Ouverture" Neruda recounts the final defeat of the hero and then writes, "But on the island the boulders burn, / the hidden branches speak." What do you think these lines mean?

7. In "Pastoral" Neruda sees the poet as verbally creating a scene from nature that he will later step into. What strange occurrence does this idea produce? What comment might Neruda be making about the way poets view their creations?

8. The essay "A Pinecone, a Toy Sheep . . ." begins with a short epigraph that describes a poet as "an interminable artichoke." What is the writer suggesting with this comparison?

9. If you were producing a movie about Pablo Neruda's childhood, which scenes from "A Pinecone, a Toy Sheep . . ." would you include? What kind of person would you try to show the young Pablo to be?

SUGGESTION FOR WRITING

In "A Pinecone, a Toy Sheep . . ." Neruda creates a loosely-organized account of some of the memorable events and people of his childhood. Like the petals of an artichoke, these events are not connected, but they accumulate to form a unique structure of memories.

Create your own artichoke of early memories, briefly recounting four or five events, objects, or people that, for one reason or another, made an impact during your early years. Concentrate on helping the reader share the flavor of these experiences.

HORACIO QUIROGA
(1878–1937)

A short story writer famous for his tales of terror and tragedy, Quiroga was plagued by illness and misfortune all his life. The early death of his father in a shooting accident, followed a few years later by his stepfather's suicide, had an enormous impact on him. Quiroga became a teacher in Buenos Aires, but a manic-depressive disorder began to interfere with his work, giving rise to depression, anxiety, and nameless terrors. He turned to alcohol to relieve his anxiety and, during a drinking bout, accidentally killed a friend while inspecting a gun. Overcome with grief, he left Buenos Aires and headed for the wild tropical regions of northern Argentina.

Quiroga was enchanted with primitive life and decided to buy land in a remote part of Argentina, where he became a cotton planter. In 1909 he married and eventually had two children. His wife, unable to tolerate the harsh jungle conditions, killed herself, and the two children also committed suicide. Quiroga began publishing short stories during this period, his most famous collections being *Tales of Love, Madness, and Death* and *The Exiles*. In 1937 Quiroga became ill and returned to Buenos Aires to visit a clinic. When he learned that he had cancer, he killed himself.

Quiroga's stories, which were strongly influenced by the writings of Edgar Allan Poe, are usually stark, terse tales of impending doom. They often portray abnormal mental states and illusions, which are seen as human attempts to escape from fate. These stories repeatedly demonstrate the helplessness of man and the relentlessness of fate. ■

THE SON

Translated by Linda Wilson and Willis Knapp Jones

It is a magnificent summer day in Misiones, with all the sun, heat, and calm that the season can offer. Nature seems satisfied with itself.

Like the sun, the heat, and the calm atmosphere, the father also opens his heart to nature.

"Be careful, youngster," he says to his son, summarizing in that remark all his observations and advice, and his son understands perfectly.

"Yes, papa," the child replies, while he takes his rifle and loads his shirt pockets with cartridges.

"Come back by lunch time," his father adds.

"Yes, papa," repeats the boy. He balances the rifle in his hand, smiles at his father, kisses him on the forehead, and off he goes.

His father follows him a short distance with his eyes and then returns to his task for that day, happy because of his little son.

He knows that his son, brought up since his tenderest childhood to take precaution against danger, can use a rifle and hunt anything.

Although he is very tall for his age, he is only thirteen years old. And he would seem to be younger, judging by the clearness of his blue eyes, still naive with childish astonishment.

The father doesn't need to raise his eyes from his task to follow his son's progress in his mind. By now the boy has crossed the red trail and is walking across the clearing straight toward the forest full of birds.

To hunt fur-bearing game in the forest requires more patience than his small son possesses. After crossing that isolated section of forest, his son will go along the cactus border as far as the swamp, looking for doves, toucans, or perhaps a couple of herons like those his friend John discovered a few days before.

Alone now, the father smiles faintly at the thought of the two boys' passion for hunting. Sometimes they hunt only a *yacútoro* bird or a *surucuá* that is still smaller, and return triumphant, John to his hut with the 9-millimeter rifle that he gave him, and his son to the house on the hill with a large .16-caliber St. Etienne shotgun with a quadruple lock and white gunpowder.

He had been the same way. At thirteen, he would have given his life to possess a shotgun. His son, at that same age, owns one and the father smiles. It is not easy for a father who has lost his wife, to bring up a son. Danger is always at hand for a man, but even more if he has always to depend on himself. It has been a constant worry. Sometimes he has even suffered hallucinations like the fright he once had because of his weak vision, seeing the boy hammering on a bullet at the workshop bench when really he was polishing the buckle of his hunting belt.

Suddenly, at no great distance, he hears a gunshot.

"The St. Etienne!" thinks the father, recognizing the report. "Two less doves in the forest."

Without paying any more attention to the unimportant incident, the man concentrates again on his task.

The sun, already very high, continues ascending. Wherever one looks, at the rocks, the land, or the trees, the air, rarefied as in a furnace, vibrates with the heat. The father glances at his watch; it is noon. He raises his eyes toward the forest.

His son ought to be returning. In the mutual confidence that they place in each other, the father with silvery temples and the son of thirteen, they never deceive each other. When his son answers, "Yes, papa," he will do what he promises. He said that he would return before twelve, and the father smiled upon seeing him depart.

And the boy has not returned yet. Suddenly he realizes that for three hours he has heard no more shooting. A shot, a single shot has sounded, long ago. Since then, the father has heard no other sound, has seen no bird.

Bareheaded and without his machete, the father runs out. He cuts across the clearing, enters the forest, and hurries along the cactus border without finding the least trace of his son. By the time he has covered the game trail and explored the swamp in vain, he is sure that every step is taking him fatally and helplessly toward the spot where he will find the body of his son, killed while crawling through a fence.

"Son!" he suddenly exclaims. If the voice of a man of character is capable of weeping, let us cover our ears in pity in the presence of the anxiety apparent in that voice.

No one has replied. Nothing! Along the trail red in the sunlight, aged ten years hurries the father, looking for his son who has just died.

"Son! Oh, son!" he shouts, with a surge of affection that rises from the depths of his soul.

Once before, in the midst of complete happiness and peace, the father had suffered the hallucination of seeing his son, fallen with his forehead pierced by a bullet of chrome nickel. Now, in every dark corner of the forest he sees flashes of wire; and at the foot of a post, with his musket discharged nearby, he sees his . . .

"Sonny! . . . My son! . . ."

The strength of a poor father subjected to such a frightful hallucination has its limits, and the father in our story feels he is approaching his, when suddenly he sees his son coming abruptly out of a side path.

The sight, even at a distance of fifty meters, of his father, distraught and unarmed is enough to make a child of thirteen hasten his steps.

"My little boy!" murmurs the man. And exhausted, he drops onto the white, sandy soil, throwing his arms around the youngster's leg.

The child remains standing, with his father's arm around his knees, and as he understands his father's anguish, he slowly strokes his head:

"Poor papa!" . . .

By then, time has passed. It is already going on three. Together now, father and son start back to the house.

"How did it happen that you didn't notice the sun and see how late it was?" murmurs the father again.

"I did notice, papa . . . But when I started to return, I saw John's herons and followed them . . ."

"What anxiety you cause me, my boy!"

"Papa!" also murmurs the young boy. After a long silence:

"What about the herons? Did you kill them?" asks the father.

"No . . ."

That really doesn't matter, after all. Under the blue sky and the shimmering heat, through the clearing, the man returns home with his son, over whose shoulders, almost on a level with his own, rests the happy father's arm. He gets back drenched with perspiration and although upset in body and soul, he smiles happily. . . .

He smiles with a happy hallucination. . . . The father is walking alone. He has found no one and his arm encompasses empty space. Because behind him, at the foot of the post with his legs in the air, entangled in barbed wire, his beloved son lies in the sun, dead since ten o'clock that morning.

DISCUSSION QUESTIONS

1. How did you feel about the ending to this story? Did you feel tricked, or was there adequate preparation and justification for such an ending?

2. Three hallucinations are present in this story. What are they? How is the father's last hallucination different from the earlier two?

3. How does Quiroga communicate the father's deep affection for his son?

4. Does the author give any clue that the father's mind has, in effect, snapped just as the final hallucination begins?

SUGGESTION FOR WRITING

"The Son" is narrated entirely from the father's point of view until the last paragraph. Write the final scene, in which the father goes looking for the boy, from the point of view of an outside observer. Then explain why the story's impact is dependent on having the story presented from the father's point of view.

ALFONSINA STORNI
(1892–1938)

Born in Switzerland, Storni worked as a traveling actress in her youth and then went to Argentina, where she began a career as a teacher and journalist. Her first volume of poetry, entitled *Sweet Danger,* was published in 1918 and was extremely well received. Two other notable collections include *World of Seven Wells,* a book of highly symbolic poetry, and *Mask and Trefoil,* published shortly before her death. In 1938 Storni, disappointed by the cold reception of her recent poems and suffering from cancer, drowned herself.

Storni is known primarily for her poems expressing resistance to male domination, but she also had an unquenchable yearning for love. These two impulses created strong inner conflicts that often appear in her poems. Other frequent themes in her poetry are an intense love of nature, criticism of conformity and materialism, and death. ■

SHE WHO UNDERSTANDS
Translated by Alice Stone Blackwell

Her dark head fallen forward in her grief,
The beauteous woman kneels in suppliant fashion—
A woman past her youth; the dying Christ
From the stern rood[1] looks on her with compassion.

5   A burden of vast sadness in her eyes,
Beneath her heart a child, a burden human.
Before the white Christ bleeding there she prays:
"Lord, do not let my child be born a woman!"

---

1. rood: the cross on which Christ was crucified.

INHERITANCE
Translated by Jessie Reed Wendell

You said to me: "My father did not weep,
Nor my grandfather weep." I heard you say:
"No man of all my race has ever wept;
Of steel were they."

5   And thus upon my trembling mouth I felt
The poison of your bitter teardrop fall,

Worse potion than my lips have ever quaffed
From a cup so small.

Weak woman, born all grief to comprehend,
10   I drank the pain of ages infinite;
But oh, my wretched soul cannot support
The weight of it!

SQUARES AND ANGLES
Translated by Willis Knapp Jones

Houses in a line, in a line,
In a line there,
Squares, squares, squares,
In a line there.
5   Even people now have square souls,
Ideas in file, I declare,
And on their shoulders, angles wear.
Just yesterday I shed a tear and it
Oh, God, was square!

I AM GOING TO SLEEP
Translated by Willis Knapp Jones

Oh, kindly nurse, you with the teeth of flowers,
With hair of dew and open hands of grass,
Lend me, I beg, some earthy sheets and quilt
Of plucked-out moss, in place of eiderdown.
5   For I would sleep, dear nurse. Put me to bed
And at my head gently set down as lamp
A constellation. Any one will do.
They're all so lovely. Turn it down a bit.

Leave me alone where I can hear things grow.—
10   "A heavenly foot will rock you to and fro.
A bird will sing a constant lullabye
So you'll forget."—Oh, thanks! One more request:
If he should telephone to me again,
Tell him not to persist. I have gone out.

DISCUSSION QUESTIONS

1. In "She Who Understands" what is the meaning of the title—why is it *she* who understands? What similarities does the woman seem to see between her role and Christ's?

2. In "Inheritance" who is the person referred to as "you"? What kind of an inheritance is the poet describing?

3. In "Squares and Angles" what kind of life is Storni criticizing? How does she use hyperbole (exaggeration) to make her point?

4. In "I Am Going to Sleep" who is the "kindly nurse"? Support your answer with evidence from the poem.

5. All of these poems involve some sort of protest. If Storni were alive today, what attitude, convention, or activity do you think she might choose as the subject of a protest poem?

SUGGESTION FOR WRITING

Select an aspect of contemporary life that Storni did not live to see. (She died in 1938.) It could be television, E-mail, call waiting, remote control, answering machines, the Internet, or anything else that has changed our way of life. Write a short poem in which you attempt to capture the effect, either positive or negative, of this innovation on the way we live. Use Storni's "Squares and Angles" as a model.

LUIS TABLANCA

(1883–1965)

Tablanca was born in El Carmen, Santander, Colombia, the area that serves as the setting for the story that follows. His thorough knowledge of this coffee-growing region is evident in the lavish details that he provides as a background for "Country Girl." Tablanca, whose real name was Enrique Pardo Farelo, received no education beyond that given to him by his parents. However, he taught himself to be an accountant and did expert work in that field for many years. When he was nineteen years old, he began writing for some of the Colombian newspapers as well as for several literary magazines. Among his published works are novels, short stories, and poetry collections. ■

COUNTRY GIRL

Translated by Alida Malkus

In this fierce land of the tropics, the rainy season begins in the early days of October. The months of August and September are clear and dry; not the lightest fleece of a cloud is seen to cross the wide heavens. But at this time the blue loses its purity and depth; it seems as though a rosy dust, resembling the splendor of distant fire, floats in the air. The earth is parched, the vegetation decays and vanishes, the little rivulets shrink and disappear.

It is the time when the shepherds of the burning pampas drive their cattle forth and search for a little pasturage and coolness upon the banks abandoned by the rivers. One day, when October has already begun, and when the heat is most suffocating, a cloud appears above the mountains; it grows, it becomes dark. Another cloud, equally black and heavy, sweeps up by the same road and advances with the noise of a hundred war chariots. The two clouds meet, they collide and blend, and from their mysterious womb a livid splendor bursts suddenly. The zigzag of a lightning shaft darts downward to strike the highest tree of the forest. The thunder resounds with threats as if it would rend the earth apart. Fat drops of rain fall, they slant across the sound-filled air with the crack of a whiplash as they strike the thirsty earth. And it rains; it rains one day after another, without stopping, as if the forty days of the Flood had returned. . . .

At this season in the extreme north of Santander[1] the coffee begins to ripen and the coffee grower must redouble his efforts to gather in the precious beans. Many poor people flock out from the villages, looking for a

---

1. **Santander:** province in northeast Colombia.

few days' work, eager to eat until they are full once more, and to pass a merry time in the coffee plantations. Neither cooks nor servants remain in the houses; in the streets there are no porters, nor any of the barefooted ne'er-do-wells who lounge about in the sun in every village plaza. All of them set out on a great excursion to hire out as day laborers at the haciendas. Young and old, men and women, find jobs with good pay in these days. They all know the work. The coffee branches are heavy and drooping, and must be relieved of their burden before the berries fall and are lost. Whoever presents himself is hired at once, without question as to who he is or where he comes from. And thus for some weeks the most widely assorted and strange people from the poor of country and village are gathered together.

Old Juan Cuevas had a coffee plantation. He had planted it in his youth with his own hands. It was not very large, nor very good; but when the crop began to ripen, he had to hire at least twenty laborers to gather it in. The harvest, helped out with other small crops which a good farmer always knows how to obtain from the tireless earth, brought Juan enough to live in sumptuous ease according to his notions, with enough left over for his little savings.

His whole family consisted of one daughter, who worked tirelessly. She cooked, she washed, she served the meals, mended the clothes, and raised a few chickens, which laid no golden eggs but did lay one egg each and every day, as much as any mistress of the house could desire for the honor of her chicken yard. This girl was called Vicenta; she was in her early youth, and all, except her father, who saw her were filled with admiration that so pretty a flower should have budded from so ugly a trunk. He was of Indian blood, short and bowlegged; the color of tobacco, with a shock of bristly and rebellious gray hair. She, although somewhat brown, like a gypsy, was fine and sparkling, with a tall, slender body. He had small, inexpressive eyes, and she, below her long brows, two black suns between a hedge of curly lashes. The one beauty they shared was a fine show of white, even, and well-placed teeth.

On Sundays they went down to the village to hear Mass and to shop. When they had walked for a while up and down the almost vertical hills with the wind blowing in their faces and the sun scorching them, it was something to see how the girl's cheeks flamed. She would throw her handkerchief over her head, cross the ends on her chest, and hold them there with one hand, a hand spread there without coquetry, brown, dimpled, weighted with old rings. Old Juan wore his new blanket of blue woolen stuff, his fine straw hat, with its high crown of creamy white mellowed by time, and sandals with wool toe pieces, the color of which seemed to have been taken from the wings of a macaw. As they walked—the daughter went ahead and the father followed—the men opened a path before them, raining compliments and burning glances upon her. But she, very honest and not wishing to encourage them, behaved as if she were deaf and blind; she would not even smile.

Among the laborers whom the old Cuevas brought to his coffee plantation in that month of October was a man born in the little village of Burbura. He said he was a native of Ocaña, being one of those men who deny their humble cradle and claim another which they believe lends them more honor and importance; as if each man were not the child of his own deeds. This man was somewhat blond, he had honey-colored eyes, a little mustache like brown silk, and the air of a fine cock, of the sort that cannot see a female without dragging a wing. Papa Cuevas was not a man who was friendly to conversation; but the workman made him curious and he detained him for a time in the corridor asking him questions. As was natural, he began with politics, which is an obsession with these good people.

"Don't tell me," answered the boy. "In my family from the beginning we've all been liberals to the very bones, and just you let a war come and watch me. When the revolution came I wasn't born, but my papá took arms and made his mark. He was the last to surrender, and this only because they had already signed the peace, and there was no other course. My grandfather also was a guerrilla"—the man spoke in the dialect of the hilltown from which he came, dropping his final syllables, slurring his *d*'s and *r*'s. "I, if the hour should come, would do even better than they, because I know the militia. Last year I did my military service in Pamplona. When you like I shall show you the passbook, which always goes with me. I am a good marksman and I can judge distances better than anyone . . . There, it says so in the passbook."

"Can you work?"

"I am a demon for work. I don't know what laziness is, you will see. And I have the advantage that I know a little of everything. I am a mason, I am a carpenter, a farmer, and a blacksmith; I can turn my hand to anything. I say that a man has to know about everything."

"And where did you work last?"

"I come from Gamarra; but that port didn't suit me, in spite of the good money I made. The fevers struck me, and I said, No! I'd better look for a cold climate, and I left."

"You did well. Here you can be easy and earn good money too. With me everyone does cleverly; I give good food and good treatment. The only bad thing we have now is the weather, which is pure water. See what a curtain of clouds. Hear that thunder!"

This was Sunday afternoon, and the youth still wore around his neck the rose-colored kerchief with which he had dressed up. Old Cuevas said, "Before it starts raining again I am going to try to finish my work."

He retired to his afternoon duties, which consisted of giving a thought to the cows and shutting up the calves. The wind swept by at a great speed, carrying on its wings pennants of mist and drops of rain. In the ravine the winter-swollen torrent roared, and the hills which filled the landscape displayed all shades of green.

More than a half hour later, when already the afternoon light was beginning to fade and become sad, the old man came out from the palm-thatched shed where he kept his animals, and saw that the laborer, whose name was Elías Cañas, was talking at great length with the disdainful Vicenta. This did not please the old man, as he was not accustomed to seeing his daughter chatting with the peons; for the girl, though rustic and simple, was both womanly and dignified and knew by instinct how to maintain the decorum of a landowner, and, if necessary, of the mistress of the house. Her father wanted to hear their talk. Pretending that he had noticed nothing, he took a turn around the house, and entered craftily by the back door, walking in such a way that his clay-hardened sandals made no noise whatsoever.

"Believe me," said Elías to Vicenta, "hardly had I set eyes on you than I felt a heart throb no other woman has caused me in all the years I have been running around the world. For every man born there is a woman destined for him only, and one can walk from one land to another, and even if this woman is hidden, in the end he meets up with her; it may be for her good luck, it may be for her ill fortune. I wager that when you saw me come to your house, you also felt something strange. . . ." As Vicenta denied this with a shake of the head, the youth argued: "Don't deny it, when the eyes are the mirror of the soul; and in your eyes, in the way that they look at me, I knew it from the beginning. I don't pretend that you are going to tell me this minute that you like me, but it is certain that you and I were not born to be indifferent to each other. My heart tells me this. Your father is old, he will soon die, God forbid, and you will be alone in the world. . . . You must marry, and if you have to make a match with someone, why not with me, who hardly saw you when I fell so in love with you? Who knows what I shall do if you refuse me?"

The wily youth had arrived at this point when a cough betrayed the old man before he could hear another word, and Elías went on talking of other things in order to put him off the track.

"Here's what I shall do! I shall have patience and keep my mouth shut. We came up from the level country and passed some days at Cucuta, which is a very progressive and very pretty city, but with a very hot climate. The streets are wide, with trees . . . And what stores!"

"In the streets of Cucuta," old Juan put in, coming nearer, "they killed the son of my compadre Mamerto Arias during the last war. He was a boy of much promise . . ."

The house had one small sleeping room with irregular walls and a low roof, over the timbers of which cockroaches and other predatory creatures ran all night. Vicenta's bed was at one end of the room, her father's at the other. The beds were hard as if designed for penance, mere mats and a blanket laid over creaking wooden frames. But on them they slept better than on feathers. Every night father and daughter talked, seated each one in his bed, said their prayers together, put out the little oil lamp, and undressed in the darkness for the sake of their modesty.

At the head of old Juan's bed stood a poorly made little walnut chest where he kept his savings, the bottle of camphorated brandy, the blue wool poncho, and certain possessions of Vicenta, as well as other things of great value. Vicenta's possessions consisted of little tambourines with cheap ornaments, filigree earrings, six or eight old rings with very showy stones, and a collar of the so-called duck's tail. This jewelry was inherited in part, and in part acquired by purchase; the girl wore all of it when she went down to the parish, to the feast of the Virgin of Carmen, or during Holy Week.

The savings consisted of Peruvian soles, or dollars, half a gold condor, like a fried egg, some smaller coins, and a good bundle of bills, tightly folded and moldy, all the fruit of many privations and much effort. On days when old Juan was in a happy humor he would turn the treasure out upon a shawl to count it, and Vicenta, with the back of each hand upon a hip, would watch smiling, eyes shining with pleasure. It was her inheritance, her fortune, a sacred thing which she had to guard carefully and to preserve.

On that night old Juan asked his daughter this untimely question:

"What was that fellow talking to you about this afternoon?"

"Which of them, papá—Elías Cañas?"

"Ah, you already know his name?"

"I know the names of all the workers, papá."

"What was be talking about, I ask you?"

"Oh, of the lands that he has known. He spoke to me of Pamplona, he spoke to me of Cucuta, of the military service . . ."

A thought occurred to the old man and he forgot the subject. "Now they are calling the boys up for the draft. In the old days they gathered them in by force. When they decided to begin collecting men, one could not go down to the parish."

They said their prayers, put out the light, pulled the blankets over them, and after a while the old man spoke again.

"Awake, Vicenta?"

"Yes, papá; I am not very sleepy tonight."

"What sleep are you going to get, child of God, if your head is turned with the lies of that fraud! I never have been a man who permitted myself to deceive anyone. I see and understand everything that happens to you. He says he is in love and you believe him! I say that he is leaving here not later than tomorrow. For an adventurer who tramps from place to place, doing day labor, no match could be better than you, an only daughter, brought up in your father's house with honor, with good land that sooner or later will be in your own hands. Besides all this treasure here that is yours when I am dead—add to that the money in the stocking in the little chest at the head of your bed. For this I have brought you up with so much care," he went on, "and for this I have killed myself working, so that between night and morning Don Elías Cañas may come, and with one look at you he feels a heart throb, and he believes himself already owner of the saint and of the alms. How easy, and how fine for him, if I weren't here to stop him!"

He talked a long time with lowered voice, as if he were afraid that some stranger might be listening outside the little window. Vicenta, huddled into a ball beneath the bedclothes, did not dare to say a single word.

When the old man was hoarse with talking, he lay down again, and it now being well into the middle of the night, they both slept.

In that region the cleaning of the coffee is done in a very primitive way. The workmen grasp the branches, and closing the hand they strip into the basket, which they carry tied to the belt, all the fruit green or ripe, many times even with the leaves. They carry it to the drying courts and turn it over, forming mounds. The rains then are incessant, and in a few days the husks begin to rot, the pulp falls away, and thus continues decomposing until the good weather that December brings finishes drying the beans that remain, and they can be taken to the sorting troughs.

That October was the rainiest ever known. The peons, soaked to the bones, had to give up work for half-days at a time to come in search of dry clothes to the house, where they had their sleeping-quarters and kept their trunks and small bundles. It happened that one day Elías Cañas, instead of getting under the shed with his companions, remained all huddled up in the shelter of the eaves, with his clothes stuck to his flesh, trembling with cold like a dog.

"It's going to hurt you to be wet, Elías. Change your clothes as the others are doing; for today, with this weather, there will be no more work." It was Vicenta who concerned herself for the poor peon, and the tone of her voice held a maternal sweetness.

Elías, looking at her with feverish and hungry eyes, answered: "Never think, my girl, that one who has lived the life of a soldier in the open field can pass his days inside a well without feeling the change. But a man can get used to anything." He smiled and made visible efforts to appear in the best of spirits, although his muscles did not obey him, and he trembled as if he had a fit of the ague.[2]

The girl, knowing the truth, asked in a low voice, "Haven't you got any dry clothes?"

"Just what I carry on my back, if the truth must be told; but there is no shame in being poor."

"Well, wait a moment."

She ran away and returned in a little while, flushed with happiness, bringing an armful of old Juan's washed and much-mended garments. She offered them hurriedly, stooping over to hand them to him, her face betraying her emotion.

"Hurry and put on these things. They are my papá's and they are clean and dry, and go on inside so that no one will notice. Hurry, or you'll be sick with this dampness."

She felt the deep satisfaction of the naturally charitable soul, and she would have liked to confide her rapture to everyone. On meeting her papá in the living room and having to face the keen scrutiny which the old man turned upon her, she grew deathly pale and lowered her eyes. It seemed to her that the wise old countryman had found out about the act

---

2. **ague:** a fever, such as malaria, characterized by bouts of chills, fever, and sweating.

of charity which she had done at his expense, and that he was going to scold her. But when he spoke his words were not at all terrible.

"What is the matter, child? You look like a dead person!"

"Nothing, papá," she said, and gathering courage she went up to him and threw her arms around his neck. "What frightfully rainy weather we are having! These poor people who get so wet every day are going to be sick."

"And poor Juan Cuevas, paying them by the day, and feeding them even when they don't work, is going to come out loser this year."

"Is there still much coffee on the bushes?"

"More than half."

"Then there won't be room enough in the drying-yards. What a fine crop!"

"Whatever the yield, we'll find a place to dry it."

On Thursday the old man called a laborer whom he knew, who had worked for him on other coffee harvests, and he said to him as if he had thought deeply about the plan: "I have to go down tomorrow to the parish to bring silver for the pay, and as I am taking Vicenta I am going to make you boss for the day. See that you look after the place as if it were your own. Watch over the house; and see that the peons don't get the day's wages for nothing."

Vicenta was astonished. "Leave the plantation in charge of a stranger?" How could such an extraordinary notion occur to her papá, who was prudence personified?

The old man explained it plausibly at least. "At other times I left you in charge and I went away with an easy mind, for then you ran no risk. But now a dangerous enemy has got in among us, and it is not safe to leave you alone."

Vicenta, ashamed, hung her head and reddened like a poppy.

"I know how to take care of myself, don't worry . . ." she murmured.

"And I know that it is best to avoid temptations."

At dawn the two set out downhill. The narrow road twisted among the thickets, wet with dew, and as they brushed against the branches drops fell and the birds flew up. The cold air was filled with the odor of wild flowers and with indefinable murmurings. The sun came out and gilded the farthest hills.

Old Juan made observations as he walked. "I see my old friend Lucas over there in his patio. Poor man! this year all his crop is ruined.

"The road is very bad. As soon as the winter season settles down, we'll have to come out and give it a good sweeping.

"See what a narrow entrance this field has; yonder is that good-natured reddish cow. The Devil's own breed!"

Before eight, when the bells called to Mass, they saw the thatched roofs of the pueblo standing out against the green background of the mountain. That pueblo is El Carmen, in the province of Ocaña, a small place, charming as a bowl of flowers. Their road led by the Hill of Hoyito, at that hour deserted. Before starting the ascent the old man waited, seated on a stone, while the girl devoted some moments to her hair. She was a simple country-bred girl; but she was a woman, and without even knowing it her heart was full of feminine instincts.

As she had never seen any other more important village, El Carmen was all she could imagine for size, for beauty, for desirability, in this world. She seated herself, therefore, at the edge of the Quebradita, a chattering stream which flows down foaming among the round stones, and washed her feet so that she could put on some new cloth slippers which she brought in a kerchief for the occasion. She filled her hands with water and washed the sweat of the journey from her face. She shook out her skirt, which she had looped up in her belt in order not to soil the hem; she ran the comb through her hair and looked to see if the braid had become loosened. Powder she had never used. She had brought her kerchief folded over her arm, and now she put it on, gathering it on her breast with the plump brown hand.

Italian and Turkish merchants came out to the doors of their stores with an inviting air.

"Holá,[3] old Juan, come on in here; don't go on by."

In the glass showcases of the counters they had a thousand gewgaws which fascinated the girl: combs set with stones, handkerchiefs with verses, little bottles of perfume, brilliant rings, pins inscribed with the words "forget me not." While she was gazing, her father finished his business. The merchants were counting out to him a pile of bills, the enormous price of who knows how many arrobas[4] of coffee which he had promised to deliver by January, two months away. To celebrate the deal the merchants gave each one half a glass of wine.

They went in to hear Mass and gave the padre a good alms. In a house in Atras Street they ate a plate of yucca, meat, and plantains with hot pancakes. They bought salt, meat, soap . . . and, at the stroke of noon, before the rain hanging ready to fall from the black clouds could begin, they started back up the hill.

The girl had bought a little flask of Cologne water, and there trailed behind her a wake of intense perfume; but her heart was filled with the intenser sweetness of her illusions.

On Saturday afternoon old Juan had his accounts made ready to pay the day laborers. The men approached one after another; they counted on their fingers the days they had worked, received what was owing them, and tying it in a corner of their handkerchiefs, they went off to one side to count it again, and to make corrections. Old Juan, without knowing one thing about arithmetic, but without making a single mistake, paid off the vouchers; Vicenta herself handed over the money, taking it from a square of cloth laid across her lap.

---

3. **Holá:** hello.

4. **arroba:** unit of weight equal to about twenty-five pounds.

When Elías Cañas drew near (he happened to be the last), the old man said to him, in a low voice:

"As the season is about finished, and the coffee groves nearly cleaned out, after tomorrow I have no more work for you."

"Very well," said the youth. After a long silence he raised his eyes, fearing to meet the gaze of all his companions fastened on him. In a moment he ventured to reply.

"But is there no more work for me only? Because you have more than twenty men on the plantation and no other has been dismissed. I have worked with the best; I have earned the money honorably."

Vicenta's bosom rose and fell painfully, like a trapped pigeon; her throat closed, the tears gathered in her eyes, and it was only with great difficulty that she kept them from falling.

Taking advantage of old Juan's silence, Elías Cañas put forth new arguments in his own favor.

"Work, there is work everywhere, and for a man who knows how to do everything, one place is as good as another. The money is worth the same anywhere. But this, which will set everybody talking, is shameful. They see me discharged and will say I was thrown out for something evil. And there will always be someone who will believe it and discredit me. It is true that the coffee harvest is about finished, but there is work for all the coming week. Then after this week we could all leave together, each one with honor."

The old man waited until he had finished, then got up without answering. He took the cloth with the money from Vicenta's hands, and went to put it away, meaning to show that his mind was made up, and would not change.

The young man then walked up to Vicenta and said, in a disturbing voice, "He throws me out because he has seen that I care for you."

"Be quiet!"

"Because for sure he has already arranged to get you a husband with money, and it won't matter whether he pleases you or not."

"Hush, for God's sake! He will hear you."

"You, what you can do is to come with me to the parish church and we will be married. After we are married he will pardon us and we will return."

"Don't believe it. He is terrible; what he says once he sticks to always."

"Think about it. I am not going without you."

They separated as the old man returned from the work shed. Vicenta followed her father. He went by the road of the washing-place, beneath the tall fig trees that had let fall their leaves upon the be-puddled earth. The gushing spring, swollen by the rains, rushed with a crystalline noise which, in the loneliness of the hour, in that gray twilight, sounded like the furious sobbing of a broken-hearted woman. White clothes were spread out on the little meadows of forest grass, and the frogs hidden among the watercress croaked, lured to the nocturnal mysteries of love. Old Cuevas and his daughter saw each other only as two shadows in the early darkness of the night.

"What do you want of me that you have come along?" asked the old man ill-humoredly.

Vicenta did not hesitate. "You should have let him stay here until the crop was finished. He has worked honorably . . ."

"I don't want him here; he is after you, and you do not have to take that young fool; throughout the countryside there are many boys who are known here, and men of means, so that you may choose a husband whenever you have a mind to. See yourself clearly, look around, consider; remember that you are a country girl, and that for you a town idler, full of evil tricks and of unbridled love, is not fitting. The old have much experience and we know what we are doing. It was an evil hour that brought that fellow here."

"I love him, papá . . ."

"Then the quicker he goes, the better, if that's the way things stand. The unseen saint gets no prayers. Let him go. I give the orders here!"

He walked on beneath the banana branches and Vicenta returned to the house slowly, crying. She went to the kitchen, primed the old lamp, and taking a burning stick from the hearth she blew on the hot coal until it burst into flame and with this she lit the lamp. Returning to the living room she thought she saw a shadow which came out from the sleeping quarters and glided rapidly toward the patio.

She asked in fright, "Is that you, Elías?"

"Yes, I was looking for you. Your voice trembles. Were you frightened?"

"My papá does not consent."

"He will give in once we are married. Tonight I will wait for you. Let him go to sleep, then come out and we will go. Tomorrow we will be married, and then there will be nothing left for him but to pardon us. It always happens like that. Have you made up your mind?"

"I do not dare . . . My papá would die of anger."

"He won't die at all. The old ones are in their dotage and there is no use paying any attention to them. Nobody does. And as we are going to marry, anyhow . . ."

"I don't dare. It is a very grave thing . . . going from the house like a bad woman."

"We shall go straightaway to the church. I shall not lie down this night; I shall sit here on a stone and wait for you."

"Holy God! . . ."

"Your mind is made up?"

"Yes."

In a little while old Juan came in and folded himself up on the bed to smoke a pipe slowly. The lamp was turned low, and seated very near him Vicenta pretended to mend, but she was really lost in thought, her eyes fastened on the stitches as the needle moved between her fingers. From a neighboring shed rose the noise of laughter and the voices of the peons.

"Now they have money, they'll play cards or dice all night. That's why some of them have nothing left to buy a change of clothes."

Vicenta kept silent; she lifted her work and cut the thread with her teeth.

"Are those my king's cloth slippers?"

"Yes, papá."

"I have seen my old friend Manuel Gonzalez wearing the very same kind. And that man is rich; the least that he will gather this year is forty loads. If the price keeps up, what more could you want! The trouble is, he lives hand to mouth with his sons; none of them has any sense, they spend all they make. The girls, yes, they have turned out very well and, I have heard tell, the eldest is married, very well married."

Vicenta remained silent, without paying any attention to what the old man was saying.

"Another who does well also is my old friend, Araos; but what helps him out is his cattle. What beautiful animals he has! One young heifer I tried to buy—which cost one grain of gold—so that you might have four . . . Hi there, daughter, are you listening?"

"No, I knew that already."

"You are wool-gathering and do not know what I am saying. You have Elías on the mind and do not even hear what I am telling you. Lie down and go to sleep; rest will take away all your troubles. And forget all this foolishness, for now that he is going, and you shan't see him any more, you'll forget him, and that's the end of it."

Vicenta tried to smile, without speaking. She got up stiffly and carried the lamp to a bracket near her bed. She placed some matches ready and asked, with a tearful voice, "Shall we say our prayers together?"

"That's the very thing; then all the bad thoughts will leave you."

He went to lay his pipe on the small chest and seeing the key in the lock asked in surprise: "What is this? I could swear that this afternoon, after the pay-off, I closed the chest well and put the key in my small purse . . . no sir, the key, the key is hanging here caught in the lock. What a head I have on me! Lucky for us these people are very honest . . ."

They said all their accustomed prayers, and then Vicenta blew out the dim little lamp. In the silence that followed one might have heard the swift heartbeats of the poor girl, who did not know what road to take. She struggled between her desire to go away with the man who had made love to her and sorrow at abandoning the poor old man who until then had been her all in this world. Time seemed to her to fly and she thought of Elías outside waiting for her. Should she go?

After all, the opposition of old Juan was no more than an unjust whim, since the natural law of life is that a man chooses a woman and a woman takes her husband, and who can be better judge than one's own heart to choose this companion for a whole life? She slipped from her bed, listening acutely. Her papá slept, and his measured breathing was like a light murmur in the room. She pushed open the door and went out without making any noise.

Elías was waiting for her.

"Let us go," he said quickly.

"Let us go," she murmured.

The night was bright, for the clouds were passing and the moon shone;

the road opened up between the trees like a mysterious tunnel. The breeze rustled the leaves of the willows, and the bats flew round and round squealing sharply. The two dogs, Faithful and Vigilant, wanted to follow their mistress, whining softly, like children threatening to weep. But with forbidding gestures Vicenta made them go back. She hurried along, frightened of the shadows and of the ghostly trees beside the road. Suddenly she sat down, overcome, looked up at her abductor, and whimpered.

"If he catches us he will kill us."

"By the time he wakes up we shall be far away."

"What is going to happen to us?"

"What is going to happen? Whatever we want to happen." And as he bent over to kiss her he confessed shamelessly. "I have brought all your own money with me—everything that is yours. With this we shall be kings anywhere."

Vicenta freed herself from Elías's arm and put her hands to her head.

"You have stolen the silver that was in the chest? That was what you were doing in the bedroom?"

"Stolen, no; it is your money and you have the right to take it with you. And as you are going with me, you go only with what is your own."

Disillusioned with shocking suddenness, she seized him by his sleeves and cried out: "Thief! You are a thief, Elías!"

Her love turned to hate. That ancestral feeling, transmitted from generation to generation, of holding sacred, untouchable, the fruits of the labor of a whole lifetime; that well of secret avarice which sleeps in the heart of every countryman, moving his hand to knot up in the corner of his handkerchief the money which represents so many days of bending over the furrows under the blazing sun, awoke in the girl with unexpected fierceness. She was no longer enthralled in the madness of love; here were the gold rings, relics of her dead mother, here the Peruvian dollars and the half-condor, the treasure fondled and counted so many times, between smiles and dazzling visions, which this vagabond was taking for himself. She would never let it happen.

"You are a barefaced thief! Shameless! A thief!"

She snatched the knapsack and cried out, calling to Faithful and Vigilant. The dogs leaped forward with terrible fury. A troop of the laborers aroused by the cries rushed toward them, and old Juan also came running, half-enveloped in his red blanket, brandishing a formidable club.

"What does this mean, daughter?" cried the old man threateningly. "What are you doing here? What happened?"

Frightened by the girl's cries, and intimidated by the strength with which she snatched the money from his bands, Elías had fled across the country, and was lost among the shadows of the night. Vicenta, alone in the middle of the road, wept, hiding her face in the crook of her arm. To their questions she could only say, sobbing, "He was no better than a thief . . ."

"Who?"

"Elías."

"And what has he taken?"

"Nothing—after all. I am here. Our treasures are here with me. He gave me a frightful look when I snatched them away from him . . . Thief! He was no more than a thief, that Elías!"

Poor country girl! In this adventure she lost nothing except the flower of her first and only illusion. When she is older she will marry honorably but without love. She will bear many sons, she will see her grandchildren multiply; and she will be one of those austere old ladies who wear many long starched petticoats, who go down from the country to hear Mass on feast days, and who pass by clutching their kerchiefs on their breasts with a hand brown and weather-beaten, a hand which has worked hard, but its fingers are covered with antiquated rings.

DISCUSSION QUESTIONS

1. What do you think of the way Juan handled the situation with his daughter? Did he do the right thing? Why or why not?

2. What hints does the author give us about the untrustworthy character of Elías Cañas even before the theft?

3. Vicenta was born into a family with very strong values and traditions. How does Tablanca make it clear that Vicenta cherishes these values, even as she defies her father's instructions?

4. When Vicenta realizes that Elías Cañas has taken the contents of the chest, she responds with "unexpected fierceness." Perhaps her response is just as unexpected to her as it is to him. What does she realize at that moment?

5. Tablanca closes the story with a vision of Vicenta in the distant future, and this vision ends with a curious detail: her fingers are covered with "antiquated rings." What is the significance of this detail?

SUGGESTION FOR WRITING

"Country Girl" is filled with fascinating details about the rural culture of northern Colombia. Imagine that you have been asked to contribute an article to *National Geographic* about the coffee growers and the local customs of the area. Using information gleaned only from this story, write a vividly descriptive article on the coffee growers' way of life.

FERNÁN SILVA VALDÉS
(1887–1975)

Valdés is known primarily for founding a poetic movement called Nativism, a manner of writing that emphasizes regional characteristics of the land and its people. This type of writing is usually vivid and highly descriptive. Valdés' most important volume of Nativist poetry is *Water of Time*, in which he celebrates the lifestyles of Indians, gauchos (South American cowboys), and Creoles (in this case, people of mixed Spanish and Indian ancestry).

In the first poem below, Valdés associates the gauchos with the troubadours of France. The troubadours were traveling poets of the twelfth and thirteenth centuries who sang the verses they composed, usually with instrumental accompaniment. ■

THE GAUCHO TROUBADOUR
Translated by Willis Knapp Jones

I. EVOCATION

Troubadour, with your mane like the Nazarene,[1]
Poet of the desert vast,
Not yet does paint or stone your glory immortalize,
In your progress through the world you've reached America at last.
Your race first saw the light in far Provence,[2]
And in the Pampas[3] finally closed its eyes.

II. NORTH

Lord of the four-fold compass points.
Adventure-loving, free of habitat,
You used to wander aimlessly,
Yet one by one all routes would finally sweep
Beneath the wide brim of your ragged hat.

III. LIKE THE BIRDS

You did not need much urging to display your art:
A drink, a rival (if he sang well, you'd rejoice).

---

1. **mane like the Nazarene:** long-haired, like the usual pictorial representations of Jesus of Nazareth.

2. **Provence:** region in southeast France where the troubadours originated.

3. **Pampas:** dry, flat grasslands of southern South America.

As birds have song bubbling in their throats,
You used to have your verse ready in your voice.

IV. THE GUITAR

Your guitar in your arms was like a daughter,
    Tiny and motherless,
And you would croon to it so drowsily.
Your guitar in your arms was like a mother
Whose milk, seeping through warm arteries,
Has come even to me!

V. SINGING

Your hat, pushed back with pride upon your head,
Pulled tight against your jaw its leather thong,
And where your beard against your moustache pressed,
Each time you raised your voice in song
Your lips peeped out like a cardinal in its nest.
The whitened skull of cattle used to serve you as a throne,
Or if you'd rise about the earth, a counter was your seat;
An unsophisticated audience squatting on its heels
Would sit around you solemnly in speechlessness complete,
Though from the hitching post outside
A chorus of bridle rings was your accompaniment,
With the metallic tinkle of their beat.

VI. REWARD

No matter where you sang, trailed merriment a-wing.
You used to pass, with festive gayness at your back
And afterward lay silence over the countryside,
Harmonious as a copper kettle, used and black.

Unheeded beauty girt you which you never knew.
Nature, being blind, mingles the good with the bad.
It showers, wetting you, dirtied your skies, it's true,
Yet reared a rainbow arch of triumph over you.

THE INDIAN

Translated by Willis Knapp Jones

He came
Who knows from where
With headband like a *benteveo* bird,[4]
And crested like a cardinal.

---

4. *benteveo* bird: a brown and yellow South American bird with a white spot on its head.

Little he knew of native land, although he loved his home.
The Spaniards found him rooted deep
Fishing in rivers, hunting in forests, ranging wide.

His ringing war cry served to keep
Eternal obstacles, eternal checks between them and
The vast horizon's sweep.

Molded in clay of stubbornness his slim, sly body passed
Swift as a naked shadow, ever on the run,
Along his well-known hillside steeps,
Its color, copper fused with red; its brawn surpassed by none.
At noise of war, his sharpened instincts tensed,
And in his veins, instead of blood, ran liquid sun.

Instinctive slave of beauty he;
Upon his face he traced a mass of brilliant hues, none pale.
His plumed war bonnet made him no more Indian,
Yet more of color made him more the male.

Master of all the region,
Over trifling hunting quarrel with some neighboring chief
He'd brandish in the wind his courage, keen-edged as a sword;
Like Uruguayan trees he, too, was tough,—trunk, stem, and leaf,
Within, without; his only softness was his uttered word,
The heart of him, as in the hardiest *pitanga* tree,[5]
A sweet and trembling flower seemed to be.

How often his canoe would cut the streams;
One was he with the wildest animal
As he would roam for months on end,
Lured by the never-reached horizon's call,—
His copper hide tanned by the elements;
Reddened by sun or soaked by rainy splash,—
Through those hot, dreary days when locusts chirp,
Or through the long nights bright with lightning's flash.

The Spanish conquest checked his wanderings,
And tribes who widely roamed in any weather
Came clustering in a bunch about a chief,
Boleadora[6]-like, going round together.

He had no skill at laughter or at tears;
The puma-bellow at the killing was his only cry,
And when his end came, he passed on without a sound,
His feathers trembling, dying as the wild birds die.

———
5. *pitanga* tree: a kind of cherry tree with violet or purple blossoms.

6. *Boleadora*: a weighted lariat used by South American cowboys to twist around an animal's legs.

DISCUSSION QUESTIONS

1. In "The Gaucho Troubadour" Valdés describes a way of life that he regards as relatively carefree and happy. Does he mention any drawbacks of the gaucho life? Can you imagine any drawbacks to this way of life that are not mentioned?

2. Valdés sees the gauchos as spiritual descendants of the troubadours of the Middle Ages. In what ways are gauchos and troubadours similar?

3. In "The Indian" the metaphors and similes compare the Indian to several animals and, at one point, to a tree. Discuss the impact of these images.

4. The Indians' loss of liberty after the Spanish conquest is described by a single image. What effect does this image have on the reader's response to the poem?

SUGGESTION FOR WRITING

Indians are often presented as colorful and fascinating people who aroused both the interest and the fear of the white people who first saw them. Unfortunately, we know little of how these Indians viewed the first white people who appeared on their land.

Imagine that you are an Indian from any area in North or South America and that you have spotted a group of Europeans. They could be English colonists, Spanish conquistadors, French fur traders, or any other group appropriate to the area you have chosen. Decide what you want to tell the members of your tribe about this discovery. Write out your report, describing the appearance and behavior of these newcomers. Speculate on what you think can be expected from these people. (For example, do they appear menacing or peaceable?)

CÉSAR VALLEJO

(1892–1938)

The son of a small-town mayor, Vallejo grew up in a large Peruvian family of mixed Spanish and Indian ancestry. After earning a degree in literature, he taught for a short time. In 1918 he published his first book, *Black Heralds,* a pessimistic collection of poems about rural life. His passionate political activities on behalf of Indians led to a prison sentence on trumped-up charges in 1920. In prison he wrote his second book of poetry, *Trilco,* which reflects his deepening interest in political issues. Shortly after his release from prison, he left Peru, never to return, and moved to Paris.

In Paris Vallejo dedicated himself to socialist ideals and joined with activist groups in promoting social reform. Believing that literature could change society, he continued to write poetry but was unable to publish any of his Paris poems during his lifetime. He lived in extreme poverty, eventually dying a lonely death at a relatively young age.

After Vallejo's death, most of his Paris poems were finally published under the title *Human Poems.* These poems reveal his disillusionment and despair, his view of the world as a menacing place, and his yearning for social justice. They are notable for their bold diction and their highly original imagery. ■

BLACK STONE ON TOP OF A WHITE STONE

Translated by Thomas Merton

I shall die in Paris, in a rainstorm,
On a day I already remember.
I shall die in Paris—it does not bother me—
Doubtless on a Thursday, like today, in autumn.

5   It shall be a Thursday, because today, Thursday
As I put down these lines, I have set my shoulders
To the evil. Never like today have I turned,
And headed my whole journey to the ways where I am alone.

César Vallejo is dead. They struck him,
10   All of them, though he did nothing to them.
They hit him hard with a stick and hard also
With the end of a rope. Witnesses are: the Thursdays,
The shoulder bones, the loneliness, the rain and the roads. . . .

DISCUSSION QUESTIONS

1. In this poem Vallejo anticipates and describes some of the circumstances of his own death. Do you think he is simply wallowing in self-pity, or does the poem move beyond these narrow, personal concerns?

2. The stones mentioned in the title are not referred to again in the body of the poem, and so their meaning is never directly explained. White stones were used in ancient times as a symbol of something fortunate. What might the black stone represent? What is suggested by the black stone on top of a white stone?

3. What does Vallejo mean when he writes, " . . . I turned/ And headed my whole journey to the ways where I am alone"?

4. Why does Vallejo think that Thursday and autumn are likely times for his death?

5. In the final stanza, to whom do you think the words *they* and *them* refer?

6. Whom does the poet expect to witness his death? What does this say about the kind of death he expects?

SUGGESTION FOR WRITING

Imagine that you have been given the task of writing an epitaph for Vallejo's tombstone. Concentrate on capturing something significant about his life and work and try to create the kind of epitaph that he would have wanted. You may write in either poetry or prose.

JOSÉ VASCONCELOS
(1882–1959)

Born in Oaxaco, Mexico, Vasconcelos was a politician, statesman, and writer who was active in the Mexican Revolution of 1910. After the revolution he was appointed president of the National University of Mexico and, a year later, became Secretary of Public Education. During this period he established libraries, organized public schools, and encouraged the arts.

Vasconcelos' most famous work is probably *The Cosmic Race,* which advocates a united Latin American nation comparable to those of Canada and the United States. Another important work is *A Mexican Ulysses,* an autobiography that gives an account of Mexico before, during, and after the revolution. In general, Vasconcelos' writings are historical and sociological rather than fictional, but he occasionally wrote short stories and plays. The following story is a tale of adventure. ■

THE BOAR HUNT

Translated from the Spanish by Paul Waldorf

We were four companions, and we went by the names of our respective nationalities: the Colombian, the Peruvian, the Mexican; the fourth, a native of Ecuador, was called Quito[1] for short. Unforeseen chance had joined us together a few years ago on a large sugar plantation on the Peruvian coast. We worked at different occupations during the day and met during the evening in our off time. Not being Englishmen, we did not play cards. Instead, our constant discussions led to disputes. These didn't stop us from wanting to see each other the next night, however, to continue the interrupted debates and support them with new arguments. Nor did the rough sentences of the preceding wrangles indicate a lessening of our affection, of which we assured ourselves reciprocally with the clasping of hands and a look. On Sundays we used to go on hunting parties. We roamed the fertile glens, stalking, generally with poor results, the game of the warm region around the coast, or we entertained ourselves killing birds that flew in the sunlight during the siesta hour.

We came to be tireless wanderers and excellent marksmen. Whenever we climbed a hill and gazed at the imposing range of mountains in the interior, its attractiveness stirred us and we wanted to climb it. What attracted us more was the trans-Andean region: fertile plateaus extending on the other side of the range in the direction of the Atlantic toward the immense land of Brazil. It was as if primitive nature called us to her

---

1. **Quito:** the capital of Ecuador.

breast. The vigor of the fertile, untouched jungles promised to rejuvenate our minds, the same vigor which rejuvenates the strength and the thickness of the trees each year. At times we devised crazy plans. As with all things that are given a lot of thought, these schemes generally materialized. Ultimately nature and events are largely what our imaginations make them out to be. And so we went ahead planning and acting. At the end of the year, with arranged vacations, accumulated money, good rifles, abundant munitions, stone- and mud-proof boots, four hammocks, and a half dozen faithful Indians, our caravan descended the Andean slopes, leading to the endless green ocean.

At last we came upon a village at the edge of the Marañón River.[2] Here we changed our safari. The region we were going to penetrate had no roads. It was unexplored underbrush into which we could enter only by going down the river in a canoe. In time we came to the area where we proposed to carry out the purpose of our journey, the hunting of wild boars.

We had been informed that boars travel in herds of several thousands, occupying a region, eating grass and staying together, exploiting the grazing areas, organized just like an army. They are very easy to kill if one attacks them when they are scattered out satisfying their appetites—an army given over to the delights of victory. When they march about hungry, on the other hand, they are usually vicious. In our search we glided down river between imposing jungles with our provisions and the company of three faithful Indian oarsmen.

One morning we stopped at some huts near the river. Thanks to the information gathered there, we decided to disembark a little farther on in order to spend the night on land and continue the hunt for the boars in the thicket the following day.

Sheltered in a backwater, we came ashore, and after a short exploration found a clearing in which to make camp. We unloaded the provisions and the rifles, tied the boat securely, then with the help of the Indians set up our camp one half kilometer from the river bank. In marking the path to the landing, we were careful not to lose ourselves in the thicket. The Indians withdrew toward their huts, promising to return two days later. At dawn we would set out in search of the prey.

Though night had scarcely come and the heat was great, we gathered at the fire to see each other's faces, to look instinctively for protection. We talked a little, smoked, confessed to being tired, and decided to go to bed. Each hammock had been tied by one end to a single tree, firm though not very thick in the trunk. Stretching out from this axis in different directions, the hammocks were supported by the other end on other trunks. Each of us carried his rifle, cartridges, and some provisions which couldn't remain exposed on the ground. The sight of the weapons made us consider the place where we were, surrounded by the unknown. A slight feeling of

---

2. **Marañón River:** one of the Amazon's main sources in Peru.

terror made us laugh, cough, and talk. But fatigue overcame us, that heavy fatigue which compels the soldier to scorn danger, to put down his rifle, and to fall asleep though the most persistent enemy pursues him. We scarcely noticed the supreme grandeur of that remote tropical night.

I don't know whether it was the light of the magnificent dawn or the strange noises which awakened me and made me sit up in my hammock and look carefully at my surroundings. I saw nothing but the awakening of that life which at night falls into the lethargy of the jungle. I called my sleeping companions and, alert and seated in our hanging beds, we dressed ourselves. We were preparing to jump to the ground when we clearly heard a somewhat distant, sudden sound of rustling branches. Since it did not continue, however, we descended confidently, washed our faces with water from our canteens, and slowly prepared and enjoyed breakfast. By about 11:00 in the morning we were armed and bold and preparing to make our way through the jungle.

But then the sound again. Its persistence and proximity in the thicket made us change our minds. An instinct made us take refuge in our hammocks. We cautiously moved our cartridges and rifles into them again, and without consulting each other we agreed on the idea of putting our provisions safely away. We passed them up into the hammocks, and we ourselves finally climbed in. Stretched out face down, comfortably suspended with rifles in hand, we did not have to wait long. Black, agile boars quickly appeared from all directions. We welcomed them with shouts of joy and well-aimed shots. Some fell immediately, giving comical snorts, but many more came out of the jungle. We shot again, spending all the cartridges in the magazine. Then we stopped to reload. Finding ourselves safe in the height of our hammocks, we continued after a pause.

We counted dozens of them. At a glance we made rapid calculations of the magnitude of the destruction, while the boars continued to come out of the jungle in uncountable numbers. Instead of going on their way or fleeing, they seemed confused. All of them emerged from the jungle where it was easy for us to shoot them.

Occasionally we had to stop firing because the frequent shooting heated the barrels of our rifles. While they were cooling we smoked and were able to joke, celebrating our good fortune. The impotent anger of the boars amazed us. They raised their tusks in our direction, uselessly threatening us. We laughed at their snorts, quietly aimed at those who were near, and Bang! a dead boar. We carefully studied the angle of the shoulder blade so that the bullet would cross the heart. The slaughter lasted for hours.

At 4:00 P.M. we noticed an alarming shortage of our ammunition. We had been well supplied and had shot at will. Though the slaughter was gratifying, the boars must have numbered, as we had been informed previously, several thousands, because their hordes didn't diminish. On the contrary, they gathered directly beneath our hammocks in increasing groups. They slashed furiously at the trunk of the tree which held the four points of the hammocks. The marks of the tusks remained on the hard bark. Not without a certain fear we watched them gather compactly, tenaciously, in tight masses against the resisting trunk. We wondered what would happen to a man who fell within their reach. Our shots were now sporadic, well aimed, carefully husbanded. They did not drive away the aggressive beasts, but only redoubled their fury. One of us ironically noted that from being the attackers we had gone on the defensive. We did not laugh very long at the joke. Now we hardly shot at all. We needed to save our cartridges.

The afternoon waned and evening came upon us. After consulting each other, we decided to eat in our hammocks. We applauded ourselves for taking the food up—meat, bread, and bottles of water. Stretching ourselves on our hammocks, we passed things to each other, sharing what we needed. The boars deafened us with their angry snorts.

After eating, we began to feel calm. We lit cigars. Surely the boars would go. Their numbers were great, but they would finally leave peacefully. As we said so, however, we looked with greedy eyes at the few unused cartridges that remained. Our enemies, like enormous angry ants, stirred beneath us, encouraged by the ceasing of our fire. From time to time we carefully aimed and killed one or two of them, driving off the huge group of uselessly enraged boars at the base of the trunk which served as a prop for our hammocks.

Night enveloped us almost without our noticing the change from twilight. Anxiety also overtook us. When would the cursed boars leave? Already there were enough dead to serve as trophies to several dozen hunters. Our feat would be talked about; we had to show ourselves worthy of such fame. Since there was nothing else to do, it was necessary to sleep. Even if we had had enough bullets it would have been impossible to continue the fight in the darkness. It occurred to us to start a fire to drive the herd off with flames, but apart from the fact that we couldn't leave the place in which we were suspended, there were no dry branches in the lush forest. Finally, we slept.

We woke up a little after midnight. The darkness was profound, but the well-known noise made us aware that our enemies were still there. We imagined they must be the last ones which were leaving, however. If a good army needs several hours to break camp and march off, what can be expected of a vile army of boars but disorder and delay? The following morning we would fire upon the stragglers, but this painful thought bothered us: they were in large and apparently active numbers. What were they up to? Why didn't they leave? We thus spent long hours of worry. Dawn finally came, splendid in the sky but noisy in the jungle still enveloped inwardly in shadows. We eagerly waited for the sun to penetrate the foliage in order to survey the appearance of the field of battle of the day before.

What we finally saw made us gasp. It terrified us. The boars were painstakingly continuing the work which they had engaged in throughout the entire night. Guided by some extraordinary instinct, with their tusks they were digging out the ground underneath the tree from which our hammocks hung; they gnawed the roots and continued to undermine them like large, industrious rats. Presently the tree was bound to fall and we with it, among the beasts. From that moment we neither thought nor talked. In desperation we used up our last shots, killing more ferocious beasts. Still the rest renewed their activity. They seemed to be endowed with intelligence. However much we concentrated our fire against them, they did not stop their attack against the tree.

Soon our shots stopped. We emptied our pistols, and then silently listened to the tusks gnawing beneath the soft, wet, pleasant-smelling earth. From time to time the boars pressed against the tree, pushing it and making it creak, eager to smash it quickly. We looked on hypnotized by their devilish activity. It was impossible to flee because the black monsters covered every inch in sight. It seemed to us that, by a sudden inspiration, they were preparing to take revenge on us for the ruthless nature of man, the unpunished destroyer of animals since the beginning of time. Our imagination, distorted by fear, showed us our fate as an atonement for the unpardonable crimes implicit in the struggle of biological selection. Before my eyes passed the vision of sacred India, where the believer refuses to eat meat in order to prevent the methodical killing of beasts and in order to atone for man's evil, bloody, treacherous slaughter, such as ours, for mere vicious pleasure. I felt that the multitude of boars was raising its accusing voice against me. I now understood the infamy of the hunter, but what was repentance worth if I was going to die with my companions, hopelessly devoured by that horde of brutes with demonlike eyes?

Stirred by terror and without realizing what I was doing, I hung from the upper end of my hammock, I balanced myself in the air, I swung in a long leap, I grasped a branch of a tree facing the one on which the boars were digging. From there I leaped to other branches and to others, reviving in myself habits which the species had forgotten.

The next moment a terrifying sound and unforgettable cries told me of the fall of the tree and the end of my companions. I clung to a trunk, trembling and listening to the chattering of my jaws. Later, the desire to flee gave me back my strength. Leaning out over the foliage, I looked for a path, and I saw the boars in the distance, marching in compressed ranks and holding their insolent snouts in the air. I knew that they were now withdrawing, and I got down from the tree. Horror overwhelmed me as I approached the site of our encampment, but some idea of duty made me return there. Perhaps one of my friends had managed to save himself. I approached hesitantly. Each dead boar made me tremble with fear.

But what I saw next was so frightful that I could not fix it clearly in my mind: remains of clothing—and footwear. There was no doubt; the boars had devoured them. Then I ran toward the river, following the tracks we had made two days before. I fled with great haste, limbs stiff from panic.

Running with long strides, I came upon the boat. With a great effort, I managed to row to the huts. There I went to bed with a high fever which lasted many days.

I will participate in no more hunts. I will contribute, if I have to, to the extermination of harmful beasts. But I will not kill for pleasure. I will not amuse myself with the ignoble pleasure of the hunt.

DISCUSSION QUESTIONS

1. Do you think "The Boar Hunt" was intended as simple entertainment, or does the story also carry a "message"? Support your position.

2. How does the hunters' attitude toward the boars change in the course of the story? Why do you think Vasconcelos selected boars as the target of the hunt? (Think about how the mood of the story might have been different if the target had been bears or jaguars?)

3. What techniques does Vasconcelos use to build suspense in "The Boar Hunt"?

4. After the hunters set up camp, the author describes their tired feelings in this way: "Fatigue overcame us, that heavy fatigue which compels the soldier to scorn danger . . . and to fall asleep though the most persistent enemy pursues him." Explain how this description serves as a foreshadowing of events to come.

5. Vasconcelos could easily have arranged for the narrator to see his companions' horrible death, but he chose to keep the narrator at a distance. Do you think the story would have been more effective with the narrator as a direct witness, or do you prefer the ending as it stands now? Explain your thinking.

SUGGESTION FOR WRITING

Imagine that you are the narrator of "The Boar Hunt" and that you have just received a letter from Ms. Sylvia Flores, a well-known naturalist in the area. She is about to investigate the intelligence of wild boars and has heard about your encounter with them. She would appreciate any observations you can make about the boars' general intelligence and their ability to carry out purposeful activities. Please respond to her letter as accurately as you can, offering specific examples to support your conclusions.

Acknowledgments

xii "Life Is a Dream" by Pedro Calderón de la Barca, translated by Arthur Symons from *Poems.*

3 "The Launch" by Max Aub, translated by Elizabeth Mantel from *Great Spanish Short Stories,* ed. Angel Flores. Reprinted by permission of the Estate of Angel Flores.

8 "The First Prize" by Emilia Pardo Bazán, translated by Armando Zegri from *Great Stories of All Nations,* ed. Maxim Lieber and Blanche Colton Williams.

14 "They Closed Her Eyes" by Gustavo Adolfo Bécquer, translated by John Masefield from *The Story of a Round House* by John Masefield. Reprinted by permission of The Society of Authors as the Literary Representative of the Estate of John Masefield.

18 "The Village Idiot" by Camilo José Cela, translated by Beatrice P. Patt from *Great Spanish Short Stories,* ed. Angel Flores. Reprinted by permission of the Estate of Angel Flores.

21 "The Lament" by Federico García Lorca, translated by Stephen Spender & J. L. Gili, from *The Selected Poems of Federico García Lorca.* Copyright © 1955 by New Directions Publishing Corp. Reprinted by permission of New Directions Publishing Corp.

22 "Song" by Federico García Lorca, translated by Stephen Spender & J. L. Gili, from *The Selected Poems of Federico García Lorca.* Copyright © 1955 by New Directions Publishing Corp. Reprinted by permission of New Directions Publishing Corp.

22 "The Guitar" from *Obras Completas* by Federico García Lorca, trans. Stephen Spender and J. L. Gili.

23 The Arrest of Antoñito el Camborio on the Road to Seville" from *Lament for the Death of a Bullfighter and Other Poems* by Federico García Lorca, trans. A. L. Lloyd. Copyright 1962 by A. L. Lloyd.

25 "The Death of Antoñito el Camborio" by Federico García Lorca, translated by Stephen Spender and J. L. Gili from *The Selected Poems of Federico García Lorca.* Copyright © 1955 by New Directions Publishing Corp. Reprinted by permission of New Directions Publishing Corp.

26 "The Dawn" by Federico García Lorca, translated by Rolfe Humphries, from *The Selected Poems of Federico García Lorca.* Copyright © 1955 by New Directions Publishing Corp. Reprinted by permission of New Directions Publishing Corp.

27 "New York (Office and Arraignment)" from *Obras Completas* by Federico García Lorca, trans. Rolfe Humphries.

29 "Seville" by Federico García Lorca translated by Rolfe Humphries, from *The Selected Poems of Federico García Lorca.* Copyright © 1955 by New Directions Publishing Corp. Reprinted by permission of New Directions Publishing Corp.

31 "What Happens to a Melody" from *Juan Ramón Jiménez: Three Hundred Poems 1903-1953* by Juan Ramón Jiménez, translated by Eloise Roach. Austin: University of Texas Press, 1962.

32 "I Shall Not Return" from *Juan Ramón Jiménez: Three Hundred Poems 1903-1953* by Juan Ramón Jiménez, translated by Eloise Roach. Austin: University of Texas Press, 1962.

32 "Hand Against the Light" from *Juan Ramón Jiménez: Three Hundred Poems 1903-1953* by Juan Ramón Jiménez, translated by Eloise Roach. Austin: University of Texas Press, 1962.

33 "Is It I, Pacing My Room" from *Juan Ramón Jiménez: Three Hundred Poems 1903-1953* by Juan Ramón Jiménez, translated by Eloise Roach. Austin: University of Texas Press, 1962.

33 "Forgers of Swords" from *Juan Ramón Jiménez: Three Hundred Poems 1903-1953* by Juan Ramón Jiménez, translated by Eloise Roach. Austin: University of Texas Press, 1962.

34 "The Lamb Baaed Gently" from *Juan Ramón Jiménez: Three Hundred Poems 1903-1953* by Juan Ramón Jiménez, translated by Eloise Roach. Austin: University of Texas Press, 1962.

34 "This Other I" from *Juan Ramón Jiménez: Three Hundred Poems 1903-1953* by Juan Ramón Jiménez, translated by Eloise Roach. Austin: University of Texas Press, 1962.

35 "I Fired at the Ideal" from *Juan Ramón Jiménez: Three Hundred Poems 1903-1953* by Juan Ramón Jiménez, translated by Eloise Roach. Austin: University of Texas Press, 1962.

35 "I Wish My Book Might Be" from *Juan Ramón Jiménez: Three Hundred Poems 1903-1953* by Juan Ramón Jiménez, translated by Eloise Roach. Austin: University of Texas Press, 1962.

37 "The Return" by Carmen Laforet, translated by Martin Nozick from *Great Spanish Short Stories,* ed. Angel Flores. Reprinted by permission of the Estate of Angel Flores.

42 "The Crime Was in Granada" from *Eighty Poems* by Antonio Machado, translated by Willis Barnstone. Reprinted by permission of Willis Barnstone.

45 *The Olives* by Lope de Rueda, translated by Angel Flores from *Spanish Drama*. Copyright © 1962 by Bantam Books, Inc. Reprinted by permission of the Estate of Angel Flores.

50 *Fuente Ovejuna* by Lope de Vega, translated by Angel Flores and Muriel Kittel. Copyright 1962 by Bantam Books. Reprinted by permission of the Estate of Angel Flores.

103 "The Stone and the Cross" by Ciro Alegría, translated by Zoila Nelken. From *Short Stories of Latin America,* translated by Zoila Nelken and Rosalie Torres-Rioseco, edited by Arturo Torres-Rioseco. Copyright 1963 by Las Americas Publishing Company. Reprinted by permission of Rosalie Torres-Rioseco.

111 "Handbill for Green" by Jorge Carrara Andrade, translated by John Igo from *Poet Lore* 60:1. Reprinted by permission of John Igo.

112 "A Man from Ecuador Beneath the Eiffel Tower" by Jorge Carrara Andrade, translated by Thomas Merton, from *The Collected Poems of Thomas Merton*. Copyright © 1948 by New Directions Publishing Corporation. Reprinted by permission of New Directions Publishing Corp.

113 "The Weathercock of the Cathedral of Quito" by Jorge Carrera Andrade, translated by Thomas Merton, from *The Collected Poems of Thomas Merton.* Copyright © 1963 by The Abbey of Gethsemani, Inc. Reprinted by permission of New Directions Publishing Corp.

115 "Pilgrimage" by Armando Arriaza, translated by Alis De Sola from *Fiesta in November, Stories from Latin America,* ed. Angel Flores and Dudley Poore. Copyright 1942 by Houghton Mifflin. Reprinted by permission of the Estate of Angel Flores.

121 "The Garden of Forking Paths" translated by Helen Temple and Ruthven Todd from *Ficciones* by Jorge Luis Borges. Copyright © 1962 by Grove Press, Inc. Used by permission of Grove / Atlantic, Inc.

130 "Hengest Cyning" from *Jorge Luis Borges Selected Poems 1923-1967* by Jorge Luis Borges. Copyright © 1968, 1969, 1970, 1971, 1972 by Jorge Luis Borges, Emece Editores, S. A. and Norman Thomas Di Giovanni. Used by permission of Delacorte Press / Seymour Lawrence, a division of Bantam Doubleday Dell Publishing Group, Inc.

131 "Afterglow" from *Jorge Luis Borges Selected Poems 1923-1967* by Jorge Luis Borges. Copyright © 1968, 1969, 1970, 1971, 1972 by Jorge Luis Borges, Emece Editores, S. A. and Norman Thomas Di Giovanni. Used by permission of Delacorte Press / Seymour Lawrence, a division of Bantam Doubleday Dell Publishing Group, Inc.

131 "The Dagger" from *Jorge Luis Borges Selected Poems 1923-1967* by Jorge Luis Borges. Copyright © 1968, 1969, 1970, 1971, 1972 by Jorge Luis Borges, Emece Editores, S. A. and Norman Thomas Di Giovanni. Used by permission of Delacorte Press / Seymour Lawrence, a division of Bantam Doubleday Dell Publishing Group, Inc.

134 "Cross Over, Sawyer!" by Jesús del Corral, translated by Harry Kurz from *A World of Great Stories* by Hiram Haydn. Reprinted by permission of the Estate of Harry Kurz.

141 "The Birth of the Sun" by Pablo Antonio Cuadro, translated by Thomas Merton, from *The Collected Poems of Thomas Merton.* Copyright © 1963 by The Abbey of Gethsemani, Inc. Reprinted by permission of New Directions Publishing Corp.

142 "The Jaguar Myth" by Pablo Antonio Cuadro, translated by Thomas Merton, from *The Collected Poems of Thomas Merton.* Copyright © 1963 by The Abbey of Gethsemani, Inc. Reprinted by permission of New Directions Publishing Corp.

143 "Meditation Before an Ancient Poem" by Pablo Antonio Cuadro, translated by Thomas Merton, from *The Collected Poems of Thomas Merton.* Copyright © 1963 by The Abbey of Gethsemani, Inc. Reprinted by permission of New Directions Publishing Corp.

143 "The Secret of the Burning Stars" by Pablo Antonio Cuadro, translated by Thomas Merton, from *The Collected Poems of Thomas Merton.* Copyright © 1963 by The Abbey of Gethsemani, Inc. Reprinted by permission of New Directions Publishing Corp.

145 "The White Wind" by Juan Carlos Dávalos, translated by Angel Flores from *Fiesta in November, Stories from Latin America,* ed. Angel Flores and Dudley Poore. Copyright 1942 by Houghton Mifflin. Reprinted by permission of the Estate of Angel Flores.

156 "Ballad of Life" by Gaston Figueira, translated by Willis Knapp Jones from *Spanish-American Literature in Translation,* ed. Willis Knapp Jones. Reprinted by permission of Continuum Publishing Company.

156 "The Pineapple" by Gaston Figueira, translated by Willis Knapp Jones from *Spanish-American Literature in Translation,* ed. Willis Knapp Jones. Reprinted by permission of Continuum Publishing Company.

158 "The Life Line" by Carlos Fuentes, translated by Lysander Kemp. Originally published in *Evergreen Review,* Vol. 2, No.7. Reprinted by permission of the Estate of Lysander Kemp.

166 "The Farm Magnate" by Monteiro Lobato, from *Great Stories of All Nations,* ed. Maxim Lieber. Copyright 1934 by Tudor Publishing.

177 "Tuesday Siesta" from *No One Writes To The Colonel* by Gabriel García Márquez. Copyright © 1968 in the English translation by Harper & Row Publishers, Inc. Reprinted by permission of HarperCollins Publishers, Inc.

183 "Rocking" by Gabriela Mistral from *Selected Poems of Gabriela Mistral,* translated by Doris Dana. Reprinted by arrangement with Doris Dana, c/o Joan Daves

Agency as agent for the proprietor. Copyright © 1971 by Doris Dana.

183 "If You'll Only Go to Sleep" by Gabriela Mistral from *Selected Poems of Gabriela Mistral*, translated by Doris Dana. Reprinted by arrangement with Doris Dana, c/o Joan Daves Agency as agent for the proprietor. Copyright © 1971 by Doris Dana.

184 "The Sad Mother" by Gabriela Mistral from *Selected Poems of Gabriela Mistral*, translated by Doris Dana. Reprinted by arrangement with Doris Dana, c/o Joan Daves Agency as agent for the proprietor. Copyright © 1971 by Doris Dana.

184 "Fear" by Gabriela Mistral from *Selected Poems of Gabriela Mistral*, translated by Doris Dana. Reprinted by arrangement with Doris Dana, c/o Joan Daves Agency as agent for the proprietor. Copyright © 1971 by Doris Dana.

186 "Ode to My Socks" by Pablo Neruda, translated by Robert Bly. Reprinted from *Neruda and Vallejo: Selected Poems*, edited by Robert Bly, Beacon Press, Boston, 1971, 1993. Copyright 1971, 1993 by Robert Bly. Reprinted with his permission.

188 James Wright's translation of Pablo Neruda's "Some Beasts" from *Above the River: The Complete Poems* © 1990 by Anne Wright, Wesleyan University Press, by permission of University Press of New England.

189 "Cristobal Miranda" by Pablo Neruda, translated by Robert Bly. Reprinted from *Neruda and Vallejo: Selected Poems*, edited by Robert Bly, Beacon Press, Boston, 1971, 1993. Copyright 1971, 1993 by Robert Bly. Reprinted with his permission.

190 "The United Fruit Co." by Pablo Neruda, translated by Robert Bly. Reprinted from *Neruda and Vallejo: Selected Poems*, edited by Robert Bly, Beacon Press, Boston, 1971, 1993. Copyright 1971, 1993 by Robert Bly. Reprinted with his permission.

191 "Toussaint L'Ouverture" by Pablo Neruda, translated by James Wright from *Neruda and Vallejo: Selected Poems*. Copyright © 1971, 1993 by Robert Bly. Reprinted with his permission.

192 "Pastoral" by Pablo Neruda, from *Selected Poems of Pablo Neruda*, edited and translated by Ben Belitt. Copyright © 1958 by Pablo Neruda; English translation copyright © 1961 by Ben Belitt. Used by permission of Grove / Atlantic, Inc.

193 "A Pinecone, a Toy Sheep . . ." by Pablo Neruda, translated by Ben Belitt from *The Evergreen Review*. Reprinted by permission of Ben Belitt.

204 "The Son" by Horacio Quiroga, translated by Linda Wilson and Willis Knapp Jones from *Spanish-American Literature in Translation*, ed. Willis Knapp Jones. Reprinted by permission of Continuum Publishing Company.

208 "She Who Understands" by Alfonsina Storni, translated by Alice S. Blackwell from *Some Spanish American Poets*, University of Pennsylvania Press, 1937.

208 "Inheritance" by Alfonsina Storni, trans. by Jessie Reed Wendell. From *Translations from Hispanic Poets*. Reprinted by permission of The Hispanic Society of America.

209 "Squares and Angles" by Alfonsina Storni, translated by Willis Knapp Jones from *Spanish-American Literature in Translation*, ed. Willis Knapp Jones. Reprinted by permission of Continuum Publishing Company.

209 "I Am Going to Sleep" by Alfonsina Storni, translated by Willis Knapp Jones from *Spanish-American Literature in Translation*, ed. Willis Knapp Jones. Reprinted by permission of Continuum Publishing Company.

211 "Country Girl" by Luis Tablanca, translated by Alida Malkus from *Fiesta in November, Stories from Latin America*, ed. Angel Flores and Dudley Poore. Copyright 1942 by Houghton Mifflin. Reprinted by permission of the Estate of Angel Flores.

224 "The Gaucho Troubador" by Fernán Silva, translated by Willis Knapp Jones from *Spanish-American Literature in Translation*, ed. Willis Knapp Jones. Reprinted by permission of Continuum Publishing Company.

225 "The Indian" by Fernán Silva Valdés, translated by Willis Knapp Jones from *Spanish-American Literature in Translation*, ed. Willis Knapp Jones. Reprinted by permission of Continuum Publishing Company.

228 "Black Stone on Top of White Stone" by César Vallejo, translated by Thomas Merton, from *The Collected Poems of Thomas Merton*. Copyright © 1963 by The Abbey of Gethsemani, Inc. Reprinted by permission of New Directions Publishing Corp.

230 "The Boar Hunt" by José Vasconcelos, translated by Paul Waldorf from *The Muse in Mexico: A Mid-Century Miscellany*, edited by Thomas Mabry Cranfill, Copyright © 1959. By permission of the University of Texas Press.

Pronunciation Key

a	bat	ėr	her	oi	soil	ch	change		a	in along
ā	cage	i	hit	ou	scout	ng	song		e	in shaken
ä	star	ī	nice	u	up	sh	shell	ə	i	in stencil
â	dare	o	cot	u̇	put	th	think		o	in lemon
au	law	ō	old	ü	tube	TH	there		u	in circus
e	bet	ô	for			zh	pleasure			
ē	me									

Index of Authors, Titles and Translators